DEFENDING THE FIRST

LEA's Communication Series
Jennings Bryant/Dolf Zillmann, General Editors

Selected titles in Mass Communication (Alan Rubin, Advisory Editor) include:

Alexander/Owers/Carveth/Hollifield/Greco • *Media Economics: Theory and Practice, Third Edition*

Bryant/Bryant • *Television and the American Family, Second Edition*

Harris • *A Cognitive Psychology of Mass Communication, Fourth Edition*

Kundanis • *Children, Teens, Families, and Mass Media: The Millennial Generation*

Moore • *Mass Communication Law and Ethics, Second Edition*

Palmer/Young • *The Faces of Televisual Media: Teaching, Violence, Selling to Children, Second Edition*

Perse • *Media Effects and Society*

Russomanno • *Speaking Our Minds: Conversations With the People Behind Landmark First Amendment Cases*

Valkenburg • *Children's Responses to the Screen: A Media Psychological Approach*

Van Evra • *Television and Child Development, Third Edition*

For a complete list of titles in LEA's Communication Series, please contact Lawrence Erlbaum Associates, Publishers at www.erlbaum.com

DEFENDING THE FIRST

COMMENTARY ON FIRST AMENDMENT ISSUES AND CASES

Edited by

Joseph Russomanno
Arizona State University

LAWRENCE ERLBAUM ASSOCIATES, PUBLISHERS

2005   Mahwah, New Jersey   London

*Dedicated to the spirit of
freedom of expression
and to those willing to fight for it
yesterday, today, and tomorrow.*

Lawrence Erlbaum Associates, Inc., Publishers
10 Industrial Avenue
Mahwah, New Jersey 07430
www.erlbaum.com

Cover design by Sean Sciarrone

Library of Congress Cataloging-in-Publication Data

Defending the First : commentary on First Amendment issues
and cases / edited by Joseph Russomanno

    p. cm.

Includes bibliographical references and index.
ISBN 0-8058-4925-4 (cloth : alk. paper)
1. United States. Constitution. 1st Amendment. 2. Freedom of
speech—United States. 3. Freedom of the press—United
States. I. Russomanno, Joseph.

KF4770.D44 2004
342.7308'53—dc22   2004056425
                                            CIP

Books published by Lawrence Erlbaum Associates are printed on
acid-free paper, and their bindings are chosen for strength and
durability.

Printed in the United States of America
10 9 8 7 6 5 4 3 2 1

CONTENTS

v

     U.S. Supreme Court Takes on the Challenge of a New
     Communication Medium
     Paul M. Smith

9 The Past, Present, and Future of Internet Censorship   185
     and Free Speech Advocacy
     John B. Morris, Jr.

     Table of Cases   203

     Index   207

FOREWORD

Nadine Strossen[1]

Defending the First is an enlightening collection of fascinating first-hand accounts of some recent major free speech cases. Each essay is a compelling narrative in its own right, and together, they all underscore important conclusions and ongoing questions about First Amendment principles, especially when viewed through the lens of Joseph Russomanno's thought-provoking introductions to each chapter. Each of these introductions manages to frame complex legal questions with remarkable conciseness—this book should provide an exciting introduction for the First Amendment neophyte. Additionally, for First Amendment experts, this work offers a stimulating re-examination of timeless concerns. Although I was thoroughly familiar with the cases and issues discussed—because I have taught them in my constitutional law classes, and the ACLU was directly involved in almost all of the cases, I still gained valuable new insights from each chapter and its thoughtful introduction. In short, no matter how little or how much First Amendment background any reader might bring to this book, he or she should find it illuminating, as well as engaging.

NO FIGHT FOR FREE SPEECH EVER STAYS WON

The ACLU's principal founder, Roger Baldwin, observed that "No fight for civil liberties ever stays won."[2] *Defending the First* underscores that important insight in the free speech context. For example, Dan Johnston's chapter explains how the case of *Tinker v. Des Moines Independent Community School District*[3] (in which he was acting as a "cooperating attorney" for the ACLU's

---

[1]Professor of Law, New York Law School; President, American Civil Liberties Union.

[2]Lindsey Gruson, *Second Thoughts on Moments of Silence in the Schools*, N.Y. TIMES, Mar. 4, 1984, at 6E.

[3]393 U.S. 503 (1969).

Iowa affiliate) constitutes not a new victory for students' free speech rights in wartime, but rather a reaffirmation of earlier such victories. Even so, *Tinker* still deserves its usual accolade as a "landmark" case, because we can never take for granted that the Supreme Court will uphold basic constitutional liberties, including free speech rights, in times of war or other national crisis—especially when the speakers are politically powerless, as is the case with students too young to vote.

Consistent with our nation's historical pattern of suppressing dissenting voices during wartime, *Tinker's* reaffirmation of students' right to criticize the government's war policies has not "stayed won" in the nation's ongoing post-9/11 "War on Terrorism," as indicated by a more recent ACLU case, on behalf of Michigan high school student Bretton Barber. In 2003, Bret Barber was disciplined for wearing a T-shirt with a message criticizing President Bush's Iraq policies, despite the fact that Bret expressly cited the *Tinker* precedent to his school officials. Although Bret Barber's rights were ultimately vindicated in court,[4] it is still disturbing that his school authorities did not voluntarily honor the longstanding First Amendment principles at stake. Accordingly, Dan Johnston's comment concerning the *Tinker* student plaintiffs remains true today concerning Bret Barber and other student plaintiffs: "The failure of their school authorities...to recognize [their free speech rights] demonstrates the fragility of the rule of law in times of war."

In addition to Dan Johnston's chapter, the chapters by Marjorie Heins, Edward J. Cleary, Rodney A. Smolla, Bruce Rogow, Paul M. Smith, and John B. Morris, Jr., also all bear witness to the necessity of regularly refighting old free speech battles so that they can "stay won" in new circumstances. For one thing, the Heins, Smith, and Morris chapters illustrate the constant struggle to ensure that courts and other government officials will apply the First Amendment's guarantee of "the freedom of speech" to new media for conveying speech. As Marjorie Heins reminds us, when the Supreme Court first considered a challenge to censorship of the then-new film medium in 1915, the Court concluded that movies did not constitute "speech" that is sheltered by the First Amendment.[5] Even more astonishing, from our current vantage point, is the fact that the Court did not overturn that ruling until four decades later, in 1952, when it finally acknowledged that cinema is "a significant medium for the communication of ideas"[6] and hence subject to First Amendment protection.

Likewise, Paul Smith and John Morris remind us that when the Internet burst onto the public and political radar screen little more than a decade ago, the government strongly argued that it constituted only second-class speech, subject to strict government regulation of its content, similar to that imposed on the broadcast media. Although the Supreme Court resound-

---

[4]Barber v. Dearborn Public Schools, 286 F. Supp. 2d 847 (E.D. Mich. 2003).
[5]Mutual Film Corp. v. Industrial Comm'n of Ohio, 236 U.S. 230 (1915).
[6]Burstyn v. Wilson, 343 U.S. 495, 505-06 (1952).

ingly rejected that government argument in its unanimous ruling in *Reno v. ACLU*[7] that ruling was not at all a foregone conclusion, given the Court's past reluctance to bring new media fully into the First Amendment fold, as evidenced by its treatment of both film and broadcasting.

The Heins chapter illustrates the constant struggle to protect free speech not only in emerging new media, but also from religiously motivated censorship. Although her chapter focuses on the suppression of film content from the 1930s until the 1950s, in response to pressure from the Catholic Church, she also cites several much more recent examples—from 1988 through 2002—of religiously inspired suppression of artistic expression.

Even more recently, in 2004, the Federal Communications Commission actually incorporated religious concepts into its broad, vague description of *indecent* expression that is barred from the broadcast media. The FCC's standards for forbidden broadcast *indecency* now proscribe anything that is *profane*. This term explicitly harks back to notions of *blasphemy* or *sacrilege*, such as those that animated the 1951–1952 crusade against Roberto Rossellini's acclaimed film *The Miracle*, which Heins recounts. Moreover, the ban on broadcast *profanity* was adopted in response to a concerted campaign by leaders of the so-called "Religious Right" for the FCC to crack down on broadcast expression that offends their religious and moral sensibilities. This campaign was stimulated by the brief flash of Janet Jackson's breast during the January 2004 televised Super Bowl halftime show.

Still more recently, in the wake of the 2004 elections, with some polls indicating that "moral values" may have played a decisive role in many voters' minds, "Religious Right" organizations and spokespersons have renewed their calls for further restrictions on expression that they deem inconsistent with their moral or religious values. Therefore, the kinds of religiously inspired threats to free expression that Heins describes are likely to be of as much concern in the immediate future as they have been in the more distant past.

Bruce Rogow's chapter cites many examples of government officials violating what former Supreme Court Justice William Brennan termed the *bedrock principle*[8] of our free speech law: the concept of *content neutrality* or *viewpoint neutrality*, which holds that government may never limit speech just because any listener—or even, indeed, the majority of the community—disagrees with or is offended by its content or the viewpoint it conveys. Accordingly, as Rogow's chapter chronicles, he repeatedly had to fight for this fundamental free speech precept in cases involving expression that was offensive to particular politically powerful, vocal constituencies, ranging from Republican Party leaders who were offended by David Duke's white supremacist statements, to Cuban-Americans who were offended by

---

[7]521 U.S. 844 (1997).
[8]Texas v. Johnson, 491 U.S. 397, 414 (1989).

artistic expression emanating from Cuba. (Rogow handled many of these important First Amendment cases as a "cooperating attorney" for the ACLU of Florida.)

As Rogow noted, all of these cases should have been "easy" in light of the government's responsibility to adhere to the core First Amendment commands of content and viewpoint neutrality. "Easy" as those cases should have been in light of these established constitutional law principles, it is nevertheless hard for members of the public and politicians to understand or accept such principles, and even some judges sometimes depart from them, as Rogow's chapter illustrates.

In particular cases involving expression that is unpopular at the time, and in the circumstances in which it is conveyed, courageous attorneys such as Bruce Rogow constantly have to stand up for "freedom for the thought we hate," to quote former Supreme Court Justice Oliver Wendell Holmes.[9] Similarly principled—and "politically incorrect"—stances have been taken by Edward Cleary and Rodney Smolla, whose chapters describe their efforts to uphold neutral free speech tenets in the context of an especially vilified form of expression, cross-burning. These brave free speech advocates recurrently have to remind both courts of law, and the court of public opinion, that what is at stake is not only the freedom of the specific client in the specific case, but also, more fundamentally, the overall freedom of all mature individuals to make our own decisions about the (de)merits of any idea or expression.

It is a positive testament to our contemporary society's widespread rejection of racist ideology that one of the most reviled forms of expression is the burning cross, given its association with the Ku Klux Klan. However, in opposing laws that broadly stifled cross-burning, as they vividly recount, both Cleary and Smolla were standing up for neutral free speech principles that have been essential for combating racist and other discriminatory ideologies. Thus, any apparent "victory" in terms of suppressing even such a hated symbol as the flaming cross might well in fact be a pyrrhic victory for civil rights, because—as Cleary and Smolla explain—it empowers the government selectively to suppress certain ideas, a power that could well be unleashed against not only political minorities, but also racial and other minority groups.

DEFENDING THE FIRST AMENDMENT: PRIVATE SECTOR AND GOVERNMENT THREATS

In addition to reminding us about the constant need to refight old free speech battles in new factual contexts and new historical circumstances, *Defending the First* also reminds us that free speech is constantly threatened by

---

[9]United States v. Schwimmer, 279 U.S. 644, 654-55 (1929) (Holmes, J., dissenting).

many strategies—not only traditional, direct government censorship, but also more subtle yet equally dangerous government strategies, as well as efforts by many kinds of nongovernmental actors. In that sense, the fight for free speech is one that must invoke not only First Amendment law, which directly constrains only government conduct, but also the more general values that underlie the First Amendment, cherishing the free flow of ideas and information and resisting any inhibition by anyone, including private sector actors.

As noted previously, Marjorie Heins' chapter describes the dramatic negative impact that certain religious groups had in stifling free expression in films during the first half of the last century, leading to suppression of not "only" particular words and images—itself an enormous cost to free speech—but also entire subjects and themes, ranging from racial desegregation to women's rights. Heins also describes the significant contributions toward this repression of film content that were made by other nongovernmental actors, including: investment bankers who threatened to withhold financing from films with certain content; and film company executives, who capitulated to threats of audience boycotts, quite likely exaggerating the real danger posed by such threats, as Heins suggests.

John Morris's chapter provides a potent current example of private power to suppress—or to enhance—free speech in the still-evolving realm of online communications. He stresses the increasingly critical role that is being played by the computer scientists and others in the private sector who are developing the Internet's technical parameters, in ways that will either facilitate or thwart free speech.

In their respective chapters, Jerome Barron and Elliot Rothenberg explain how even private sector entities that are committed to First Amendment values in most contexts—the news media—can themselves at least potentially undermine the free speech of others. Because newspapers have the First Amendment right to print unfavorable (and also inaccurate) commentary about individuals without affording the individuals any "right of reply," doesn't that deter individuals from expressing their views on matters of public concern, as Barron maintains? And isn't the same problem posed by newspapers' asserted First Amendment right to breach confidentiality pledges to sources, which they pressed in *Cohen v. Cowles Media Co.*,[10] as described in Rothenberg's chapter? Wouldn't that asserted right deter potential whistleblowers and other sources of information of public concern from stepping forward, influencing them not to provide such information to newspapers, as Rothenberg posits? When one entity or individual asserts a free speech right that adversely affects the free speech interests of other

---

[10]501 U.S. 663 (1991).

entities or individuals, which should prevail? As Jerome Barron noted in his chapter, "the difficulty of the access issue is that it presents competing First Amendment rights."

NEW MEDIA, ONGOING ISSUES

Given the proliferation of media outlets, thanks to the burgeoning of the Internet and other "new media," conflicts between competing free speech rights and interests will also continue to proliferate. For example, is an investigator's online dissemination of private information about someone, which is obtained from online databases, a protected exercise of that investigator's free speech-based rights to obtain and convey information, in furtherance of the public's right to receive information? Or is it a violation of the free speech-based right of the subject of the private information to withhold it from the public, consistent with the right not to speak? Likewise, Elliot Rothenberg's contention that the media should not be immunized from generally applicable laws also takes on new urgency in the Internet age, when any individual with a Weblog or Website can plausibly claim to be a member of "the media."

The foregoing issues arising from the expansion of cybercommunications are only a sample of the important unresolved issues and problems to which this book points. Among the other ongoing problems are what Jerome Barron terms the Court's "schizophrenic" treatment of broadcast media and other media; the Court's seemingly anomalous treatment of "commercial" speech as a First Amendment stepchild, which Rogow questions; and the Court's failure, in its four major cyberspeech cases, to specify clearly the extent to which government may regulate Internet content, in ways that make it less accessible to adults, for the sake of shielding minors from certain expression, which Smith stresses. Just as each case described in this book constitutes an essential building block of our current free speech law and culture, consistent with the common-law "case method," each cases also raises at least as many questions as it answers.

Along with other constitutional guarantees, the First Amendment is not self-executing, but can only be enforced at the behest of individuals who actually assert and defend the rights it guarantees in the abstract. The Supreme Court, as well as other courts, can only resolve First Amendment cases that are initiated by individuals who are willing to stand up for their free speech rights—and, by extension, the free speech rights of everyone else in this country. Therefore, the continued enforcement and expansion of these rights will continue to depend on not only vigorous enforcement of free speech principles by Supreme Court Justices and other judges, but also, at least as much, on vigorous advocacy by lawyers who follow in the fine footsteps of the lawyers who have contributed to this book, as well as the courageous clients they represented. These essential efforts are, appropriately, lauded in Joseph Russomanno's dedication of *Defending the First* to "those willing to fight for" freedom of expression "yesterday, today, and tomorrow."

I hope and trust that these collected narratives by and about principled, dedicated free speech advocates will go beyond informing the readers of this book, and will also inspire them to stand up for their own—and, thereby, others'—free speech rights. As the early 20th century free speech philosopher Zechariah Chafee declared, "In the long run, in this country people will have as much freedom of speech as they want."[11]

New York, New York
January 1, 2005

---

[11]ZECHARIAH CHAFEE, Jr., FREE SPEECH IN THE UNITED STATES 500 (4th ed. 1948).

Preface

It didn't matter that a bitterly cold December rain—wind-driven and icing the streets outside—had already been pelting Washington, D.C. for hours early that morning. It didn't matter that most local schools were closed for the day. It really didn't matter that most of the people present inside had gone to great effort just to be there, many of them lined up and bundled up outside for hours before the doors opened. All that mattered for the next hour were the words that would be spoken by a dozen people situated inside within a few feet of one another.

"Oyez! Oyez! Oyez! All persons having business before the Honorable, the Supreme Court of the United States, are admonished to draw near and give their attention, for the Court is now sitting...." It is difficult to imagine any American who values justice not being moved upon hearing those words as the most powerful jurists in the land enter the room. It is equally difficult to imagine any attorney about to argue before the U.S. Supreme Court whose pulse doesn't quicken as those words are uttered.

The accounts on the pages that follow were each authored by individuals who have stood in those shoes, many as the primary litigator, others as members of a team of attorneys before the Court. On that wet December morning, as on many other days, that room housed a clash of constitutional rights and values.

Those who face the Court are required to handle a barrage of information as they deal with the ebbs and flows of the arguments. "Like a quarterback using all his powers of feel and experience and peripheral vision to desperately read a defense in the midst of a furious blitz," writes Rodney A. Smolla in chapter 6 about his encounter, "my every advocate's sense and instinct took in all that was happening in the adrenal rush of the crisis."

Like others who have faced the Supreme Court justices, Mr. Smolla could observe a wall painting high above them. It depicts a battle between Good and Evil. It is reminiscent of Milton's celebrated reference to truth: "Let her and falsehood grapple ... in a free and open encounter."[1] Perhaps the quintessential example of such grappling on this planet occurs in this "marble palace." Values, ideals, and principles oppose one another. But here, truth and falsehood, good and evil, are often barely discernible, hardly ever clear and unambiguous. Those are among the reasons cases reach this level. They are difficult, demanding, and replete with thorny issues, with resolution a challenging assignment. They are cases that merit deliberation and reflection by the nation's supreme judicial arbiters.

It is those nine individuals who become a major focus of the Supreme Court attorney. As some of those attorneys discuss in the pages that follow, the art of persuasion in this venue is not an easy task. Beyond that, understanding one's own case, its lineage, and its likely impact all become part of the formula for success. The reader of this volume's essays—and that includes the Foreword—is provided the unique perspective of those who have been on the front lines of some of this era's most important First Amendment cases. Some have written about their experiences at the Supreme Court many years after being there, and with the perspective that affords. Other experiences are analyzed from a more recent vantage point. One Supreme Court attorney offers a historical analysis of a case replete with a variety of First Amendment issues, both deep-rooted and contemporary.

In summary, wherever readers turn in this volume, they will be taken into a realm of First Amendment analysis that is unique—told by some of those at the forefront of the battle to defend "the First."

—*Joseph Russomanno*

---

[1] John Milton, *Areopagitica, reprinted in* THE STUDENT'S MILTON 751 (Frank Allen Patterson ed. 1933)(1654).

Creating a New First Amendment Right

Miami Herald Publishing Co. v. Tornillo and the Story of Access to the Media

Jerome A. Barron*

EDITOR'S INTRODUCTION

"I don't have time for any cases."

"You will want this one."

Thus began Jerome Barron's journey to the U.S. Supreme Court. Actually, as he describes in chapter 1, the journey's roots extend to his interest in the right-of-access issue. And to his seminal 1967 Harvard Law Review *article on the topic.*

Professor Barron had concluded that there were inconsistencies in First Amendment law. It protected ideas once they entered the marketplace, but little in the way of assuring entry into the marketplace initially. In an era when the tip of the iceberg of concentration of media ownership was just emerging, this seemed to make sense. The idea was that the First Amendment could be construed as a safeguard for making a variety of ideas public. But instead of the idea making sense for many, it was a catalyst for criticism.

Allowing the free market to operate and govern the system would be fine—if only the market was free. Instead, it is not open to all. Just try to buy a major newspaper or station. The extremely wealthy dominate the media scene. The sentiment against government involvement with the media—for example, providing citizens a right of access—is

---

*Jerome A. Barron is Harold H. Greene Professor of Law, George Washington University Law School, Washington, D.C.

deep within our national DNA. For more than two centuries the First Amendment has been equated with the notion that the media cannot be regulated or restricted. That's a false assumption. The First Amendment has become a mechanism for protecting class privilege rather than the interests of the public, such as promoting democracy.

One of the great First Amendment philosophers in America was Alexander Meikeljohn. He believed that the primary purpose of the First Amendment is that all citizens shall, so far as possible, understand the issues that bear upon our common life. That is why, he said, no idea, no opinion, no belief, no counter belief, no relevant information may be kept from them.

Is the First Amendment serving that end? The First Amendment stands for a free flow of ideas. Debate on issues of public importance should be "uninhibited, robust, and wide open" (New York Times v. Sullivan). Is that happening? Or has media content become little more than spending-friendly, mood-establishing background noise between advertisements?

Who does the First Amendment serve? The public? Owners of the media? As the U.S. Supreme Court has said in justifying broadcast regulation that may infringe on the privileges of station owners, "It is the right of the viewers and listeners, not the right of the broadcasters, which is paramount" (Red Lion Broadcasting Co. v. FCC, 395 U.S. 367, 390 (1969)).

Broadcast regulation has been justified by the U.S. Supreme Court because broadcasting is a scarce, limited resource. Today, it is arguable the same can be said of all news media. Not only is the information provided to the citizenry scarce, so too are the news outlets themselves. Their numbers have increased, but the concentration of ownership has grown exponentially. Like wealth, in general, the biggest part of the pie is in the hands of a relative few. Entry into the privileged club is made more difficult by the day. True access would enhance the possibility of the news being a forum for a diverse marketplace of ideas.

Five years after his Harvard Law Review *article was published, the phone in Professor Barron's office rang. When he answered, a door was opened to a path that would eventually lead him to the U.S. Supreme Court.*

*   *   *

This is the story of a Supreme Court case that had its origin in a law review article. *Access to the Press—A New First Amendment Right* appeared in the *Harvard Law Review* in 1967.[1] Seven years later, the Supreme Court considered the ideas expressed in that article. Typically, law review articles discuss, an-

---

[1] Jerome A. Barron, *Access to the Press—A New First Amendment Right*, 80 HARV. L. REV. 1641 (1967).

alyze, and criticize Supreme Court cases after they have been announced. But a law review article that generates a Supreme Court case is more unusual. When I wrote *Access to the Press—A New First Amendment Right*, I did not have litigation in mind—much less a Supreme Court case. My goal, instead, was to call attention to what I saw as a fundamental shortcoming in the law. Once ideas managed to secure entry to the so-called marketplace of ideas, existing First Amendment law protected them to a substantial extent. But suppose the media marketplace erected barriers to the entry of ideas in the first place? The plain fact was that entry to the media marketplace was at the sufferance of its owners and managers.

FIRST AMENDMENT LAW AND THE ACCESS PROBLEM

I first began to understand the nature of this problem when, as a law school teacher, I started to teach and write in the areas of First Amendment law and broadcast law. In so doing, I found myself confronting at least three basic inconsistencies in the law. First, at that time—the 1960s—broadcasting law provided some measure of access for ideas of individuals to be heard and seen on broadcasting. Yet in the print media no such rights existed. This seemed to me both illogical and wrong. The second inconsistency was that First Amendment law was entirely directed to the protection of speech once it had entered into the marketplace. But it was quite indifferent to the obstacles that obstruct the entry of ideas and individuals into the marketplace of ideas in the first place. The third inconsistency was that First Amendment law was extremely sensitive to government restraints on expression but quite indifferent to media restraints on expression. I began to see the need for a right of access to the media. I believed that it was entirely consistent with First Amendment to allow those whom the media attacked to respond. This prompted me to write—and to urge—the recognition of a new First Amendment right—a right of access to the press.

The article drew much more attention than I would have ever dreamed possible. In fact, it drew immediate fire. Clifton Daniel of the *New York Times* argued that it would be impossible to write an access law that would not in the end result in government control of the press.[2] Ben Bagdikian, journalist and press critic, lampooned the idea of a right of access to the press. *Editor & Publisher,* the voice of the print media, he contended, would have to print the press releases of the National Association of Broadcasters praising the virtues of the electronic media. Anti-regulation *Broadcasting* magazine, the organ of

---

[2]Clifton Daniel, *Right of Access to Mass Media-Government Obligation to Enforce the First Amendment*, 48 TEX. L. REV. 783 (1970).

the broadcast industry, would have to give equal time to pro-regulation FCC (Federal Communications Commission) commissioners.[3]

To understate the matter, the American newspaper press was not enchanted with the idea of a legally enforceable right of access to the press. The *St. Louis Post-Dispatch* took up the battle and wrote a dismissive editorial about *Access to the Press—A New First Amendment Right:*

> The newspaper (which is in no way licensed by the government as [is] a broadcast station) has an obligation to the community in which it is published to present fairly unpopular as well as popular sides of a question. *Enforcing such a dictum by law is constitutionally impossible, and should be.* As a practical matter, a newspaper which consistently refuses to give expression to viewpoints with which it differs is not likely to succeed, and doesn't deserve to.[4]

In a speech in 1968 before the American Civil Liberties Union (ACLU), I responded to the criticism of the *St. Louis Post-Dispatch* and others that a right of access should not be legally enforceable. "Whether it is true," I said, "as the *Post-Dispatch* suggests that the wicked do not prosper," I did not want to take the chance that they might. I wanted to show that a right of access was valid under the Constitution and that it was practically feasible.[5] Yet even though I truly believed in it, I did not expect the Supreme Court to recognize a legally enforceable right of access, based on the First Amendment, to occur very soon.

SOME SUPREME COURT VICTORIES FOR A RIGHT OF ACCESS TO THE MEDIA

Events moved faster than I had anticipated. In 1969 the Supreme Court decided a case, *Red Lion Broadcasting v. FCC*[6] that represented a very significant advance for the cause of access to the media. That case upheld two FCC policies that were addressed to achieving fair debate within the media, the fairness doctrine and the personal attack rules. The fairness doctrine required that broadcasters offer a balanced presentation of controversial issues of public importance during the license period.[7] The FCC's personal-attack rules

---

[3]Ben Bagdikian, *Right of Access: A Modest Proposal*, COLUM. JOURN. REV., Spring 1969.

[4]*St. Louis Post-Dispatch*, August 24, 1967, at 2E (emphasis added).

[5]These comments were part of a speech given at the 1968 (June 20–25) Biennial Conference at the University of Michigan, Ann Arbor. The speech became the basis of a law review article: Jerome A. Barron, *An Emerging First Amendment Right of Access to the Media?* 37 GEO. WASH. L. REV. 487, 498 (1969).

[6]395 U.S. 367 (1969).

[7]The FCC announced the fairness doctrine in the *Report on Editorializing By Broadcast Licensees*, 13 F.C.C. 1246 (1949). The FCC declared that broadcast licensees could editorialize but they were obliged to provide in their overall programming a balanced presentation of controversial ideas of public importance. They were also obliged to seek out and cover the issues that concerned their communities. Subsequently, in the 1980s, in keeping with its new policy of deregulation, the FCC abolished the fairness doctrine. Syracuse Peace Council, 2 F.C.C.R. 5043 (1987). That decision was upheld by the federal court of appeals in Washington. Syracuse Peace Council v. FCC, 867 F.2d 654 (D.C. Cir. 1989).

enabled persons or groups whose character or integrity was attacked during discussions of controversial issues of public importance to respond on the same broadcast station where they were attacked as a matter of right. And at no cost to them.[8] The Supreme Court resoundingly upheld both policies. These policies, the Court ruled, were not only consistent with the First Amendment; they were in furtherance of the principles underlying the First Amendment. Access to the electronic media was becoming a reality.

Two years later another decision provided additional support for the idea that a right of access to the media, based on the First Amendment, would be recognized by the Supreme Court of the United States. The case, *Rosenbloom v. Metromedia*,[9] involved a suit by a magazine dealer, George Rosenbloom, whose newsstands, a local radio station reported, had been closed down by the police on the ground they sold obscene publications. The magazine dealer had also been referred to by the radio station as a smut peddler. After Rosenbloom was acquitted of criminal obscenity charges, he sued the Philadelphia radio station that had made the offending broadcast for libel. The case reached the Supreme Court. In a plurality opinion for three Supreme Court justices, Justice Brennan, joined by Chief Justice Burger and Justice Blackmun, gave a surprise endorsement to a right of access to the media.

To understand how three Justices of the Supreme Court came to favor a right of access to the media, one has to go back to what is the Supreme Court's most famous defamation decision, *New York Times v. Sullivan*.[10] The case arose out of the long and sometimes bloody struggle for civil rights that transformed the American South during the 1960s. The *Times* had provided extensive coverage to that struggle. At one point, the *Times* published an editorial advertisement paid for by civil rights organizations protesting the treatment of student civil rights demonstrators by Alabama law enforcement personnel in that state. The advertisement contained some inaccuracies. Because the ad criticized law enforcement in the city of Birmingham, Alabama, one of the responsible law enforcement officials in that city, commissioner L. B. Sullivan, claimed he had been libeled. He sued the *Times* as well as some civil rights leaders and obtained a judgment in the state courts for $500,000. Three other libel suits based on the same editorial advertisement sought damages against the *Times* for a total of $2,000,000.

---

[8]The personal-attack rules, a corollary of the fairness doctrine, provided that if the "honesty, character or integrity" of an individual or a group was attacked over a broadcast station in connection with a controversial issue of public importance, the broadcaster had to inform the person attacked and give her an opportunity to respond at no cost to the person attacked. *See Personal Attack Rules*, 47 C.F.R. Sec. 73.1920. The FCC was ordered to repeal the personal-attack rules by the federal court of appeals in Washington after the FCC commissioners failed to agree on whether to keep or abolish the personal attack rules. *See* RTNDA v. FCC, 229 F.3d 269 (D.C. Cir. 2000).

[9]403 U.S. 29 (1971).

[10]376 U.S. 254 (1964).

Justice Brennan believed that criticism of public officials should not be easily stifled by defamation suits. The citizen-critic of government was to be encouraged, not thwarted. Accordingly, the Supreme Court ruled that where, as in the *Times* case, the plaintiff was a public official, the ability to secure damages against media criticism should be more limited than in the past. A public official would now be able to recover damages for a defamatory falsehood relating to his official conduct only if he could prove by clear and convincing evidence that the statement was made with "actual malice." In other words, the plaintiff would have to prove that the defamation was published with knowledge of its falsity or with reckless disregard of whether it was true or false. Justice Brennan explained why the Court ruled that the First Amendment required this change in the law of defamation: The central meaning of the First Amendment was to encourage vigorous criticism of government. The design of the First Amendment was to protect and stimulate debate: "Debate on public issues should be uninhibited, robust and wide-open."[11]

I applauded these sentiments. But I was concerned that although protecting free debate was the very purpose of the *Times* case, the Court had done nothing to assure that in fact more debate would be the result of that decision. Indeed, I feared an unintended side effect of the decision might well be to retard debate instead of furthering it.[12] The *Times* case and the law that developed around it made it much more difficult for public officials and public figures to recover for defamation.

Even though the chances for public persons to get libel damages for defamation were slimmer after the *Times* case, many public persons still had a remedy left. After all, public persons are by definition players in the public discourse of the nation. If they give a press conference, the press will come. Generally, public persons can count on access to the media. If the police commissioner of the city of Birmingham is attacked by a newspaper, the press will want to hear his response. If he wants a to call a conference, the press will want to be there. The police commissioner is a newsmaker.

By contrast, someone like George Rosenbloom, the magazine dealer charged with selling obscene magazines by a radio station, is in an entirely different situation. He is neither a public figure nor a public official. For the

---

[11]New York Times v. Sullivan, 376 U.S. 254, 270 (1964).

[12]"The irony of *Times* and its progeny lies in the unexamined assumption that reducing newspaper exposure to libel litigation will remove restraints on expression and lead to an 'informed society.' But in fact the decision creates a new imbalance in the communications process. Purporting to deepen the constitutional guarantee of full expression, the actual effect of the decision is to perpetuate the freedom of a few in a manner adverse to the public interest in uninhibited debate. Unless the *Times* decision is deepened to require opportunities for the public figure to reply to a defamatory attack, the *Times* decision will merely serve to equip the press with some new and rather heavy artillery which can crush as well as stimulate debate." Barron, *supra* note 1, at 1657.

three Justices who formed the plurality opinion for the Court in the *Rosenbloom* case, this state of affairs wasn't fair. The key to whether the press should be given new protection against defamation suits should not depend on their status—whether the person attacked was a public official or a public figure. The test for relaxing the defamation laws should depend on whether the content of the defamation involved a public issue. Reporting on the enforcement of the obscenity laws by the police was certainly a public issue. Justice Brennan, joined by Chief Justice Burger and Justice Blackmun, suggested that instead of damages for defamation, a right of reply might be the a more desirable remedy where the person attacked was not given an opportunity to respond to a media attack. The Court elaborated on this point:

> One writer, in arguing that the First Amendment itself should be read to guarantee a right of access to the media not limited to a right to respond to defamatory falsehoods, has suggested several ways the law might encourage public discussion. Barron, Access to the Press—A New First Amendment Right, 80 Harv. L. Rev. 1641, 1666–1678 (1967). It is important to recognize that the private individual often desires press exposure either for himself, his ideas, or his causes. Constitutional adjudication must take into account the individual's interest in access to the press as well as the individual's interest in preserving his reputation.[13]

This sympathetic account of a First Amendment–based right of access by Justice Brennan was certainly a source of great encouragement to those of us who believed that in an age of increasing media concentration of ownership, a right of access to the media would keep the public discourse open. All in all, the legal events I have just described gave me hope to believe that eventually a right of access might one day be recognized as an enforceable First Amendment right.

PAT TORNILLO, *THE MIAMI HERALD*, AND THE FLORIDA RIGHT OF REPLY LAW

In the meantime in 1972, I accepted an offer to become the Dean of Syracuse University Law School. I was still committed to establishing a right of access to the media. But I was now embarked on what would be for me a new adventure. I expected that for a while my time would be pretty well filled with the responsibilities of administering a law school. And indeed it was. But the opportunity to fight for a right of access came much sooner that I had anticipated. On a gray November day I was sitting in my office going over some law school budget figures when my phone

---

[13]Rosenbloom v. Metromedia, Inc., 403 U.S. 29, 47 (1971).

rang. The person on the other end of the line was an exuberant and passionate lawyer from Miami, Florida, Tobias Simon. Known to all who knew him as Toby, Tobias Simon was both a civil rights lawyer and a labor lawyer. His friendly and intense voice on the other end of my phone line said, "I have a case for you." I said, "I don't want any cases; I don't have time for them." He said, "You will want this one."

Simon explained that, because of my Harvard article and my work on access to the media, this was a case I must take. He went into the facts of the case in detail. I was impressed with Toby Simon's enthusiasm and commitment. Nevertheless, I told I him I was a new dean and that I simply would not have the time to join him in the case he was describing. At that point, Toby said, "Suppose I fly up to Syracuse from Miami to explain to you the significance of this case? Would you at least see me?" I replied, "Anyone dedicated enough to exchange a warm, sunny day in Miami for a cold, cloudy November day in Syracuse, New York, in late November is someone I would surely see."

Toby Simon was as good as his word. A few days later, he flew up to Syracuse from Miami, sat down with me and explained the facts of the case he wanted me to take. Toby had a feisty client, Pat Tornillo, head of the Dade County Classroom Teachers Association. In 1968 Tornillo had led the public school teachers in Dade County in a strike. There was nothing remarkable about a union leader leading his union in a strike except that strikes by public school teachers were illegal in the state of Florida. A few years later Tornillo decided to present himself as a candidate for the Florida state legislature. If corporation presidents could sit in the state legislature, there was no reason a union leader could not do so as well.

But Pat Tornillo's candidacy ran into a formidable obstacle; the *Miami Herald*, then as now the dominant newspaper in the state of Florida, opposed his candidacy. On September 20, 1972, the *Miami Herald* published the following editorial.

The State Law and Pat Tornillo
LOOK who's upholding the law!

Pat Tornillo, boss of the Classroom Teachers Association [CTA] and candidate for the State Legislature in the October 3 runoff election, has denounced his opponent as lacking the knowledge to be a legislator, as evidenced by his failure to file a list of contributions to and expenditure of his campaign as required by law.

Czar Tornillo calls violation of this law inexcusable. This is the same Pat Tornillo who led the CTA strike from February 19 to March 11, 1968, against the school children and taxpayers of Dade County. Call it whatever you will, it was an illegal act against the public interest and clearly prohibited by the statutes. We cannot say it would be illegal but certainly it would be inexcusable of the voters if they sent Pat Tornillo to Tallahassee to occupy the seat for District 103 in the House of Representatives.

On September 27, 1972, Pat Tornillo submitted a reply to the *Miami Herald*'s September 20 editorial and asked them to publish it:

Pat Tornillo and the CTA RECORD

Five years ago, the teachers participated in a statewide walkout to protest deteriorating educational conditions. Financing was inadequate then and we now face a financial crisis. The Herald told us that what we did was illegal and that we should use legal processes instead. We are doing just that through legal and political action. My candidacy is an integral part of this process.

During the past four years:

• CTA brought suit to give Dade County its share of state money to relieve local taxpayers.
• CTA won a suit which gave public employees the right to collectively bargain.
• CTA won a suit which allowed the school Board to raise $7.8 million to air-condition schools and is helping to keep this money. Unfortunately, the Herald dwells on past history and ignores totally legal efforts of the past four years. We are proud of our record.

The *Herald* did not print this relatively mild reply. Instead, it fired another volley at Tornillo. A new editorial attack appeared in the paper on September 29, 1972. This one was nastier than its predecessor. Here is part of it:

For years now he [Pat Tornillo] has been kicking the public shin to call attention to his shakedown statesmanship.... Give him public office, says Pat, and he will no doubt live by the Golden Rule. Our translation reads that as more gold and more rule.

On September 30, 1972, Tornillo submitted this reply pursuant to the Florida state right of reply law:

We have attempted to obey all the laws of the state, not intentionally violating any, while continuing our efforts to alert the public to the impending financial crisis facing the schools. We have, however, also retained our belief in the right of public employees to engage in political activity and to support the candidate of our choice, as is the right of any citizen in this great country of ours.

When the *Miami Herald* refused to publish the replies Tornillo had submitted, Simon brought suit under a unique and little known Florida law—a law that was going to have a great impact on the future of a right of access to the media. The Florida right-of-reply law had been sleeping in the Florida sun since 1913. The law provided that if any newspaper attacks the personal character of a political candidate running for election or charges that person with "malfeasance or misfeasance" or otherwise attacks his official record, that newspaper shall on request publish free of charge any reply that candidate should make in "as conspicuous a place and in the same kind of type" as the matter that called for the reply in the first place.[14]

The trial court judge quickly dismissed Tornillo's complaint under the Florida right-of-reply law as a violation of the First Amendment. The case was dismissed even though the *Miami Herald* had not yet filed a motion to dismiss. Toby Simon believed that the Florida right-of-reply law did not violate the First Amendment in any way. He was convinced that the right-of-reply law implemented the debate and controversy that the First Amendment was designed to protect.

Simon emphasized the attractive features of the case. The *Miami Herald* was the dominant newspaper not only in the metropolitan Miami area but also in the entire state. Here was the kind of David-and-Goliath situation I had been writing about. Newspapers properly insisted on their right to publish without censorship but yet they wished to act as censors. But in this case there *was* a remedy. Florida's right-of-reply law specifically provided that a political candidate who was attacked by a newspaper was entitled to a right of reply at no cost to the candidate. In order for Tornillo to be successful a court would not have to take the rather radical step of fashioning a right of reply on its own on a theory the new right was based on the First Amendment. All the court would need to do is simply hold that the existing right-of-reply law was consistent with the First Amendment.

The courts were unlikely to create a right of reply on their own where no such right had existed before in state law. Validating a law that a state legislature had already passed was far more likely to meet with success in the courts. Moreover, the Florida right-of-reply law was not some new development born out of the activism and radicalism of the 1960s. The Florida state right-of-reply law had been enacted as far back as 1913. It was part of the Florida state electoral code, the theme of which was government-in-the-sunshine. All things governmental should be done in the open. The citizenry should be able to see at all times what the government was up to. Today, we call this transparency. With respect to political candidates, the legislature believed that newspapers should be able to criticize and even attack political candidates. But they also believed the candidates should have the opportunity to respond. In short, the Florida right-of-reply law ensured debate rather than monologue. That way the electorate would get both sides of the story.

---

[14]F.S. Sec. 104.38.

TORNILLO V. MIAMI HERALD PUBLISHING CO. IN THE SUPREME COURT OF FLORIDA

I decided to join Toby Simon in his suit on behalf of Pat Tornillo's right to reply. We obtained review in the Supreme Court of Florida. In the spring of 1973, Toby and I appeared for the oral argument before the Supreme Court of Florida. We split up the oral argument. Toby handled the Florida law issues and I handled the First Amendment issues. The Court seemed sympathetic to our argument. In our briefs and argument, we stressed that the Supreme Court of the United States in *Red Lion* and in *Rosenbloom* supported our view that a right of reply was a way of implementing First Amendment values such as free and untrammeled debate. When we left the courthouse in Tallahassee after the oral argument, our mood matched that of the Florida sunshine. We were optimistic that the trial court would be reversed and that the Supreme Court of Florida would conclude that the Florida right of reply did not violate the First Amendment.

A cloud soon appeared on the horizon. On May 29, 1973, the Supreme Court of the United States announced a new access decision, *CBS v. Democratic National Committee* (1973).[15] This case constituted a setback for the cause of access to the media. Two organizations, the Democratic National Committee and an organization of business people opposed to the Vietnam War, sought to buy time from the broadcast networks in order to present their ideas to the public. These organizations reasoned that if one could buy time on television to sell soap or cars, one ought to also be able to buy time to discuss ideas. The networks didn't agree.

The networks took the position that they had a blanket policy of declining to sell time for the presentation of social and political ideas. Why did they have this policy? Their reasoning was that they, unlike the public, were broadcast journalists. The networks contended that the development of programming on the issues of the day was *their* exclusive responsibility. The two organizations turned to the FCC for relief. They asked the FCC to rule that the networks could not, consistent with the First Amendment, maintain a blanket policy that they would never sell time segments for the development by people other than themselves of programming about political and social ideas. The two organizations believed their access claims were quite strong. After all, in the *Red Lion* case, the Supreme Court had said that it was "the right of the viewers and listeners, not the right of the broadcasters, which is paramount."[16] Nevertheless, the FCC ruled that the networks were not obliged to sell the requested time. The FCC was horrified at the thought of trying to administer a system of access;

---

[15]412 U.S. 94 (1973).
[16]Red Lion Broadcasting Co. v. F.C.C., 395 U.S. 367, 390 (1969).

the problems inherent in such a task were simply too formidable.[17] The access claimants went to the court of appeals. There they met a measure of success. Judge Skelly Wright, speaking for the Court of Appeals, ruled that it was a violation of the First Amendment to have a flat ban on paid public issue announcements while at the same time paid announcements of a commercial nature were accepted.[18] To have a policy of accepting commercial advertisements but not editorial advertisements constituted impermissible and unconstitutional discrimination. The Court of Appeals did not require that the networks accept the proffered advertisements. Instead, they sent the matter back to the FCC so that it could develop regulations that would permit a system of access for political advertisements.

The networks appealed to the Supreme Court. At oral argument and in their briefs the networks particularly attacked the position of the access claimants that they had a First Amendment right of access to the electronic media. The networks argued the First Amendment supported them, not the access claimants. The right of access, the networks contended, was completely at odds with the exercise of editorial judgment, which was certainly protected by the First Amendment. It did not occur to the network lawyers that both the access claimants and the networks might each have a claim to First Amendment protection. The significance and the difficulty of the access issue lies in the fact that it presents a case of competing First Amendment rights. Nonetheless, Chief Justice Burger, in an opinion for the Court, agreed with the networks. "Editing," he wrote, is "what editors are for."[19]

Justice Brennan, joined by Justice Marshall, dissenting, observed that "broadcasters generally tend to permit only established—or at least moderated—views to enter the broadcast world's 'marketplace of ideas.'"[20] Citing the works of many access advocates,[21] Justice Brennan emphasized the failure of our legal system to offer any way for new ideas to enter the media marketplace.[22] For me, it was a matter of real concern that Justice Brennan's position was not a majority position but a dissenting one. The *CBS* case was worrisome. There had been a media barrage against both the wisdom and

---

[17]*See* Democratic National Committee, 25 F.C.C. 2d 216 (1972); Business Executives' Move for Vietnam Peace, 25 F.C.C. 2d 242 (1972).

[18]Business Executives' Move for Vietnam Peace, 450 F.2d 642, 646 (D.C. Cir. 1971).

[19]*Id.* at 124.

[20]*Id.* at 188.

[21]*Id.* at fn.24.

[22]"Indeed, the failure to provide adequate means for groups and individuals to bring new issues or ideas to the attention of the public explains, at least to some extent, 'the development of new media to convey unorthodox, unpopular and new ideas. Sit-ins and demonstrations testify to … the inability to secure access to the conventional means of reaching and changing public opinion. [For by] the bizarre and unsettling nature of his technique, the demonstrator hopes to arrest and divert attention long enough to compel the public to ponder his message.' Barron, *supra* note 1, at 1647; cf. Adderley v. Florida, 385 U.S. 39, 50–51 (1966) (Douglas, J., dissenting)." *Id.* at 190.

the constitutionality of the right of access. Perhaps the *CBS* case was a harbinger that the Supreme Court's interest in a right of access was momentary rather than enduring.

THE SUPREME COURT OF FLORIDA UPHOLDS THE FLORIDA RIGHT-OF-REPLY LAW

Our fears about the impact of the *CBS* decision notwithstanding, on July 18, 1973, the Supreme Court of Florida held, 6 to 1, that the Florida right-of-reply law not only did not violate the First Amendment, but that it implemented the First Amendment.[23] The Court observed that "news corporations are acquiring monopolistic influence over huge areas of the country."[24] The Court then rather pointedly noted that the *Miami Herald* had the largest newspaper circulation of any newspaper in the state of Florida. The Court then declared:

> Freedom of expression was retained by the people through the First Amendment *for all the people* and *not merely for a select few.* The First Amendment *did not create a privileged class* which through a monopoly of instruments of the newspaper industry would be able to *deny to the people the freedom of expression* which the First Amendment guarantees.[25]

In its opinion, the Supreme Court of Florida relied on the cases we had emphasized in our oral argument and briefs—*Red Lion* and its holding that the First Amendment protected a right of access to ideas, and the plurality opinion for the Court in *Rosenbloom*, which had expressed sympathy and support for a right of access to the media for those otherwise excluded from the public discourse. In upholding the Florida right-of-reply statute, the Supreme Court of Florida limited the reach of the statute to editorial attacks. A newspaper would not have to offer a reply every time a reporter criticized a political candidate in a news story.[26] So limiting the statute reduced the burden on editorial autonomy and hopefully improved the chances that the case would be affirmed if the Supreme Court of the United States decided to review the case. The Court also made it clear that civil remedies, including money damages, would be available under the statute. We took this to mean that if the *Miami Herald* did not wish to publish Tornillo's replies, they could, as an alternative, respond in money damages.

To decide a case against the dominant newspaper in a state where judges are elected, and thus dependent on newspaper endorsements and coverage,

---

[23]Tornillo v. Miami Herald Publishing Co., 287 So. 2d 78 (Fla. 1973).
[24]*Id.* at 83.
[25]*Id.*
[26]*Id.* at 86.

took no small amount of courage. Significantly, no one justice took the primary responsibility for the decision upholding the right of reply against the
objection of the *Miami Herald*. An indication that the Justices of the Supreme
Court who upheld the Florida right-of-reply law realized that they might be
putting their futures on the line is found in the fact that the majority opinion
did not bear the name of any one of the justices who comprised it. Instead,
the opinion was a *per curiam* opinion, a device courts sometimes use when no
single judge wishes to bear the primary responsibility for the decision.

The judges who joined in the majority opinion of the Supreme Court of
Florida in the *Miami Herald* case were well aware of the *CBS* case decided
several months before. Each of the judges who joined in the majority opinion joined in a special concurring opinion by Justice Roberts. The point of
the concurrence was to make it clear that although the majority was well
aware of the *CBS* decision, they did not believe it was relevant to a case involving the First Amendment validity of the Florida right-of-reply law. The
concurring Justices declared that *CBS* did not diminish the importance of
the earlier *Red Lion* case, which gave First Amendment validation to not one
but two affirmative responsibilities of broadcasters. Furthermore, *CBS* was
just not applicable to the facts of the *Miami Herald* case. Instead, *CBS* was
limited to the special field of broadcasting and the unique problems and responsibilities that flow from the finite character of the electromagnetic
spectrum. Furthermore, the concurring opinion pointed out that in *CBS*
the Court had noted broadcasters were obliged by the fairness doctrine to
present the broadcast audience with access to a balanced presentation of
controversial issues of public importance. Even if a First Amendment right
of access to the electronic media was not accepted, access would still be
available because of the fairness doctrine. That would not be true in Florida
with respect to newspapers in the absence of a right-of-reply law. Also, the
nature of the access issue was different in *CBS* than the right-of-reply issue
before the Supreme Court of Florida. For example, the Supreme Court in
CBS was particularly concerned that the end result of requiring broadcasters to accept paid political or issue advertisements would be that the views of
the affluent would prevail. The Florida right-of-reply law gave the candidate who was attacked by a newspaper a free right of reply.

There was a fundamental distinction between the *Miami Herald* case and
the *CBS* case that the Supreme Court of Florida failed to make. This was the
point that Toby Simon made to me on that gray November afternoon in
Syracuse. *Miami Herald* involved the interpretation of a statute; *Red Lion* involved the interpretation of statute as well as FCC policy and regulation. In
CBS, on the other hand, the Court was being asked to say that the First
Amendment itself compelled broadcasters to accept paid political advertisements. This was a large and novel request and it was not surprising the
Supreme Court of the United States declined to take it. In the *Miami Herald*

case the access proponents made a much more modest request. They wanted the Supreme Court of Florida only to rule that a state law that afforded political candidates a right to reply to newspaper attacks during an election campaign did not violate the First Amendment

There was one dissent in the Supreme Court of Florida on the First Amendment validity of the right of reply. Justice Boyd accepted the vigorous arguments of Dan Paul, the lawyer for the *Miami Herald*. The statute was so vague on its face as to create doubts in anyone who read it as to its meaning. For example, the Florida law contained no criteria to indicate when a newspaper had to publish a reply: "When the publisher knows his statements are true, must he publish a statement from the candidate which he knows to be false?"[27] Finally, just as government could not censor the news and editorial columns of a newspaper, so government could not require a newspaper to publish that which it did not wish to publish. But Justice Boyd aside, all the other Justices of the Florida Supreme Court believed that the Florida right-of-reply law advanced rather than weakened the values of debate and dialogue, which the First Amendment protected.

THE SUPREME COURT OF THE UNITED STATES STRIKES DOWN THE FLORIDA RIGHT-OF-REPLY LAW

When the decision of the Supreme Court of Florida upholding the Florida right-of-reply law was announced, the decision was reported in the media as a victory for a new and rising First Amendment right of access to the media. For those who believed that the recognition of such a right implemented rather than thwarted freedom of expression, the Florida Supreme Court's right-of-reply decision was both groundbreaking and exciting. Reality set in when the *Miami Herald* sought and obtained review in the Supreme Court of the United States. The fact that the Supreme Court of the United States had only recently rejected a First Amendment–based right of access to the media in the *CBS* case was disturbing. But, as has been noted, we thought the Florida right-of-reply situation was entirely different. However, there were other troubling developments as well. In the midst of his Watergate troubles, President Nixon's popularity was in rapid decline. He saw the press as the source of many of his problems. Therefore, practically on the eve of the oral argument in the Supreme Court in the *Miami Herald* case, President Nixon declared that he favored the enactment of a federal right-of-reply law. Senator McClellan of Arkansas, known for his law-and-order views, spoke on the floor of the Senate in favor of the enactment of such a law. With such friends, one did not need enemies. From my point of view, such support from those who were not generally identified with the cause of civil liberties or freedom of expression was not

---

[27]*Id.* at 89.

helpful. Furthermore, I thought it far more likely that a right-of-reply law would be upheld if it were seen simply as an experiment by a single state rather than a right that was now going to exist throughout the country.

On June 25, 1974, the Supreme Court decided the case of *Miami Herald Publishing Co. v. Tornillo*.[28] The Court was unanimous in holding that the Florida right-of-reply law violated the First Amendment. Yet, on examination, the opinion was surprisingly ambivalent. I have described the decision in the past as having two ends but no middle.[29] The first part of Chief Justice Burger's opinion for the Court restated with remarkable fidelity the arguments in favor a right of access to the media that we had made at the oral argument and in our briefs. The alarming pattern of concentration of ownership in the media, the near universality of one-newspaper cities, and the ability, therefore, of a few owners to shut out voices that displeased them was impartially set forth. Indeed, the Chief Justice summarized, "this trend toward concentration of control of outlets to inform the public" in substantial detail and in a manner which left no doubt that the Court was deeply concerned with the size and scope of the problem.[30]

Yet nothing in the opinion was offered to counter our arguments that the problems presented were serious and increasing. On the contrary, the Court's account of the situation indicated that diversity of expression might indeed be in jeopardy. The Court stressed the pattern of elimination of competing newspapers in most American cities and the general and ever-increasing pattern of concentration of ownership of the nation's media outlets. The consequence of all this was not left in doubt: "The result of these vast changes has been to place in a few hands the power to inform the American people and shape public opinion."[31] Yet the Court came down entirely on the side of the protection of editorial autonomy despite the consequences to diversity of expression.

After completing the portion of his opinion dealing with the arguments of access to the media, the chief justice addressed himself to resolving the issues in the case. If a right of access to the press were to be enforced by government, coercion would be necessary and that would run counter to the First Amendment. Chief Justice Burger turned to a theme that he had discussed in his opinion in *CBS* the year before. This was the absolute nature of the editorial autonomy enjoyed by the newspaper press: "The power of a privately owned newspaper to advance its own political, social and economic views is bounded only by two factors: first, the acceptance of a sufficient number of readers—and hence advertisers—to assure financial success; and, second, the journalistic integrity

---

[28]418 U.S 241 (1974).
[29]JEROME A. BARRON, PUBLIC RIGHTS AND THE PRIVATE PRESS 3 (1981).
[30]Miami Herald Publishing Co. v. Tornillo, 418 U.S. 241, 249–50 (1974).
[31]*Id.* at 255.

of its publishers."[32] When I read this paean to editorial autonomy, I recalled that in oral argument in the *Miami Herald* case I had asserted that the great newspaper chains that often owned the only daily newspaper in many American cities should not be allowed to treat that newspaper as a private plantation. This was particularly so, I argued, when the plantation was treated as private property open only to those whom the owner chose to admit. Justice Rehnquist interjected at that point and asked, "Is that such a naive idea?" I was later to learn, to my regret, that it was not a naive idea; in fact, it was going to be the law of the land.

Continuing on with this theme of the primacy of editorial autonomy, the Court declared that editors and publishers could not be compelled to publish that which reason told them not to publish. Given the monopoly status that the daily newspaper in many cities enjoyed then, and enjoys now, the question arises: Is this a fair result? Chief Justice Burger had a ready response: "A responsible press is an undoubtedly desirable goal, but press responsibility is not mandated by the Constitution and like many other virtues it cannot be legislated."[33]

In addition to the theme of editorial autonomy as the primary First Amendment value at stake in the access issue, the Court sounded another theme as well. This was the idea that compulsory replies exacted a penalty from the press in terms of the costs associated with affording space to compulsory replies when the press would have otherwise chosen to print something else in its place. Faced with this penalty, a paper might decide not to enter a particular controversy at all. In other words, if the press had to give both sides of an issue, the press might choose to give none. In retrospect, it seems strange that so childish a stance should have been accorded First Amendment protection. But so it was.

In sum, the heart of the *Miami Herald* decision was the idea that the choice of what was to constitute the content of a newspaper belonged to the editor—whether that choice was fair or unfair. It had not been shown how government regulation of the editorial process could be accomplished in a manner consistent with the First Amendment.

MIAMI HERALD AND ITS IMPACT ON THE PRESS

One of the real puzzles posed by the decision was, what happened to Justice Brennan? Only the previous year in the *CBS* case, Justice Brennan had written a dissent joined in by three other justices that asserted that the First Amendment itself provided an enforceable right of access. Why had he changed his mind? I could only guess. I think that the fact that the case was

---

[32]Columbia Broadcasting System, Inc. v. Democratic National Committee, 412 U.S. 94, 117 (1973).
[33]Miami Herald Publishing Co. v. Tornillo, 418 U.S. 241, 256 (1974).

being considered at a time when the Watergate case was front-page news throughout the nation had a good deal to do with it. The press had proved itself to be an essential monitor for government. An untrammeled press had not been afraid to expose wrongdoing at the highest levels of government. Perhaps, it was best not to impose any responsibilities on the press.

Yet despite the result in the *Miami Herald* case, the decision has had an impact on the print media that has served the values associated with a right of reply. For example, it became good newspaper practice to check with the subject of a story or an editorial before publication. Along the same lines, some of the leading newspapers in the country like the *Washington Post* created the position of press ombudsman so that those who had problems with newspaper fairness or coverage would have someone on the staff of the paper to whom they could turn with their complaints. Often the press ombudsman would discuss in the newspaper the nature of some of those complaints and the manner in which they had been resolved. Finally, in the aftermath of the *Miami Herald* case, some newspapers instituted the op-ed page. This was a page opposite to the editorial page where a spectrum of views—not necessarily those of the editorial page—could be presented. All these developments helped to compensate—but only partially—for the lack of legal remedies such as rights of access and reply.[34]

In addition, it should be noted that the *Miami Herald* case did not terminate all mandatory obligations of the newspaper press. Many states have enacted right-of-retraction laws. These retraction laws usually provide that if the newspaper will retract a particular statement, the retraction will mitigate the assessment of punitive damages. Justice Brennan wrote a short concurring opinion in the *Miami Herald* case to the effect that nothing in the Court's opinion should be read to suggest the invalidity under the First Amendment of retraction statutes. Of course, there is a big difference between retraction statutes and right-of-reply statutes. In a right of reply, the person attacked writes the reply. In the case of a retraction statute, the newspaper writes the retraction. In that sense, retraction still leaves editorial control with the newspaper.

MIAMI HERALD AND ITS IMPACT ON THE BROADCAST MEDIA

A surprising feature of the *Miami Herald* decision was that it did not even mention the *Red Lion* case. The silence about *Red Lion* was not due to the fact that the Court had forgotten about it. One media amicus brief after another asked the Court to strike down the Florida right-of-reply law and reverse *Red Lion*. Instead, the Court struck down the right of reply and ignored *Red*

---

[34]*See* Jerome A. Barron, *Rights of Access and Reply to the Media in the United States Today*, 25 COMMUNICATIONS AND THE LAW 1, 6 (2003).

Lion. The result was that First Amendment law was left, as it remains, in a somewhat schizophrenic state. The print media were basically freed from any obligation to provide access or reply whereas the broadcast media are still subject to some access obligations.

The *Miami Herald* decision was not the end of a right of access to the media. A limited right of access still survives in the broadcast media. Seven years after *Miami Herald,* the Supreme Court of the United States upheld Sec. 312 (a) (7) of the Federal Communications Act that provides that federal political candidates have a right of "reasonable access" to broadcasting.[35] The law was enacted to make sure that federal political candidates could not be completely denied access to television; they were given a right to buy time on broadcasting. The law was challenged on both statutory and First Amendment grounds.

The case arose out of President Carter's reelection campaign. In December 1979, his campaign committee sought to buy time from the major television networks for a 30-minute program where he could discuss the policies that he believed in. The networks took the position that they had a general policy of refusing to sell such blocks of time at so early a point because the election was not going to be held until November of the following year. The Supreme Court upheld the law.[36] Where candidates requested time under the "reasonable access" provision, such requests had to be given *individual* consideration. A blanket policy applicable to all federal candidates seeking to buy time was in violation of the statute. The networks insisted that under the *Miami Herald* case the "reasonable access" provision was in violation of the First Amendment because it impaired their editorial freedom. The First Amendment argument of the networks was also rejected. The *Miami Herald* case had involved a *general* right of reply. The *Miami Herald* case involved only a *limited* right of reply. The "reasonable access" provisions did not violate the First Amendment; it implemented the First Amendment. The Court repeated with approval the statement in *Red Lion* that "it is the right of the viewers and listeners, not the right of the broadcasters, which is paramount."[37] The "reasonable access" provision enhanced freedom of expression because it afforded federal political candidates with the right to present their views to the public thereby giving the citizenry the information it needs to make informed political choices.

Although I was delighted with the result in the "reasonable access" case, I found it hard to see why the Florida right-of-reply law was seen as a general right of access whereas the "reasonable access" provision was seen as a limited right-of-access law. Both situations involved political candidates only,

---

[35]47 U.S.C. Sec. 312 (a) (7).
[36]CBS, Inc. v. F.C.C., 453 U.S. 367 (1981).
[37]Red Lion Broadcasting Co. v. F.C.C., 395 U.S. 367, 390 (1969).

not the public at large. More persuasive was the Court's conclusion that the "statutory right of access" embodied in the "reasonable access" provision properly balanced "the First Amendment rights of federal candidates, the public and broadcasters."[38]

As we have just seen, in broadcasting some limited rights of access survive but only for a limited class of persons—political candidates.[39] But the unfortunate truth is that the public enjoys much less in the way of access rights to the broadcast media than was the case when the Supreme Court decided the *Red Lion* case 35 years ago.

CABLE TELEVISION AND PUBLIC ACCESS TO THE MEDIA

Cable television is the medium where public access flourishes today. In 1984 Congress enacted the Cable Communications Policy Act of 1984. A provision of that law provides that local franchising authorities may require the operator of a cable system, as a condition of the franchise, to reserve a certain number of channels for public access, educational, and governmental purposes.[40] These channels are often called PEG channels. Franchising authorities throughout the country have availed themselves of this authority. Public access channels are now found on cable systems throughout the nation. Public access channels have come to provide a voice for groups and ideas that might not otherwise secure admission to commercial cable television channels to obtain a channel of their own.

The Supreme Court has taken the function of public access channels very seriously. Originally, cable operators were permitted some limited editorial control over public access channels. But in *Denver Area Educational Telecommunications Consortium, Inc. v. FCC,* the Supreme Court struck down this authority.[41] Public access channels, the Court declared, do not belong to the cable operator. The cable industry argued that cable should be analogized to newspapers and that the *Miami Herald* case ought to be read to give cable operators the same kind of dominion over public access channels that newspapers had over what they chose to publish. This industry argument did not prevail. In his separate opinion in *Denver Area,* Justice Kennedy explained why: "In providing access channels under their franchise agreements, cable operators ... are not exercising their own First Amendment rights. [Public

---

[38]CBS, Inc. v. F.C.C., 453 U.S. 367, 397 (1981).

[39]In addition to 47 U.S.C .312 (a), which grants federal political candidates a right of "reasonable access," all political candidates for elective office may also use 47 U.S.C Sec. 315, the famous "equal time" rule. Sec. 315 is really an equal-opportunities rule. Thus, if a station sells time to one candidate, it must give or sell equivalent time to her opponent. Sec. 315 gives no specific rights to broadcast time to a candidate. It is only the first sale or grant of time to a candidate that triggers the statute and gives rights to her opponent.

[40]47 U.S.C. Sec. 531.

[41]518 U.S. 727 (1996).

access channels] serve as conduits for the speech of others."[42] Justice Kennedy explained, with implicit approval, how public access channels worked: "The public access channels ... are available at low or no cost to members of the public, often on a first-come, first-served basis. The programmer on one of these channels most often has complete control as well as liability for, the content of its show."[43] The public access channels truly belong to the public and not the cable operator.

THE FUTURE OF ACCESS TO THE MEDIA

At the International Communications Association Meeting in Seoul, Korea, in 2002, I attempted to summarize for an international audience the extent to which members of the public could exercise legal rights of reply or access to the various media in the United States—newspapers, broadcasting, and cable. At that time, I concluded that with respect to newspapers, the public had no rights of reply or access. With respect to broadcasting, they had limited rights. Cable, however, presented a happier picture. I concluded: "Public access channels are a contemporary success story for the cause of public access to the media."[44] In the foregoing discussion of the fortunes of a right of access to the media in the context of the newspaper press, the broadcast media, and cable television, it may be thought that I have overlooked the one new medium that perhaps presents the greatest potential for the future of a right of access to the media. This medium is, of course, the Internet. There is no question that this medium, still in the main unregulated, surely offers the most opportunities for individual access to media. The cyberspace world of blogs, Web sites, chat rooms, and e-mail are wonderful vehicles for that vigorous and robust debate that the First Amendment was designed to assure and protect.

Will the Internet Service Providers (ISPs) eventually be bought up by the giant communications empires whose number grows steadily smaller but whose reach grows steadily larger? For the moment the Internet provides great cause for hope. After all, the very mode of the Internet is access. But we have seen in the past few years media mergers on a scale undreamed of in the past. Rupert Murdoch's News America Corporation has recently acquired Direct TV, one of the two largest satellite broadcast television carriers. Just a few years ago Viacom acquired CBS. By so doing, Viacom-CBS is able to reach nearly 40% of the total television audience in the United States.[45] More recently, in a spectacular move to create yet another

---

[42]*Id.* at 793.

[43]*Id.* at 791.

[44]Barron, *supra* note 34, at 11.

[45]Paul Farhi, *Viacom to Buy CBS, Uniting Multimedia Heavyweights*, WASH. POST, Sept. 8, 1999, at A1, A7.

mega-media giant, Comcast made an unsuccessful bid to take over Disney. One journalist reported that because Comcast provides "high-speed Internet service via cable" to 5.3 million subscribers, some observers worry that "the more ominous consequence of the Comcast deal would be in controlling Internet service."[46] One cannot help but wonder if all these developments do not suggest that ultimately the same few companies which control most of the media in the United States will not end up also controlling the largest and dominant ISPs as well.

In summary, the events chronicled in this chapter describe a battle between two very different views of the First Amendment. One view looks at the First Amendment as granting exclusive protection, as against other First Amendment claimants, only to those who own the media outlet. This was the view taken in *Miami Herald* case. The competing view, the view taken in the *Red Lion* case, looks at the First Amendment as protecting both media rights of free expression and individual rights of free expression. But when the two collide, the party that courts should favor is the party whose cause is most likely to result in the greater access for free expression. Which of these views will ultimately triumph? This is the issue that is critical for the future of freedom of expression in the United States. It is my hope that an inclusive view of the First Amendment that goes beyond ownership rights to the media and that seeks to protect individual rights of expression will in the end prevail.

---

[46]Jonathan Krim, *Media Consolidation Worries Some*, WASH. POST, Feb. 12, 2004, at E1.

Chapter **2**

WHOSE FIRST AMENDMENT?

COHEN V. COWLES MEDIA CO.

Elliot C. Rothenberg[*]

EDITOR'S INTRODUCTION

The U.S. Supreme Court's ruling in Cohen v. Cowles Media Co. *remains enormously important for the limitations it placed on news media conduct. By affirming the principle of general applicability, the Court held that media organizations do not have First Amendment immunity from laws that apply to nonmedia members of the public.*

The Court held that media organizations whose agents promise anonymity to a source must keep their word. In the short term, many interpreted the ruling as a setback for press freedom. It took some degree of decision making regarding what to publish out of the hands of editors. But in the long run, the ruling may have actually enhanced the free flow of information. By requiring media organizations to keep their word, potential sources who seek anonymity may be more willing to come forward, secure in the knowledge that a promise is legally binding.

This is the premise that Elliot C. Rothenberg advocates in chapter 2. Mr. Rothenberg represented Dan Cohen and argued his case at the U.S. Supreme Court in March 1991. The litigation included a kind of inverted dynamic in which the party suing the media invoked First Amendment values to support his case, whereas the media defendants attempted to avoid them. Mr. Rothenberg contends that despite oxymoronic appearances, the defeat for news media organizations was also a victory for the First Amendment.

---

[*]Minneapolis attorney who represented Dan Cohen in *Cohen v. Cowles Media Company*; author, THE TAMING OF THE PRESS (1999).

Cohen v. Cowles Media Co.[1] is arguably the worst defeat media organizations have ever suffered in the United States Supreme Court; it is at the least, says one First Amendment scholar, "the media's most serious loss" in the Rehnquist Court.[2] Even so, it was a victory for the values represented by the First Amendment to ensure the free flow of information. It was a revitalization of the purposes of the First Amendment after almost 30 years of decisions allowing media organizations to use the First Amendment—or more to the point abuse the First Amendment—to infringe the rights of ordinary individuals.

May a First Amendment victory from a media defeat be regarded as anything other than an oxymoron? Yes, when we disabuse ourselves of the propagated notion that the commercial interests of media corporations are somehow synonymous with the interests of freedom embodied by the First Amendment.

Cohen v. Cowles Media Co. raised fundamental questions concerning the purpose of the First Amendment. The First Amendment was designed to protect the press from government censorship and coercion. Its purpose was to ensure the free flow of information to the people.

It is difficult to argue with the proposition that in a free society, newspapers should be shielded from the machinations of politicians. In any confrontation with a state unrestrained by the rule of law, the press would be the underdog.

But does the First Amendment also anoint the media industry—increasingly concentrated into a smaller and smaller number of larger and larger behemoth corporations of a gargantuan scale inconceivable even in the relatively recent past—above the laws governing everyone else by handing them swords to harm ordinary citizens? Should media organizations have a right to inflict injuries upon private persons by breaking contracts, engaging in fraud, and committing torts and even crimes with impunity?

Is it the purpose of the First Amendment to tilt the balance of the rule of law against ordinary people and negate their legal rights against huge corporations representing a special interest? Did the framers of the Constitution intend to allow—in the name of an abstraction like freedom of the press—large businesses to hurt people with impunity?

---

[1] 501 U.S. 663 (1991); 479 N.W.2d 387 (Minn. 1992); 457 N.W.2d 199 (Minn. 1990); 445 N.W.2d 248 (Minn. App. 1989); 15 MED. L. RPTR. 2288 (Minn. Dist. Ct. 1988); 14 MED. L. RPTR. 1460 (Minn. Dist. Ct. 1987). For a book-length history of this case, *see* ELLIOT C. ROTHENBERG, THE TAMING OF THE PRESS: *COHEN V. COWLES MEDIA CO.* (1999). The author's papers for *Cohen v. Cowles Media Co.* and THE TAMING OF THE PRESS comprise a special collection in the Harvard Law School Library, Cambridge, MA 02138. A study guide to the collection is available on the Internet at http://findingaids.harvard.edu/html/law00128frames.html. *See also* JOSEPH RUSSOMANNO, SPEAKING OUR MINDS (2002), ch. six, for Prof. Russomanno's interviews of participants in the case.

[2] Burt Neuborne, *Free Expression and the Rehnquist Court*, COMMUNICATION LAW 1998, vol. one (1998) at 1273, 1297.

Is it the purpose of the First Amendment to maximize the unfettered flow of information to the public, or to aggrandize the power of media conglomerates ungoverned by an overriding principle of serving the public interest? Does the First Amendment bestow power without responsibility for the harm caused in its name?

The ultimate question is, to whom does the First Amendment belong?

These questions were at the heart of the long litigation of *Cohen v. Cowles Media Co.* where the plaintiff suing two newspapers and not the media defendants served as the true guardian of the values of the First Amendment.

Cohen v. Cowles Media Co. was the culmination of a series of cases beginning with *New York Times v. Sullivan* in 1964 and continuing to 1988, the eve of the *Cohen* trial, in which media organizations claimed special First Amendment privileges not against the government, but over private individuals to harm people by defamation,[3] invasion of privacy,[4] and infliction of emotional distress.[5] In the *Cohen* case, they were claiming a right to deliberately break agreements for confidentiality, which they voluntarily and even enthusiastically entered into to obtain news to be published. The decisions to break promises occurred after the organizations had received their desired information and had made use of the benefits from the other party's full performance of his part of the bargain.

The very assertion of a First Amendment right to betray confidential sources was astonishing to begin with and became ever more self-destructive as the media parties—joined by many of the nation's largest and most prominent media organizations—pushed the case further and further up the judicial ladder.

For the media industry, at least before the transactions triggering the *Cohen* litigation, it had been axiomatic that promises of confidentiality to sources of information were sacrosanct. The preservation of freedom of the press and the public interest in assuring the maximum flow of information, so their argument went, required that government—in the form of prosecutors or legislators or judges—be prohibited from ordering media organizations to reveal the names of persons promised confidentiality.

The media have long insisted that the Constitution itself in the form of the First Amendment barred anyone in government from ordering them to disclose the names of those to whom they promised anonymity. They pressed the argument of a First Amendment journalistic privilege before the U.S. Supreme Court and lower courts.

Study after academic study supported the media's position by documenting the overwhelming percentage of news stories based on information from

---

[3]New York Times v. Sullivan, 376 U.S. 254 (1964).
[4]Time, Inc. v. Hill, 385 U.S. 374 (1967).
[5]Hustler Magazine, Inc. v. Falwell, 485 U.S. 46 (1988).

sources promised confidentiality.[6] They showed that the media must make and honor these promises or deprive themselves and the public of much of the information they obtain.

The media argument that they had a First Amendment right to honor what they regarded as solemn promises had considerable appeal on the basis of ethical principle alone. Moreover, it makes sense as a practical matter. Many media sources demand promises of confidentiality in exchange for information because they fear loss of their jobs or worse, and reprisals and retaliation from vindictive politicians to boot, should the media identify them. These sources would rely upon agreements of confidentiality only if they were assured that no one in the media organization would break or could be forced to break them. According to the argument, news sources would "dry up" unless the media could preserve confidentiality.

Integrity in keeping one's word and practical prudence, then, both required that no one on the outside be allowed to interfere with the media's confidentiality agreements. That was the argument media parties like the *New York Times* made to the U.S. Supreme Court in the 1972 case of *Branzburg v. Hayes*.[7]

In his oral argument before the Supreme Court, Branzburg's attorney urged that the First Amendment forbade any court from compelling journalists to disclose confidential sources. The failure to recognize such a right "would result in self-censorship, prior restraint, the drying up of sources of information, and would result in a total loss to the general public of the kinds and scope and extent of information which the First Amendment was designed to achieve." Disclosing sources, he said, "will destroy the ability to obtain information."[8]

The *Branzburg* case was the basis of media claims of a First Amendment privilege against state interference with their confidential sources. That interpretation of the case was tenuous at best. The actual decision did not recognize any such First Amendment right. Instead, it held that journalists have no special immunity from general laws and are under the same obligations as everyone else to testify before grand juries. However, media organizations claimed that by adding the votes of four dissenting justices and an ambivalent concurring opinion, the Supreme Court did support such a right notwithstanding what the decision itself said. Rather inconveniently, though, a later Supreme Court decision not involving journalists reaf-

---

[6]*See, e.g.*, ELIE ABEL, LEAKING: WHO DOES IT? WHO BENEFITS? AT WHAT COST? (1987); RICHARD M. CLURMAN, BEYOND MALICE: THE MEDIA'S YEARS OF RECKONING 158 (1988); John E. Osborn, *The Reporter's Confidentiality Privilege: Updating the Empirical Evidence After a Decade of Subpoenas*, 17 COLUM. HUM. RTS. L. REV. 57 (1985); *Note, Promises and the Press: First Amendment Limitations on News Source Recovery for Breach of a Confidentiality Agreement*, 73 MINN. L. REV. 1553 (1989).
[7]Branzburg v. Hayes, 408 U.S. 665 (1972).
[8]PETER IRONS, ed., MAY IT PLEASE THE COURT: THE FIRST AMENDMENT 56–57 (1997).

firmed unanimously the *Branzburg* majority's denial of a First Amendment privilege to refuse to comply with a subpoena.[9]

Using their inventive arithmetic and the ambiguity of the concurring opinion, media organizations and lawyers since *Branzburg* have asserted a First Amendment journalistic privilege barring courts and legislatures from ordering the disclosure of confidential sources. Several courts agreed.[10]

In addition, media organizations, professing a need to preserve the free flow of information, aggressively lobbied state legislatures for so-called shield laws barring courts or anyone in government from ordering journalists to disclose confidential sources. For example, Minnesota's largest newspapers drafted and pushed through the Minnesota state legislature in 1973 what they titled the "Free Flow of Information Act." The law begins, "In order to protect the public interest and the free flow of information, the news media should have the benefit of a substantial privilege not to reveal sources of information or to disclose unpublished information. To this end, the freedom of press requires protection of the confidential relationship between the news gatherer and the source of information."[11]

On the basis of all this, one would have thought that the sanctity of the promise of confidentiality was the gold standard of American journalism. One would have been wrong.

In the waning days of the 1982 political campaign in Minnesota, Dan Cohen, a worker for the Republican gubernatorial candidate, gave reporters from four media organizations copies of public court records showing that the Democratic candidate for lieutenant governor had been previously convicted of an unspecified crime of petit theft. The candidate, Marlene Johnson, had been endorsed by the *Star Tribune* of Minneapolis and was a personal friend of the executive editor of the *St. Paul Pioneer Press*. Mr. Cohen first demanded and received with alacrity promises of confidentiality from each of the reporters.

Two of the news organizations—the Associated Press and the Minneapolis television affiliate of CBS—honored their agreements. However, over the vehement protests of their reporters, editors of the *Star Tribune* and the *St. Paul Pioneer Press* deliberately broke their newspapers' promises and identified Mr. Cohen in their newspapers the next day.

After the *Star Tribune* decided to break its reporter's promise, it instructed the reporter to try to persuade Mr. Cohen to release the newspaper from what it called "their agreement." Mr. Cohen refused, but the editors did not change their decision.

---

[9]University of Pennsylvania v. EEOC, 493 U.S. 182 (1990).
[10]For an analysis of these decisions, *see* McKevitt v. Pallasch, 339 F.3d 530 (7th Cir. 2003).
[11]Minnesota Statutes sec. 595.022.

In a long, front-page article, the *Star Tribune* published a photo of Mr. Cohen and identified not only him but gratuitously named his employer as well. The newspapers portrayed Ms. Johnson sympathetically and quoted uncritically her excuse that her conviction was "only" for shoplifting. Mr. Cohen's employer fired him the same day the newspapers printed his name.

The *Star Tribune* did not let the matter rest and, in what could be described as a journalistic jihad, it followed the first disclosures with daily condemnations of Mr. Cohen for giving it public records that embarrassed a favored politician. Some of the most scathing attacks came from an influential columnist who, it was revealed only much later, was at the same time secretly writing speeches for the Democratic candidate for governor. The *Star Tribune* also published an editorial-page cartoon depicting a squat and sinister Mr. Cohen as a garbage can with slanted, beady eyes peering through two slits. After Mr. Cohen had found another job, another columnist ridiculed the second employer for hiring him. Mr. Cohen quickly lost that position, too. In three weeks, with incessant attacks continuing even after its candidate was elected, the *Star Tribune* had single-handedly gotten Mr. Cohen fired from two different jobs.

The newspapers purported devotion to the truth in publicizing their confidential source's identity was, shall we say, selective. Only after the election and weeks after entering into their agreements with Mr. Cohen—and only after all their condemnations and all the harm they had inflicted upon him—did the newspapers disclose to their readers that they had made and broken promises of confidentiality in exchange for the information they had eagerly published.

Mr. Cohen sued the newspapers for breach of contract for violating their promises to him. Right from the outset of the case, the media parties switched roles with the plaintiff suing them. The two newspapers cavalierly jettisoned the media-trumpeted doctrine of protecting promises of confidentiality at all costs. They would have had the jurors and judge believe that promises of confidentiality were a matter of little or no importance, that they used them only sparingly, and even that they discouraged their reporters from offering them. The opposing party was left to present the case of First Amendment values—usually made by media organizations wanting to prevent court-ordered disclosure of their sources—about how crucial journalistic integrity in dealing with confidential sources has been in ensuring the free flow of information to the public.

The newspapers attempted to have the trial judge, Hennepin County (Minnesota) District Judge Franklin J. Knoll, dismiss the case on First Amendment grounds that they had the right to publish the truth regardless of any agreements with a source. They went even further, appointing themselves as moral censors of the legal rights of their sources. They accused Mr. Cohen of "secreting his role in the spoliation" of their political candidate, even though they themselves had agreed to the "secreting." Their brief insisted that they not only had a right to, but were "*obligated* to print Cohen's name. The chilling effect and self-censorship that would result if the publishers could not make an editorial decision about publishing the name of a confidential source would be intolerable. Self-censorship is an evil that must be eradicated." The newspapers were announcing to everyone that their promises of confidentiality were worthless; they would take advantage of the information provided but would honor their part of the bargain only if they saw a bigger advantage for themselves to keeping rather than breaking their agreements.

Judge Knoll denied the newspapers' motion and ordered a trial of the case for July 1988.

The newspapers' trial strategy was to put Mr. Cohen, rather than themselves, on trial. Their editors and attorneys tried to excuse the dishonoring of the agreements with their source and his subsequent savaging as supposedly deserved punishment for what they charged were the source's, in their adnauseum-repeated canard, "dirty tricks."

As Mr. Cohen's attorney, my plan in contrast was to put the promises made to him in the context of how journalists gather information, demonstrating the omnipresence in the media industry of promises of confidentiality in the pursuit of information. Promises of confidentiality indeed are a major currency of the business of journalism. They are common commercial transactions by which media organizations obtain news material to supply the public for the organizations' financial benefit.

This would show the jury and judge—and ultimately the appellate courts—how seriously the newspapers' conduct departed not only from the law, but also from their own profession's ethics and business practices.

For that purpose, I collected 462 articles from the *Star Tribune* and *Pioneer Press* together with other newspapers that used confidential sources, mainly in connection with political campaigns and controversies. In particular, these articles publicized revelations from confidential sources of crimes and other transgressions by politicians. Included as well were numerous *Star Tribune* and *Pioneer Press* articles about shoplifting—perpetrated by people ranging from the obscure to prominent personalities like politicians and beauty queens—and editorials demanding that the names of shoplifters be publicized regardless of the amounts involved and regardless of the personal humiliation for those caught committing the crime.

Never before had the newspapers deliberately broken a confidentiality agreement with a source because of character assassination allegations of "dirty tricks" or for any other reason.

These articles were the heart of the case. The articles—and the examination and cross-examination of *Star Tribune* and *Pioneer Press* editors based on what they had previously published—would constitute the most damning evidence against the newspapers.

This was the first time that a party opposing the media had made such an extensive use of what the newspaper defendant itself had published. The newspapers did not welcome the strategy. Every effort to introduce one of these articles provoked a mini-war in court as their attorneys sought to suppress their clients' published writings.

Some of the most telling testimony of the newspapers concerning the nature of today's media came, however, without the need for such cross-examination. The newspapers' own expert witness helpfully testified on direct examination that the owner of the *Pioneer Press*, Knight Ridder, "is a very big communications company with annual revenues somewhere in the territory of 2.2 billion dollars."

As an expert witness for Mr. Cohen, then-University of Oregon School of Journalism Dean Arnold Ismach testified that exposing the names of confidential sources would cut off the free flow of information needed by the public:

> If sources who provide information on the basis of anonymity found that they could not trust those agreements, journalists feel that those sources would dry up. The journalist lives on reliability, on credibility, and keeping an agreement speaks to the credibility, reliability, and responsibility of the journalist. When you make a deal, you make a deal. It is a universal ethic that reporters and editors believe that there is no circumstance under which you violate the agreement.

Regarding the newspapers' breaking of their promises to Mr. Cohen after publishing for profit the information he supplied them, Dean Ismach commented pithily, "You can't eat off a source's plate and then later say you don't like the food."

On the final day of testimony, I cross-examined the vice president and former executive editor of the *Pioneer Press*, using editorial columns he had written before the *Cohen* case arose. They summed up the issues of the case. One editorial criticized a fictional reporter named Megan Carter "who has no ethics. She is not concerned about accuracy or fairness or integrity. She uses dirty tricks—carries a concealed tape recorder; she violates confidential sources; she allows herself to be used by a politician to attack an innocent man. I would not hire her."

Another entitled "The Judge Ignored the Law" criticized a judge for raising "serious First Amendment issues" by ordering a reporter to disclose his confidential sources. Shield laws allowing a reporter to protect confidential sources, the editor wrote, "are especially important in the field of investigative reporting where sources may fear for their lives, their jobs or the safety of their families if their identities were revealed, particularly in highly sensitive cases. It is clear that unless there is some protection of the right to gather news and protect sources, the quality and flow of news will be seriously impaired."

A third column censured another judge for jailing a reporter for his refusal to turn over notes relating to a Watergate witness:

> The judge dismissed the First Amendment argument and made it clear that he didn't believe that forcing newsmen to reveal sources or produce notes and tapes would hamper their ability to gather news. HIS POSITION IS RIDICULOUS. Of course, the inability of newsmen to protect their confidential sources and unpublished information will affect newsgathering operations. Sources will tend to disappear. Our democracy depends upon maintaining the free flow of information to the public. (emphasis in the original)

In the closing arguments to the jury, the issue of the case came down to whether the newspapers should be bound by their obligations under the law of contracts or whether they should have the right to punish Mr. Cohen regardless of their promises to him because of what their lead attorney thundered was a "terrible act of infamy."

I told the jurors:

> The real issue is this: Are the rules of morality, contract, honoring one's word, the ethics of persons, a man or woman's word being his or her bond, the legal rules of keeping one's agreements, rules which all of us as individuals want to live by and are required to live by—are those rules also going to bind the huge corporate entities representing the newspapers that are involved in this suit?

> These are the two largest newspapers in the state of Minnesota. They're part of publishing empires. To suggest that a person like Mr. Cohen, self-employed, barely able to survive these days, is on anywhere near an equal basis with these newspapers, in the real world, is almost laughable. But they are equal before you today. The lowliest individual has rights before you equal to the rights of the largest corporations.

> If you allow the newspapers to get away with breaking their promises to Mr. Cohen on the basis of the scurrilous personal assaults which have been leveled at him throughout this trial, all other promises made to you or any other individual will be at risk.

> And it doesn't apply only to newspapers. It applies to all large corporations able to afford the enormous cost of lawsuits.

> If they are able to evade their obligations by attacking the character of the individual who is suing them, all contracts will be at risk.

> If you find for the newspapers, you would encourage others more powerful to avoid their obligations under promises by doing what they've done here—to evade the law and concentrate on attacking the plaintiff.

> We ask you to enforce the basic morality which governs all of us, of keeping one's word as your bond. That is the basis of the law; that's the basis of journalistic ethics.

The six-person jury, by a vote of five to one, gave its verdict for Mr. Cohen. It found that the newspapers had breached contracts with him and awarded compensatory damages of $200,000. It also found that the newspapers had committed the tort of misrepresentation and awarded another $500,000 in punitive damages.

The newspapers appealed to the Minnesota Court of Appeals arguing, among other things, a violation of their First Amendment rights to publish what it called the truth. The Court of Appeals panel, by a vote of two to one, upheld the verdict for breach of contract and rejected the newspapers' First Amendment claims. However, it reversed the finding of misrepresentation and therefore the award of punitive damages, which in Minnesota a jury may not award for breach of contract alone.

Both sides appealed to the Minnesota Supreme Court.

Up until this time, all the judges and all the parties had agreed that the fundamental issue was whether rights claimed under the First Amendment took precedence over an individual's rights under the law of contracts. The newspapers had argued that they had a First Amendment right to publish what they called the truth, regardless of any promises of confidentiality. This position, of course, disdained the long-standing media claim of a First Amendment journalistic privilege to honor these promises. Despite the hypocrisy, at least the argument recognized the primacy of the First Amendment.

The abandonment of principle, however, became absolute in the appeal to the Minnesota Supreme Court when the newspapers made an about face on the role of the First Amendment in the case.

On the day of the oral argument there, the influential *National Law Journal* published an article by a *Wall Street Journal* attorney urging the court to rule in favor of the newspapers simply on the basis of the state's law of contracts.[12] The article pressed the astonishing claim—contrary to the holdings of two courts, the verdict of the jury, the voluminous evidence at the trial and all previous journalistic arguments in legal cases and academic writing—that neither journalists nor sources nor courts nor anyone else took promises of confidentiality seriously as binding agreements. They were akin, said the article, to promises to marry, the entire category of which he apparently regarded as frivolous and not as legal contracts. Court "intermeddling" with media promises of confidentiality "would damage the delicate fabric of reporter–source relationships."

The article concluded that the press should be, in its words, "apart from the law."

The thinly veiled motive of this gambit was to eliminate any federal constitutional issue and thus thwart any opportunity for U.S. Supreme Court review of a favorable decision from a friendly state court.

---

[12]Richard J. Tofel, *Under Inspection*, NAT'L L. J., Mar. 12, 1990, at 13.

To call such an anticipated "victory" pyrrhic and shortsighted would be an understatement. Who would trust media promises of confidentiality in exchange for information in the future? Not anyone in his or her right mind who feared reprisals for disclosing facts that those in political or private power did not want revealed.

If confidentiality agreements would be so trivialized, could the *Wall Street Journal* and other newspapers turn around and claim a First Amendment privilege the next time they wanted to bar interference with their confidential information? It was an issue that would come back to haunt them.

The Minnesota chief justice, a former lobbyist for the *St. Paul Pioneer Press*, had recused himself from the case on my request. That turned out to be critical.

Four of the six justices on the state supreme court agreed that promises of confidentiality were not enforceable under the state law of contracts. The strategy, however, was too clever.

Three of the four majority judges wanted no reference at all to the First Amendment to avoid any possibility of review by the U.S. Supreme Court. To one justice supporting the newspapers, however, the court could not so insouciantly eliminate the First Amendment from the case in which for several years in the trial court and Minnesota Court of Appeals the newspapers themselves had made it the principal issue.

In July 1990, after several months of internal debate, the state supreme court by a four-to-two vote issued its decision. It held that on the basis of state law alone, the newspapers had not entered into a contract with Mr. Cohen. The decision then made a murky reference to the First Amendment in a discussion as to whether promises of confidentiality formed an implied contract under a branch of contract law called promissory estoppel. The decision refused to enforce the agreement as an implied contract either, but at least the First Amendment still was in the case, if only by a thread.

The newspapers together with all the "experts" pronounced the case over and pontificated that a petition for certiorari filed on behalf of Mr. Cohen would have no chance whatsoever at the U.S. Supreme Court. They spoke too soon.

My petition to the U.S. Supreme Court argued that the First Amendment still was vital to the case and stressed that the central question was whether the media have an obligation to obey laws that bind all others. The case has "implications beyond the violation of agreements. If it is impermissible to hold the press liable for violating voluntary promises to obtain information, is it also to be granted a right to commit torts or even crimes in gathering news?"

The importance of promises of confidentiality in acquiring information for the public also made Supreme Court review imperative. "Legalizing the violation of promises of confidentiality would deter other potential sources," I submitted, "resulting in the denial of important information to the public."

Confidential sources have been ubiquitous in news stories, continued the petition. One study reported that 80% of newsmagazine articles and 50% of wire service stories rely on confidential sources.[13] Another showed that two thirds of stories nominated for Pulitzer Prizes used confidential sources.[14] Still another revealed that on a typical day the *Washington Post* and *New York Times* attribute information to confidential sources more than 100 times.[15] The individual champion of anonymity was a *Wall Street Journal* story that in a few column inches attributed information to confidential sources 42 times.[16]

The petition's emphasis on the importance of promises of confidentiality to providing news to the public was, of course, the mirror image of the argument media organizations usually make when they do not want to disclose their sources.

In opposing certiorari, the newspapers argued that the First Amendment, which they had made all important to the litigation before the trial judge and the first appellate court, now had nothing to do with the case; they pronounced the petition's "entire discussion" of the First Amendment "an exercise in obfuscation."

It was the longest of long shots. The Supreme Court accepts for review only 1% of petitions. The odds favoring review of *Cohen v. Cowles Media Co.* were considerably more infinitesimal because of the question of whether any constitutional issue remained from the Minnesota decision.

Confounding all the predictions, the Supreme Court granted review in December 1990.

My Supreme Court brief on the merits argued that the First Amendment does not give the press immunity from laws everyone else must obey. The brief quoted from *Branzburg v. Hayes*, which held that a publisher "has no special immunity from the application of general laws. He has no special privilege to invade the rights and liberties of others."[17]

Both the *Branzburg* majority and dissents supported plaintiff's case. The dissenters agreed with the *New York Times* and others that the First Amendment required protection of promises of confidentiality to ensure the free flow of information. A First Amendment right to preserve confidentiality, they said, derives from "the broad societal interest in a full and free flow of information to the public. A corollary of the right to publish must be the

[13]Note, *Promises and the Press: First Amendment Limitations on News Source Recovery for Breach of a Confidentiality Agreement*, 73 MINN. L. REV. 1553, 1563 (1989).

[14]John E. Osborn, *The Reporter's Confidentiality Privilege: Updating the Empirical Evidence After a Decade of Subpoenas*, 17 COLUM. HUM. RTS. L. REV. 57, 73–74 (1985).

[15] RICHARD M. CLURMAN, BEYOND MALICE: THE MEDIA'S YEARS OF RECKONING 158 (1988).
[16]*Id.*
[17]Branzburg v. Hayes, 408 U.S. 665, 683 (1972).

right to gather news.... The right to gather news implies, in turn, a right to a confidential relationship between a reporter and his source. Confidentiality is essential to the creation and maintenance of a news-gathering relationship with informants."[18]

Of particular pertinence to the newspapers' accusations of "dirty tricks" to attempt to excuse breaking their agreements with a source, the dissenters observed, "The First Amendment concern must not be with the motives of any particular news source, but rather with the conditions in which informants of all shades of the spectrum may make information available through the press to the public."[19]

My brief stressed that naming sources despite promises of confidentiality would discourage others from providing information and curtail the flow of news to the public. The *Star Tribune* took precisely that position in a brief filed in a 1978 New Jersey case, *Matter of Farber*,[20] in which it opposed court-ordered disclosure of confidential sources. According to the newspaper in that case, "Much information would never be forthcoming to the news media unless the persons who were the sources of such information could be entirely certain that their identities would remain secret."[21] The result, said the *Star Tribune* in that case, would be "a substantial lessening in the supply of available news on a variety of important and sensitive issues, all to the detriment of the public interest."[22]

The newspapers' briefs insisted once again that there were no First Amendment issues in the case and that the Supreme Court should rescind its grant of the petition for certiorari. Even if the First Amendment were a part of the case, they argued, they had the right to treat their sources like Mr. Cohen in any way they chose when they published the truth.

Supporting the newspapers at the Supreme Court was an amicus brief representing the major leagues of American media: Advance Publications, the Newhouse Publishing conglomerate; the American Newspaper Publishers Association; the American Society of Newspaper Editors; the Associated Press; Copley Press; Gannett Company, which publishes *USA Today* and other newspapers, and operates many television and radio stations; the Newsletter Association; the *New York Times*; and the Times Mirror Company, which publishes the *Los Angeles Times*, the *Baltimore Sun*, and other newspapers. No one entered the case to support the principle of honoring promises of confidentiality.

The newspapers and their allies in the Supreme Court took the explicit position that First Amendment rights belong to them alone and not anyone with whom they deal. Gone were the old appeals to preserve the free flow of information.

---

[18]*Id.* at 727.
[19]*Id.* at 730.
[20]78 N.J. 259, 394 A.2d 330 (1978).
[21]78 N.J. at 265, 394 A.2d. at 333.
[22]*Id.*

Their brief asserted that no court had the authority to compel a newspaper either to honor promises of confidentiality or to disclose the name of a confidential source. "The government is not permitted to intrude into the relationships between reporters and sources in this manner, any more than it should be allowed to interfere with that relationship by attempting to compel reporters to reveal the identities of their confidential sources." Throwing down the gauntlet, the representatives of the nation's most powerful media organs declared that "press responsibility is not mandated by the Constitution."

Alexander Hamilton foresaw this type of press demand for unlimited power—without responsibility for its exercise—when he warned against abuse of a guarantee of freedom of the press:

> Why should it be said, that the liberty of the press shall not be restrained, when no power is given by which restrictions may be imposed? ... It is evident that it would furnish, to men disposed to usurp, a plausible pretense for claiming that power.... What is the liberty of the press? Who can give it any definition which would not leave the utmost latitude for evasion?[23]

The amicus brief derided as "untenable" my point—only a variation of the oft-repeated media argument—that allowing newspapers to unilaterally dishonor promises of confidentiality would discourage sources from giving the press information in the future, and thus dry up the flow of news to the press and to the public. Contrary to the claims they themselves had always made before, the leaders of American media claimed that there was no "evidence whatsoever which even remotely suggests" any such consequences.

My reply brief responded that:

> [This argument] contradicts the position of many of these same organizations in cases where they sought to protect their confidential sources. For example, amicus New York Times Co. as an appellant in *Matter of Farber* argued that if confidential sources were to be exposed through a court order, "newsgathering and the dissemination of news would be seriously impaired, because much information would never be forthcoming to the news media unless the persons who were the sources of such information could be entirely certain that their identities would remain secret!"

Many of the parties to the *Cohen* amicus brief before the Supreme Court also took the exact opposite stance when they joined as amicus parties supporting the *New York Times* in the *Farber* case.

---

[23]THE FEDERALIST no. 84 (1788).

On March 27, 1991 I launched my oral argument before the Supreme Court by stressing again that the plaintiff's position and not that of the newspapers was most consistent with the values of the First Amendment.

> *Cohen v. Cowles Media* presents the question of whether newspapers have the right to inflict injuries by dishonoring voluntary promises used to obtain information. Honoring promises of confidentiality is critical in insuring the free flow of information to the public. An expert witness in the trial testified that at least one-third of all newspaper stories and 85 percent of news-magazine stories come from sources promised confidentiality.

Establishing a right to violate promises of confidentiality would cut off the flow of information to the media and public and thus disserve the interests of the First Amendment.

Media organizations, of course, had made that same sort of argument in every case where someone seeks a court order to compel journalists to identify confidential sources.

The late Justice Thurgood Marshall, usually a strong supporter of the press, in a dramatic exchange with their attorney upbraided the newspapers over their claim of "honest speech" by railing that they "didn't publish the truth" about their promises of confidentiality to Mr. Cohen.

Later oral argument dialogue resuscitated in a novel fashion the subject of the law of contracts. In response to questioning by Justice Antonin Scalia, the newspapers' counsel said that a newspaper would have the right to sue for violation of "important contract rights" over "proprietary information" a reporter who leaked confidential information that the employer did not want disclosed.

Justice Anthony Kennedy did not accept the claim that newspapers should have stronger contractual rights over the control of information than confidential sources. "It's a very odd calculus that the person closest to the truth, in this case the source, cannot protect his ability to divulge or not to divulge, but that as you get further away from the sources of truth, i.e., in the newspaper room, you say, 'Oh, then the newspaper has a right to protect its information by a contract suit.' It seems to me the calculus should be just the other way around."

In the days following the oral argument, at the same time the Supreme Court was deliberating *Cohen v. Cowles Media Co.*, a reporter in Washington, D.C., was resisting a subpoena to disclose a news source in a drug abuse case. The *New York Times* and others—who were taking the position in the Supreme Court that they had a right to identify sources, regardless of any of their promises to the contrary—were arguing in the D.C. Superior Court and Court of Appeals a few blocks away that newspapers have a First Amendment right not to disclose to a court any sources, whether or not they are confidential. Contrary to what they were saying in their Supreme Court brief, they claimed that identification of sources would violate "the important public interest in the free flow of information to the public.... A reporter cannot hope to gather controversial information if sources fear that the reporter will testify about sources despite promises to the contrary."[24]

In the end, the U.S. Supreme Court declared in June 1991 that the *Cohen* case did present important First Amendment issues. It held, by five votes to four, that media organizations had no First Amendment immunity from the consequences of violating laws of general applicability.

The case was remanded to the Minnesota Supreme Court, which then had one last opportunity to rule against Mr. Cohen on Minnesota state law or to order a new trial on the issue of promissory estoppel. In a unanimous vote, it upheld the original award of $200,000 in compensatory damages plus a substantial amount of interest. It effectively made the matter of whether the newspapers violated the law of contracts or the subcategory of promissory estoppel a distinction without a difference.

The consequences of *Cohen v. Cowles Media Co.* have extended far beyond broken promises of confidentiality into the entire subject of what, if any, special privileges the media should enjoy at others' expense.

Cohen v. Cowles Media Co. gave the strongest judicial statement yet that, notwithstanding the First Amendment, the media must obey the same laws as everyone else. In many later cases, federal and state courts have built upon the principle that media organizations pursuing their business are subject to the rule of law. Indeed, the case has spawned a new field of communications law, the law of newsgathering.

Thus, numerous decisions have cited *Cohen v. Cowles Media Co.* as not allowing First Amendment immunity for the media from liability for various forms of tortious and criminal wrongdoing such as fraud in obtaining information;[25] or trespass and breach of an employee's duty of loyalty;[26] or invasion of privacy by spying and intrusion on individuals in the name of newsgathering;[27] or hounding and harassing and ambushing subjects of stories;[28] or violations of copyright;[29] or stealing of trade secrets and intellectual property;[30] or participation in illegal wiretapping and the knowing use of

---

[24]Wheeler v. Goulart, 593 A.2d 173 (D.C. App. 1991); Daniel Klaidman, *Bad Timing for the Washington Post: Protecting Sources Gets Tougher for Reporters*, LEGAL TIMES, April 29, 1991, at 6.

[25]W.D.I.A. Corp. v. McGraw-Hill, Inc., 34 F. Supp.2d 612 (S.D. Ohio 1998), affd. without published opinion, 202 F.3d 271 (6th Cir. 2000).

[26]Food Lion, Inc. v. Capital Cities/ABC, Inc., 194 F.3d 505 (4th Cir.1999), 984 F.Supp. 923 (M.D.N.C. 1997), 951 F. Supp. 1224 (M.D.N.C. 1996), 951 F. Supp. 1211 (M.D.N.C. 1996), 887 F. Supp. 811 (M.D.N.C. 1995).

[27]Shulman v. Group W Productions, Inc., 18 Cal.4th 200, 955 P.2d 469 (1998).

[28]Wolfson v. Lewis, 924 F. Supp.1413 (E.D. Pa. 1996).

[29]Chicago School Reform Board of Trustees v. Substance, Inc., 79 F. Supp.2d 919 (N.D. Ill. 2000).

[30]DVD Copy Control Assn. v. Bunner, 31 Cal.4th 864, 75 P.3d 1 (Moreno, J., concurring) (2003).

wiretapped phone conversations;[31] or trading in child pornography in the name of newsgathering;[32] or being instrumental in causing many wrongful deaths when media people tipped off a lunatic fringe cult leader that federal agents were planning to arrest him;[33] or even intentionally publishing instructions for contract killers on how to commit and get away with murders.[34]

Even the mere threat of litigation based on *Cohen v. Cowles Media Co.* has thwarted wrongful conduct. For example, CBS television squelched an interview because the interviewee's former employer threatened to sue the network for inducing a breach of the employee's contract not to disclose confidential information. Media lawyers feared a court ruling based on *Cohen* that media organizations had no right to violate generally applicable laws against tampering with contracts.[35]

Beyond the matter of respecting confidentiality agreements of other businesses, what about the media's own promises of confidentiality of the type that precipitated the Cohen litigation? Citing *Cohen v. Cowles Media Co.*, federal and state courts have found national media organizations as diverse as *Glamour* magazine, Gannett Co., and the National Broadcasting Co. liable for broken promises to sources under the law of promissory estoppel, breach of contract, and misrepresentation.[36]

At the same time, as if they thought judges and everyone else were oblivious of the media's behavior in the case of *Cohen v. Cowles Media Co.*, media organizations have continued to demand a right to withhold from government, courts, and litigants disclosure of their sources and written materials. Moreover, the scope of the claimed privilege has expanded beyond the most elastic definition of the public interest.

The newspaper players in *Cohen v. Cowles Media Co.* in the years following the decision have rediscovered the religion of the First Amendment, at least when it applies to people they want to protect. In several unctuous editorials, of a sanctimony particularly risible in light of their behavior in *Cohen*, they have insisted upon a constitutional right to protect sources who, unlike

---

[31] Peavy v. WFAA-TV, Inc., 221 F.3d 158 (5th Cir. 2000).

[32] U.S. v. Matthews, 209 F.3d 338 (4th Cir. 2000), 11 F.Supp.2d 656 (D. Md. 1998).

[33] Risenhoover v. England, 936 F. Supp. 392 (W.D. Tex. 1996).

[34] Rice v. Paladin Enterprises, Inc., 128 F.3d 233 (4th Cir. 1997).

[35] P. Cameron Devore, Letter, *In CBS Tobacco Case, Contract Came Before First Amendment*, N.Y. TIMES, Nov. 17, 1995, at A30; David Kohler, *Blame the Laws, Mr. Wallace, not the Lawyers*, WALL ST. J., Nov. 21, 1995, A18; *CBS said to fear unusual legal challenge to report*, N.Y. TIMES, Nov. 17, 1995, at A18; William Bennett Turner, *News Media Liability for "Tortious Interference" With a Source's Nondisclosure Contract*, 14 COMMUNICATIONS LAWYER 13 (Spring 1996); Joseph A. Russomanno and Kyu Ho Youm, *The 60 Minutes Controversy: What Lawyers Are Telling the News Media*, 18 COMMUNICATIONS AND THE LAW 65, 81–83 (September 1996).

[36] Ruzicka v. Conde Nast Publications, 939 F.2d 578 (8th Cir. 1991), 999 F.2d 1319 (8th Cir. 1993); Anderson v. Strong Memorial Hospital, 573 N.Y.S.2d 828 (Sup. 1991); Veilleux v. National Broadcasting Co., 206 F.3d 92 (1st Cir. 2000), 8 F.Supp.2d 23 (D. Me. 1998), Seth Schiesel, *Jury finds NBC negligent in "Dateline" report*, N.Y. TIMES, July 19, 1998, at A19.

Mr. Cohen, have lied about others and have even violated federal criminal law. A *Star Tribune* editorial, for example, criticized a Georgia judge in a libel suit for ordering reporters to disclose sources who had allegedly committed the defamation. Although the newspaper admitted that the reporting in question was "shabby" and had "wronged" the plaintiff there, it charged that compelling disclosure of sources infringes "legitimate First Amendment values" and "undermines a free press." A contemporaneous *Star Tribune* column said that a British journalist who had identified an aide of President Clinton "committed an unpardonable sin. He broke his promise." The miscreant "had broken a cardinal journalistic rule: Never give up a source."[37] In all its 870 words on behalf of what it called the "bedrock principle of journalism that you never give up a source," the *Star Tribune* said nothing about *Cohen v. Cowles Media Co.*

Similarly, editorials in the *New York Times* and *Wall Street Journal* have supported a syndicated columnist's refusal to disclose the names of government officials who in an alleged act of political reprisal violated federal law by disclosing the name of a Central Intelligence Agency (CIA) operative.

The *New York Times* said, "There are important First Amendment issues at play" in preserving the confidentiality of sources. "As members of a profession that relies heavily on the willingness of government officials to defy their bosses and give the public vital information, we oppose 'leak investigations' in principle." The newspaper made no mention of its contrary position in *Cohen v. Cowles Media Co.*[38]

The first *Wall Street Journal* editorial, subtitled "journalists abandon their principles in the Plame affair," pounced on suggestions from some journalists that the columnist voluntarily reveal his lawbreaking sources. "The double media standard here is breathtaking," wrote the *Journal*, "not to mention depressing for those who believe in a free press.... What are we to think of journalists who invoke 'ethics' to disguise what is really a partisan disagreement?"[39] A second *Wall Street Journal* editorial, subtitled "Joe Wilson vs. the First Amendment," was even more apocalyptic about the consequences of disclosing the names of persons promised confidentiality. Journalists who urge such behavior, said the *Journal*, "don't seem to understand the First Amendment implications" and risk provoking a definitive Supreme Court pronouncement that "the First Amendment includes no privilege covering the protection of confidential sources." With all its expressed concern about breathtaking double standards and ethics and partisan disagreements and First Amendment implications of breaking promises, there was no reference to this particular newspaper's advice

[37]Commentary, *Requiring Disclosure of Reporter's Sources Undermines Free Press*, MINNEAPOLIS STAR TRIBUNE, Jun. 8, 1999, at A13; Joel Kaplan, *Never Give Up a Source, Even Blumenthal*, MINNEAPOLIS STAR TRIBUNE, Feb. 22, 1999, at A10.

[38] Editorial, *Investigating leaks*, N.Y. TIMES, Oct. 2, 2003, at A30.

[39]Review and outlook, *The Novak Exception*, WALL ST. J., Feb. 20, 2004, at A14.

to the Minnesota Supreme Court on how to hang a source out to dry without risking an appeal on the free-press clause.[40]

So, the media have been overreaching in both directions with their claims of First Amendment right to honor or dishonor promises of confidentiality at their whim. A backlash was inevitable to the media's demand for absolute power untempered by principle or responsibility. Far from accepting the media's arguments, the shaky edifice of a supposedly absolute journalistic privilege has crumbled in the wake of important recent federal court decisions. By trying to have it both ways, by trying to have it all ways, the media are having it in none.

In 2003, the Seventh Circuit U.S. Court of Appeals decision of *McKevitt v. Pallasch*[41] explicitly rejected media claims of a First Amendment journalistic privilege to withhold materials relevant in a criminal trial. Citing the authority of *Cohen v. Cowles Media Co.*, the court declared, "we do not see why there need to be special criteria merely because the possessor of the documents or other evidence sought is a journalist."[42] There was an exquisite irony in using the rapier of *Cohen* to strike down a dubious claim of journalistic privilege to hide information about a source instead of to reveal it. The court ordered the reporters there to produce materials from interviews that a criminal defendant alleged would aid in his defense. The reporters there were not claiming any promises of confidentiality. On the contrary, the source himself wanted the documents disclosed. Nevertheless, the media parties wanted to keep the materials secret for narrow commercial purposes only; they thought that secrecy now would enhance sales of a book they were writing on the case. Judge Richard Posner observed that journalists who usually appeal to a public interest of encouraging publication rather than secrecy were trying to do the very opposite—to cloak themselves in the robes of the First Amendment to restrict the flow of information for their own private financial gain.

Earlier, in the highly publicized case of *Leggett v. United States*, a federal court in Texas jailed an aspiring freelance writer for refusing to obey an order to provide certain audiotapes and notes to a grand jury investigating a notorious murder-for-hire. The Fifth Circuit U.S. Court of Appeals upheld the order on the basis of *Cohen v. Cowles Media Co.* The U.S. Solicitor General filed a brief opposing Supreme Court review, again citing *Cohen v. Cowles Media Co.* that journalists are subject to the same laws as everyone else regarding the obligation to give relevant evidence in court. The Supreme Court denied Ms. Leggett's petition.[43]

---

[40]*Id*. at A16.

[41]McKevitt v. Pallasch, 339 F.3d 530 (7th Cir. 2003).

[42]*Id*. at 533.

[43]In re Grand Jury Subpoenas, No. 01-20745, 29 Med. L. Rptr. 2301 (5th Cir. 2001); Leggett v. United States, 535 U.S. 1011 (2002); No. 01-983, Brief of the United States in opposition, March 2002.

A more recent federal court decision of 2003, *Lee v. U.S. Dept. of Justice*,[44] rebuked journalists for protecting government officials who allegedly smeared a scientist by leaking confidential employment data in violation of the federal Privacy Act. "The Court has some doubt that a truly worthy First Amendment interest resides in protecting the identity of government personnel who disclose to the press information that the Privacy Act says they may not reveal."[45] Judge Thomas Jackson ordered the journalists to disclose their sources to the plaintiff there. They have refused to comply. The judge ruled them in contempt.[46] The media parties involved were the *New York Times*, *Los Angeles Times*, and Associated Press, all of which supported the breaking of the confidentiality promises to Mr. Cohen.

Contemporaneously in 2004, another U.S. District Court judge in Washington, D.C., Thomas Hogan, held reporters from the *New York Times* and *Time* magazine in contempt for defying a court order to testify regarding their sources to a grand jury investigating the disclosure of the identity of the covert CIA agent discussed above.[47] The reporters face possible jail time. In February 2005, the U.S. Supreme Court of Appeals for the District of Columbia affirmed Judge Hogan's order. This federal appellate court again rejected media parties' claim of a First Amendment privilege to refuse to testify concerning the identity of confidential sources.[48]

New York Times editorials condemned judicial compulsion of its reporter to reveal confidential sources as a "showdown for press freedom" which "threatens grievous harm to freedom of the press."[49] A *Times* columnist avowed that "protecting confidential sources has been a sacred ethical precept in publishing" for almost 350 years.[50]

The two top executives of the *New York Times* wrote, "Without an enforceable promise of confidentiality, sources would quickly dry up and the press would be left largely with only official government pronouncements to report."[51]

Neither they nor any of the other *Times* commentary acknowledged the opposite position the newspaper pushed in *Cohen v. Cowles Media Co.*

---

[44]Lee v. U.S. Dept. of Justice, 287 F. Supp.2d 15 (D.D.C. 2003).
[45]*Id.* at 23.
[46]Lee v. U.S. Dept. of Justice, 327 F.Supp.2d 26 (D.D.C. 2004).
[47]In re Special Counsel Investigation, 332 F.Supp.2d 26 (D.D.C. 2004), 332 F.Supp.2d 33 (D.D.C. 2004), 338 F.Supp.2d 16 (D.D.C. 2004), Adam Liptak, *Reporter for Times, Silent Over Sources, Is Facing Jail Time*, N.Y. TIMES, Oct. 8, 2004, at A1, Michael Janofsky, *Time Reporter Again Held in Contempt in Leak Case*, N.Y. TIMES, Oct. 14, 2004, at A16.
[48] In re Grand Jury Subpoena, Judith Miller, No. 04-3138, D.C. Cir., Feb. 15, 2005.
[49]*Editorial, Press Freedom on the Precipice*, N.Y. TIMES, Oct. 16, 2004, at A30; *Editorial, Showdown for Press Freedom*, N.Y. TIMES, Dec. 5, 2004, at WK12.
[50]Nicholas D. Kristof, *Our Not-So-Free Press*, N.Y. TIMES, Nov. 10, 2004, at A25.
[51]Arthur Ochs Sulzberger, Jr. and Russell T. Lewis, *The Promise of the First Amendment*, N.Y. TIMES, Oct. 10, 2004, at WK11.

Nor have they and others in the media chosen to recognize, at least publicly, that they have placed all of today's journalists at risk by arguing to the Supreme Court in 1991 that the First Amendment, instead of protecting confidentiality as a "sacred ethical precept," only gives the media the absolute right to honor or dishonor promises without being subject to the restraint of any court.

Finally, also in 2004, Rhode Island U.S. District Judge Ernest Torres convicted a Providence television reporter of criminal contempt for violating a court order to identify a confidential source in an investigation of local government corruption. Without specifically citing *Cohen v. Cowles Media Co.*, the judge declared, "The First Amendment does not confer on reporters or anyone else the right to violate the law in order to get information that they might consider newsworthy."[52]

So we have come full circle from *Cohen v. Cowles Media Co.* A case where a unified national media abandoned the principle of honoring agreements for confidentiality to claim a right to deliberately break their promises has now come back to strike down the original principle itself. The media industry has been hoist with its own self-created petard.

The fault or blame does not lie with judges or with juries or with opposing parties but with the media themselves. It was the result not only of their violation of the law and their zealous and continuing support of that violation but of the deliberate flouting by media organizations of the values of the First Amendment, which they professed to hold dear, and the ethics of their own profession. They refused to act in accord with their own standards of integrity. Instead, the media parties in *Cohen* compelled the courts to implement them in the course of enforcing the law. They have paid the price ever since.

---

[52]Pam Belluck, *Reporter Convicted for Refusing to Give Identity of a Source*, N.Y. TIMES, Nov. 19, 2004, at A1; Pam Belluck, *Reporter Who Shielded Source Will Serve Sentence at Home*, N.Y. TIMES, December 10, 2004, at A21; In re Special Proceeding, C.A. No. 01-47, Dec. 9, 2004, Transcript 12. *Id.*, 373 F.3d 37 (1st Cir. 2004).

Chapter 3

FREEDOM OF SPEECH

A CASUALTY OF WAR

Dan Johnston*

EDITOR'S INTRODUCTION

Tinker v. Des Moines Independent Community School District *is a frequently mentioned case within the context of freedom of expression, particularly in the school environment. Is it any wonder? Three adolescents who disputed the right of their school district to suspend them for wearing black armbands, with the case climaxing at the U.S. Supreme Court. As one of the petitioners, Chris Eckhardt, said, "Here's this stupid little thing of just wearing an armband and all of a sudden I'm in front of the United States Supreme Court. Wow! Who thought we'd get here? Who thought a little case from Des Moines over a little piece of cloth would end up here?"*

In this chapter, Dan Johnston, the attorney for the petitioners in Tinker, *provides historical context. He reminds us that his case was largely one of reestablishing existing law. Moreover, it was a case about wartime dissent. Throughout the history of the United States, the same liberties that most people find to be precious during peaceful periods are regularly targets of abuse when the nation is at war. Among those who fall prey to this phenomenon, Mr. Johnston suggests, are judges.*

---

*Dan Johnston was counsel for the *Tinker* petitioners in the District Court, the Court of Appeals, and the U.S. Supreme Court. He has also served a term in the Iowa legislature and for 8 years was the elected county prosecutor in Des Moines. He now practices law in New York City where he has served on the Board of the Gay Men's Health Crisis and the Civilian Complaint Review Board of the Police Department. Portions of this article were contained in a speech delivered at a Drake Law School Center for Constitutional Rights Symposium marking the 30th anniversary of the U.S. Supreme Court decision in *Tinker v. Des Moines Independent Community School District,* and are published at 48 DRAKE L. REV 519 (2000).

This American "tradition" of preferring security to liberty is as old as the republic itself. To attain security, it is sometimes deemed necessary to silence dissent and criticism of government. It began with the Alien and Sedition Acts of 1798. The laws made it a crime to "write, print, utter or publish" any "false, scandalous and malicious writing or writings against the government of the United States, or either house of the Congress of the United States or the president of the United States." A series of 20th-century acts and orders followed suit: the Espionage and Sedition Acts (1917, 1918); the Smith Act (1940); the Japanese American Detainment Act (1942); the Internal Security Act (1950); the Communist Control Act (1954); and the Amended Selective Service Act (1965). In the early 21st century, the USA PATRIOT Act (2001) sustained the tradition.

Inter arma silent leges. The Latin phrase means, "In time of war, the laws are silent." Moreover, laws are enacted to encourage silence. Openness and trust diminish in wartime. This occurrence, in fact, is cyclical. Reduced government openness leads to mistrust by the people; as the people's mistrust escalates, the government trust in them fades. Measures are taken or rulings are made that reflect that distrust.

Like several cases and circumstances that had arisen before—and some since—Tinker accurately illustrates this point. Lower court federal judges chose to disregard precedent. But by doing so they gave the U.S. Supreme Court the opportunity to weigh in, and gave the rest of us the opportunity to learn from the ruling. In the pages that immediately follow, Dan Johnston opens a new door to this fascinating case.

* * *

The U.S. Supreme Court case of *Tinker vs. Des Moines Independent Community School District*,[1] decided in 1969, is often called a "landmark" freedom-of-speech case, implying that it was "new" law. But when one examines U.S. Supreme Court decisions prior to *Tinker* that apply U.S. constitutional principles to public school authorities' duties and students' rights, it is hard to see any new legal principles in *Tinker*.

The central issue in *Tinker*—whether public school officials can restrain an exercise of free expression by students in school, absent some evidence of disruption as a result of the expression—had long before *Tinker* been settled law in the United States in favor of students. *Tinker* is an example of a recurring conflict in American politics and law between a majority urge to enforce patriotism and loyalty, and a resistance to those urges when they impose requirements contrary to individual religious or political beliefs. As with *Tinker* most of these conflicts occur during times of war. As with *Tinker*,

---

[1]393 U.S. 503 (1969).

in most of these conflicts, the majority, including judges and other public officials, find it difficult to adhere to our Constitution and laws.

THE PRECEDENTS

The pertinent U.S. Supreme Court precedents of *Tinker* begin with *Minersville District v. Gobitis*[2] Children who were Jehovah's Witnesses refused a mandate from the state legislature and their public school to pledge allegiance to, and salute, the U.S. flag. They were suspended from school and their father argued that he and his children were denied their right to public education. Lower federal courts ruled for the children.[3]

There could be no doubt that constitutional protections of freedom of speech applied to public school authorities. During World War I, the Supreme Court had overturned prohibitions against the teaching of German language in public schools.[4]

But in *Gobitis* the Supreme Court, in an opinion by Justice Frankfurter, reversed lower courts and held for the school's right to suspend the students if they refused to salute and pledge allegiance to the flag. Justice Frankfurter's lengthy opinion is based in part on the conflict between the goals of "national unity" and freedom of conscience.[5]

> For us to insist that, though the ceremony may be required, exceptional immunity must be given to dissidents, is to entertain that there is no basis for a legislative judgment that such an exemption might introduce elements of difficulty into the school discipline, might cast doubts in the minds of other children which would themselves weaken the effect of the exercise.[6]

To be sure, Justice Frankfurter implies that had he been in the state assembly he might have voted on the side of conscience, and a major premise of his decision is his preference for judicial restraint and deference to the legislative branch of government.[7]

---

[2]310 U.S. 586 (1940).

[3]108 F.2d 683 (1939); 21 F. Supp. 581 (1937).

[4]Meyer v. Nebraska, 262 U.S. 390 (1923); Bartels v. Iowa, 262 U.S. 404 (1923).

[5]Minersville District v. Gobitis, 310 U.S. 586, 595 (1940).

[6]*Id.* at 599–600. The State even argued that the Jehovah's Witnesses beliefs were inconsistent with the Bible. *Id.* at 587. The Witnesses adhere to a literal reading of Exodus, chapter 20, verses 4 and 5, which says, "Thou shalt not make unto thee any graven image, or any likeness of anything that is in heaven above, or that is in the earth beneath, or that is in the water under the earth; thou shalt not bow down thyself to them nor serve them." West Virginia Board of Ed. v. Barnette, 319 U.S. 624, 629 (1943).

[7]Minersville District v. Gobitis, 310 U.S. 586, 600 (1940). So many of the world's present conflicts (e.g., Northern Ireland, Israel and Palestine, and many of the Muslim-dominated countries) involve the struggle of minorities to secure "blessings of liberty" such as the right to practice religion, engage in political activity, and own property, that the importance of a judiciary to limit the power of the majority is, perhaps, clearer than it was in Justice Frankfurter's time.

The *Gobitis* decision did not last long. Three years later, still at the height of World War II fervor, the Court decided *West Virginia State Board of Education v. Barnette.*[8] Justice Jackson wrote the majority opinion, with Justice Frankfurter now in dissent.[9] Jehovah's Witnesses were still refusing to salute and pledge allegiance to the flag, and schools were still requiring that they do so or be suspended.

After the *Gobitis* decision, the legislature in West Virginia required all schools in the state to conduct courses in history, civics, and the U.S. and state constitutions: "For the purpose of teaching, fostering and perpetuating the ideals, principles and spirit of Americanism, and increasing the knowledge of the organization and machinery of the government.[10]

To comply with the statute, the West Virginia State Board of Education resolved that:

> [It] does hereby recognize and order that the commonly accepted salute to the Flag of the United States—the right hand is placed upon the breast and the following pledge repeated in unison; "I pledge allegiance to the Flag of the United States of America, and to the Republic for which it stands; one Nation [the clause 'Under God' was not added by the U.S. Congress until 1956] indivisible, with liberty and justice for all"—now becomes a regular part of the program of activities in the public schools ... provided, however, that refusal to salute the Flag be regarded as an act of insubordination, and shall be dealt with accordingly.[11]

The Court expressly overruled *Gobitis*[12] Where Justice Frankfurter had framed the dispute in *Gobitis* as one between the consciences of the minority and the authority of the state to legislate and regulate to achieve loyalty and patriotism, Justice Jackson frames the dispute as one between individual conscience and the will of the majority. Justice Jackson wrote:

> The very purpose of a Bill of Rights was to withdraw certain subjects from the vicissitudes of political controversy, to place them beyond the reach of majorities and officials and to establish them as legal principles to be applied by the courts. One's right to life, liberty, and property, to free speech, a free press, freedom of worship and assembly, and other fundamental rights may not be submitted to vote; they depend on the outcome of no elections.[13]

There is one rather striking factual distinction between *Gobitis* and *Barnette*. In the latter, the state went further than before to deny access to public education. An expelled child was "unlawfully absent" from school

---

[8]319 U.S. 624 (1943).
[9]*Id.* at 646.
[10]West Virginia Bd. of Educ. v. Barnette, 319 U.S. 624, 625 (1943)
[11]*Id.* at 628.
[12]*Id.* at 642.
[13]*Id.* at 628.

and could be proceeded against as a delinquent; parents could be subject to criminal prosecution, fines, and jail.[14] Perhaps it was now clear to the Court that Justice Frankfurter's doctrine of judicial restraint would not work in a society that is sincere about protecting the minority from excesses by the majority.

THE *TINKER* STORY

Just over 20 years later, *Tinker* was the next free-speech case to come to the Supreme Court in the public school context. It arose in another wartime environment—the war to save Southeast Asia from communism.

The story of *Tinker* demonstrates the burdens that dissidents must undertake in times of war to defend even clearly established rights of dissent, and the extremes to which public officials, including judges, may go to ignore settled law in behalf of the patriotism of the majority. By late fall and winter 1965, the war in Southeast Asia, and its countervailing peace movement in the United States had become a major political issue. President Johnson had committed his administration to the proposition that the war could be won by fighting it harder. Participants in the antiwar movement were accused of not supporting U.S. troops fighting the war. The antiwar dissenters thought that the best way to support the troops was to stop the war and bring them home to safety. Their pro-war opponents thought the dissenters to be traitors and not in support of "our troops."

In Des Moines, the families of the plaintiffs in *Tinker*, Christopher Eckhardt and John and Mary Beth Tinker, were at the center of antiwar activities. Chris Eckhardt's mother was active in a group that called itself the "Women's International League for Peace and Freedom." She had attended a meeting of the League in Washington, DC. Leonard Tinker, the father of John and Mary Beth, was the director of the Des Moines Regional Office of the American Friends Service Committee, which followed the Quaker tradition of pacifism.

At the Washington meeting, Mrs. Eckhardt learned of a planned effort to demonstrate opposition to the war by wearing black armbands, similar to those worn in mourning. At a meeting at the Eckhardt home, it was decided that members of the peace movement in Des Moines would join this effort, making the armbands also a symbol of their support for the suggestion of Senator Robert Kennedy that a temporary Christmas truce in the war be made open-ended.

---

[14]*Id.* at 629.

A student editorial appeared in a school newspaper, endorsing the wearing of armbands. The editorial brought to the attention of school officials the possibility that some students might attend school wearing armbands. The officials feared that disruptions of the schools might result and, so, they passed a rule prohibiting the wearing of armbands. Students who wore armbands to school would be instructed to take them off, or leave school premises.

Just before the Christmas break, Christopher Eckhardt and John and Mary Beth Tinker wore armbands to school and were sent home. After the break, they returned to school without the armbands.[15]

The Tinkers and Eckhardts asked for help from the Iowa Civil Liberties Union (ICLU). A law professor from Drake University, Craig Sawyer, went before a stormy and crowded school board meeting to argue the students' cause. The board was divided, but upheld the schools' authorities' decision.

The ICLU next voted to take the case to court, and a case was filed asking for an order restraining the school system from depriving the students of their wish to wear the armbands, and for nominal damages.

The two major parts of the Constitution that are the foundation of *Tinker*, the Bill of Rights and the Fourteenth Amendment, are the products of specific political climates: The Bill of Rights, which includes the First Amendment protection of speech, was demanded by the states as a condition to ratify the Constitution in order to protect against the kinds of specific usurpations perpetrated against the colonists by the English king.

The Fourteenth Amendment, and the statutes that were enacted to enforce it,[16] were also responsive to events at a specific time in history—the violations of the rights of U.S. citizens by their state governments, and their subsidiary local governments that led up to and followed the Civil War. The amendment makes the Bill of Rights applicable to the states as well as to the federal government. By their strict language, neither the Bill of Rights nor the Fourteenth Amendment so much give rights to people, as do they proscribe actions of the governments that had violated those rights in the recent experience of their enactments.[17]

But as the abuses of the British king during the colonial period, of the states during the time of slavery, and immediately after the Civil War slip further into history, the understanding and motivations for the legislation they generated slip further from consciousness. Several political scientists

---

[15]During the oral arguments in the Court of Appeals and the Supreme Court, the issue was raised as to why the case was not moot, as my clients had returned to school. On both occasions the issue was treated with levity. In the Court of Appeals a judge asked if I was insisting on my claim of One Dollar nominal damages in order to collect a fee: In the Supreme Court I suggested that the case was not moot because my clients still wanted to go to school with the right to wear an armband. Chief Justice Warren said, "You are assuming that these children understand this Court's decisions on mootness" to considerable laughter.

[16]*See, e.g.,* 42 USCA 1983.

[17]U.S. CONST. amend. I; U.S. CONST. amend. XIV.

have measured the attitudes of Americans to find that whereas they pro-
claim support the Bill of Rights, they do not support specific examples of
the exercise of the rights that it contains.

When issues other than the limits of government and the rights of minorities dominate the public consciousness, such as need to win a war, it becomes
more challenging to protect exercises of civil liberties that may be thought to
impede the national interest.

When the Tinker and Eckhardt children wore their armbands to school,
the law was clear that they had the right to do so, absent some kind of material disruption to the school. The failure of their school authorities and the
judges of two federal courts to recognize that demonstrates the fragility of
the rule of law in times of war.

The first *Tinker*-related people who were made to struggle to protect
clearly established civil liberties were, of course, my clients and their families.
As the opposition of the Tinkers and the Eckhardts to the war and to the
school district's prohibition against armbands became known, death threats
were scrawled on their homes and muttered over their telephones.[18] Even
school activities alienated peace activists. In school gym class, the students
were required to participate in calisthenics to the chant of "Kill Viet Cong."

Allan Herrick, the former state judge who was the lawyer for the school
board and represented the school district in federal court, particularly
abused Leonard Tinker, the father of John and Mary Beth. At various times,
Herrick implied that the elder Tinker was a communist, called him a
"Methodist minister without a church," and claimed that his children were
merely doing his bidding rather than acting from their own free will.[19]

Lorena Tinker, the mother of John and Mary Beth and a teacher at a Des
Moines college, speaks eloquently of the strength it took, and of the important support of two people—Louise Noun, who was the chair of the ICLU
and a prominent Des Moines philanthropist and feminist, and Gilbert
Cranberg, who was editorial-page editor of the *Des Moines Register*. Having
them in their corner, says Mrs. Tinker, gave the families confidence in their
position when most people in town thought them to be misguided, at best.

But it was clear, observing the experience of my clients that:

Revolt and terror pay a price.
Order and law have a cost.
What is this double use of fire and water?
The free man willing to pay and struggle and die
For the freedom for himself and others
Knowing how far to subject himself to discipline

---

[18]We did not yet have answering machines.

[19]In fact, the pacifism of the Eckhardt and Tinker families were deeply rooted in their religious faiths (Unitarian for the Eckhardts and Methodist-Quaker for the Tinkers) and the parents had done nothing more than to raise their children in the faith of their fathers.

And obedience for the sake of an ordered society
free from tyrants, exploiters and legalized frauds—
This free man is a rare bird and when you meet
Him take a good look at him and try
to figure him out because
Some day when the United States of the earth
Gets going and runs smooth and pretty there
will be more of him than we have now.[20]

No matter how sure of themselves, and how stubborn they may have seemed to their many opponents, the Tinker and Eckhardt families knew that they were engaging in a difficult enterprise, with some danger and difficulty.[21] Some of their fellow citizens made sure of it.

The next casualties of the difficult effort to maintain freedom in wartime were, of course, the school authorities. As one member of the school board later complained, her "good name" was spread all over the U.S. Supreme Court.

I believe that there were two concerns that the Des Moines school officials had when they prohibited the armbands. One was their expressed concern that other students would react angrily and disrupt the school. The principals frequently pointed out that some recent graduates of the schools had been killed in the Vietnam War.[22]

The other reason, unstated but I believe equally motivating, was the school officials' concern on behalf of parents that students might be exposed to ideas that would get them into trouble. Students throughout the United States were resisting the draft, being prosecuted, or moving to Canada. Others were burning their draft cards in public, and being prosecuted. Acting in the stead of parents, *in loco parentis,* the school officials believed that they had a duty to protect students from ideas that could lead them astray.

Law professor Sawyer, who was representing the students, and his employer Drake University were the next casualties. The university forced Professor Sawyer to withdraw from the case (which would have eventually allowed him to argue the case in the U.S. Supreme Court) out of fear of the impact of the controversy on the university.[23] He then referred the Tinkers and Eckhardts to me, then less than a year out of Drake Law School.

When I was a student at Drake Law from 1961 through 1964, the single constitutional law course was rather obviously in the curriculum only to meet accreditation standards. It amounted to nothing more than a daily recitation

---

[20]CARL SANDBURG, HARVEST POEMS 101 (1960).

[21]During the Vietnam War era, the offices of the American Friends Service Committee in Des Moines were bombed.

[22]The Supreme Court had rejected the argument that speech could be suppressed out of fear of disruptive reactions in Terminiello v. Chicago, 337 U.S. 1 (1949).

[23]To be sure, the Civil Liberties Union also felt that Professor Sawyer's impassioned presentation to the school board was unnecessarily confrontational. The Des Moines school board consists of a group of unpaid nonpartisan elected citizens who are respected as pillars of the community.

of as many black-letter paragraphs from the hornbook as could be read in each class time. No questions were entertained, no discussion allowed.

Entering law school, I had hoped to learn more about American constitutional law with its defense of individual human rights against the "tyranny of the majority," which I had discovered both as an undergraduate and in a year spent as an officer of the U.S. National Student Association. During those periods I read the like of John Stuart Mill, Hugo Black, Robert Maynard Hutchins, and Clarence Darrow.

My constitutional law class at Drake sorely disappointed and left me feeling cheated. In fact, law school left me so unprepared in constitutional law that when Professor Sawyer asked me to undertake the representation of his clients in *Tinker*, it was the first I had heard of the federal civil rights statute that provided us access to the federal courts.

In the summer immediately following the expulsion of the students, *Tinker, et al. v. Des Moines Independent Community School District, et al.*[24] was placed on the docket of Judge Roy Stephenson, the chief judge for the U.S. District Court of the Southern District of Iowa. There was no jury because the primary relief sought was an injunction and the issues to be decided were legal rather than factual.

Judge Stephenson was a highly respected jurist and for good cause. He was careful and respectful of the law and of the lawyers and litigants who appeared before him. But he was also a former Des Moines Republican County Chair, had served in combat in World War II, and had risen to the rank of Brigadier General in the Army Reserve.[25] His decision in *Tinker* is an embarrassing anomaly in his long tenure as a federal judge.

In his chambers during the trial, Judge Stephenson told me that he had much difficulty "understanding" the position of my clients. During a subsequent criminal trial of a client who was charged with violating the Selective Service Law by refusing to report for draft induction, I reminded Judge Stephenson of that and suggested that he might feel more comfortable if another judge presided. He declined to recuse himself and routinely ruled for the government in draft cases. But once the federal appellate courts ruled that the Selective Service System and its boards of volunteers were required to follow their own regulations or an induction order was void, and once the court of appeals overruled Judge Stephenson in a draft case, it seemed to me that he went to an extreme in acquitting defendants.

In the *Tinker* trial any chance that the actions of the school authorities could be reconciled with their constitutional duties, and the decision Judge Stephenson was to render, was gone when Allan Herrick failed at

[24]258 F. Supp. 971 (1986).
[25]He was also one of the few judges in Des Moines who refused to accede to Allan Herrick's conceit of demanding to be addressed as "Judge Herrick."

trial to produce any evidence whatsoever to support a finding that the wearing of the armbands disrupted orderly school processes. No teacher testified that a classroom was distracted.[26] No expert testified that the presence in the classroom of the armbands would deter learning.

The only evidence adduced by the defendants was a fear that students supporting the war might disrupt the school. But it has long been the law that fear of disorder by those who disagree with a speaker cannot be the justification for the suppression of speech.[27]

To Mr. Herrick the only issue was the fact that the students disobeyed the rule.[28] Beyond that he gave Judge Stephenson nothing to work with. In the trial record, there is simply no evidence that the armbands posed any evil, grave or otherwise.[29]

It seemed that for Mr. Herrick, disobedience to any rule of government justified government's sanction—a curious principle for a self-proclaimed conservative and even more curious in a political system that had just fought a major war against one totalitarian system and was then fighting another.

Judge Stephenson's written decision confronting the issue recognizes that the students' actions in wearing the armbands were to be afforded the protections of the First Amendment.[30]

> The abridgement of speech by a state regulation must always be considered in terms of the object the regulation is attempting to accomplish and the abridgement of speech that actually occurs. "In each case (courts) must ask whether the gravity of the 'evil', discounted by its improbability, justifies such invasion of free speech as is necessary to avoid the danger."[31]

My clients' First Amendment rights could be overridden by a "reasonable" determination by the school officials that the students' exercise of their freedom of speech might be disruptive of the school environment.[32] Judge Stephenson goes outside the record of trial evidence to observe:

---

[26]One mathematics teacher testified that he used the opportunity to discuss with his class the issues raised by the armbands.

[27]Terminiello v. Chicago, 337 U.S. 1 (1949).

[28]Punishing a citizen for disobeying a government rule, without affording an ability to challenge the rule, is the essence of totalitarianism. During a discussion of the *Tinker* decision after the Supreme Court ruling, one superintendent of schools, not from Des Moines, asserted that if he could not promulgate a rule and enforce it, he could not keep students from fornicating in the school hallways.

[29]393 U.S. 508.

[30]For years after he was reversed by the Supreme Court, I would hear Judge Stephenson's voice over a crowd at bar meetings, where he would be holding forth with young lawyers. Paraphrasing, "Dan Johnston, come over here. Tell the young lawyers that I always confront the issue. I do not avoid the issue."

[31]Tinker v. Des Moines Independent Community School District, 258 F. Supp 971, 972 (1966).
[32]*Id.*

The Vietnam War and the involvement of the United States therein has been the subject of a major controversy for some time. When the armband regulation herein was promulgated, debate over the Vietnam War had become vehement in many localities. A protest march against the war had been recently held in Washington, D.C. A wave of draft card burning incidents protesting the war had swept the country. At that time two highly publicized draft card burning cases were pending in this Court. Both individuals supporting and those opposing it were quite vocal in expressing their views. This was demonstrated during the school board's hearing in on the armband regulation.... It is against this background that the Court must review the reasonableness of the regulation.[33]

Judge Stephenson cited *Barnette,* but neither followed it nor attempted to distinguish it.[34] The case that he cited for his balancing test was *Dennis v. United States,*[35] one of the "Smith Act" cases that arose during the hysteria of the "McCarthy era."[36]

But even *Dennis* could not be authority for Judge Stephenson's decision in *Tinker. Dennis* involves a federal statute that was specifically designed to prevent advocacy with the intent to overthrow the government.[37] Moreover, the *Dennis* decision expressly distinguishes its facts from *Barnette* on the ground that the interest the government sought to protect in the latter case was too insubstantial to overcome the freedom of speech.[38] Judge Stephenson made no reference to this in his opinion.

Judge Stephenson also recognized but refused to follow the decisions in two cases that had been decided recently by the U.S. Court of Appeals for the Fifth Circuit, *Burnside v. Byars*[39] and *Blackwell v. Issaquena County Board of Education.*[40] Both cases were from the public school venue in Mississippi.

In the *Blackwell* case some students wore "Freedom Buttons" to school as a part of a drive to get African Americans to register to vote. But the court found they also acted in a disorderly manner, disrupting classrooms and disturbing other students by trying to put the buttons on those who did not want them. The court sustained enforcement of a rule against the buttons finding, "In this case the reprehensible conduct ... was so inexorably tied to

---

[33]Id. at 972–73.

[34]*Id.* at 972. *Barnette* is framed as a freedom-of-religion case. That element might have been added to *Tinker* as my clients were acting consistent with their religious beliefs as Friends and Unitarians. Justice Hugo Black, whose dissent in *Tinker* is quite hostile to Justice Fortas' majority opinion and whose participation in the oral argument of *Tinker* was quite hostile to my position, concurred in *Barnette* with Justice Douglas, who voted with the majority in *Tinker* on the grounds that the *Barnette* students were being forced to perform acts inconsistent with their religious beliefs.

[35]341 U.S. 494 (1951).

[36]*Id.*

[37]*Id.* at 496.

[38]*Id.* at 508–09.

[39]363 F.2d 744 (1966).

[40]363 F.2d 749 (1966).

the wearing of the buttons that the two are inseparable."[41] On the same day, however, the Fifth Circuit decided the case of *Burnside v. Byars*,[42] overturning the enforcement of school action prohibiting buttons bearing the slogan "One Man—One Vote" where the wearing of the buttons did not materially disrupt the school.

Judge Stephenson's decision implicitly agrees that my clients' wearing of the armbands to school did not disrupt anything when he cites from *Burnside* but refuses to follow it:

> The Court stated that school officials "cannot infringe on their students' right to free and unrestricted expression as guaranteed to them under the First Amendment to the Constitution; where the exercise of such rights in the school buildings and schoolrooms do not materially and substantially interfere with the requirements of appropriate discipline in the operation of the school."[43]

Judge Stephenson then cited his jurisdiction to rule oppositely from courts of appeals of other circuits and holds that school officials may suppress speech without a finding of a material and substantial disruption.[44] Judge Stephenson's superb record as a federal jurist became another casualty of the conflict between freedom and war.

We appealed to the U.S. Court of Appeals in St. Louis, which heard the case twice, once before a three-judge panel and then before the entire eight-judge court *en banc*.[45] The court split four-to-four, which had the effect of affirming the district court.[46] No opinion was written.

Now with the support of the American Civil Liberties Union, the ruling was appealed to the U.S. Supreme Court. It agreed to hear the case and, eventually, it reversed Judge Stephenson.

At first, Chief Justice Warren sought to rule for the students on the basis, contained in the trial record, that political symbols other than the armbands were allowed in the school. But it was Justice White who argued for a broader First Amendment holding, and his position prevailed. Justice Fortas, who had just written the Court's opinion in the case of *In Re Gault*[47] that afforded due process of law rights in juvenile court prosecutions, was assigned by Chief Justice Warren to write the majority opinion.[48]

---

[41]*Id.* at 754. The Court does not discuss why the schools could not have addressed their actions to the disorderly conduct, and allowed the wearing of the buttons.

[42]363 F.2d 744 (1966).

[43]Tinker v. Des Moines Independent Community School District, 258 F. Supp. 971, 973 (S.D. Iowa 1966), *quoting* Burnside v. Byars, 363 F.2d 744, 749 (5th Cir. 1966).

[44]*Id.* at 973.

[45]Appellate court cases are usually heard by three-judge panels. Sometimes, however, either on the court's motion or at the request of one of the litigants, the court will consider the matter by the full court. This is an "en banc" hearing.

[46]383 F.2d 988.

[47]387 U.S. 1 (8th Cir. 1967).

[48]ED CRAY, CHIEF JUSTICE 490–91 (1997).

To be sure, the eloquence of Justice Fortas' opinion for the Court advances the strength of the First Amendment. But in terms of law, it simply reinforces the earlier decisions in *Barnette, Meyer, Bartels,* and *Terminiello,* all of which must be considered casualties of the Vietnam War until Judge Stephenson and the Des Moines school system were set right.

A more restricted armband rule by the Des Moines school system might well have passed constitutional muster. During my portion of the oral argument before the U.S. Supreme Court, the following exchange between Justice White and myself occurred:

Justice White:	"What if the student had gotten up from the class and delivered a message orally what his arm band was intended to convey and insisted on doing it all during the hour?"
Johnston:	In that case we would not be here. Even if he insisted on doing it only for a second, although he would be expressing his views, he would be doing something else."
Justice White:	"Why did they wear the arm band in the class, to express the message?"
Johnston:	"Yes, sir."
Justice White:	"To everybody in the class?"
Johnston:	"Yes, sir."
Justice White:	"Everybody while they were listening to some other subject matter were supposed to also be looking at the arm band and taking in the message."
Johnston:	"Well, except that, your Honor, I believe that the method that the students chose in this particular instance was specifically designed in such a way that it would not cause that kind of disruption. None of the teachers who have testified at the hearing in the district court—"
Justice White:	"Just wearing a meaningless arm band?"
Johnston:	"No."
Justice White:	"Carrying an ineffective message?"
Johnston:	*"No, they intended to be effective."*[49]

I was trying to interpose the answer that the record contained no testimony of any teacher that a class was disrupted. Mr. Justice Thurgood Marshall, who could interrupt Mr. Justice White whereas I could not, interposed a better answer:

---

[49]Transcript of Oral Argument at pp. 7–8. The transcript and a taped recording of the oral argument, as well as other materials pertaining to the case, are available at the offices of the Iowa Civil Liberties Union in Des Moines.

Justice Marshall: "It prohibited them from wearing the arm band
                  where, in the building?"
Johnston: *"That is right. In the cafeteria, halls, anywhere in the
                  school."*[50]

Had the armband prohibition extended only to the classrooms, the result might well have been different.

THE IMPACT OF *TINKER* AND THE MYTH OF ITS EROSION

To be sure, three decades of federal judges appointed by conservative presidents have resulted in decisions that are not consistent with the opinions about the role of the First Amendment in public schools expressed so eloquently by Mr. Justice Fortas in *Tinker*. Ironically, conservatives who complained that judges appointed during the Roosevelt–Truman–Eisenhower era were not sufficiently respectful of *stare decisis*—that pre–New Deal decisions should be followed not necessarily because they were right, but because they established precedential law—now support decisions of conservative judges who fail to apply *Tinker* to comparable factual claims.

Consistency has never been the strong suit of political polemicists of either the right or the left. Federal courts since *Tinker* have upheld the disciplining of public school students for the content of speeches during an election campaign for student council president,[51] for the content of a student's valedictory speech, for selecting "the power of God" as a topic for a classroom presentation,[52] for wanting to show a videotape of a religious song in class "show-and-tell,"[53] for wearing a shirt with an anti-drug message, and for wearing T-shirts protesting school policies. Only the Ninth Circuit seems to have solidly embraced *Tinker* by reversing the discipline imposed against students for wearing "scab" buttons during a teacher strike.[54]

The two post-*Tinker* U.S. Supreme Court cases dealing with public school student rights, *Bethel School District No. 403 v. Fraser*[55] and *Hazelwood School District v. Kuhlmeier,*[56] are often cited as eroding *Tinker*. I believe they do not. Even though in both of these decisions the Court could have embraced Justice Fortas' eloquent language in *Tinker* to further expand student freedoms, *Tinker* did not mandate that they do so, and was not overruled or even significantly weakened. Despite the expansive language of Justice Fortas' opinion, the actual holding of *Tinker* was rather narrow—reaffirming the application

---

[50]*Id.*
[51]Poling v. Murphy, 872 F.2d 757, 764 (1989).
[52]Duran v. Nitsche, 780 F. Supp 1048, 1050–51 (E.D. Pa. 1991).
[53]DeNooyeer v. Livonia Pub. Sch., 799 F. Supp. 744, 755 (E.D. Mich. 1992).
[54]Chandler v. McMinnville Sch. Dist. 978 F.2d 524 (1992).
[55]478 U.S. 675 (1986).
[56]484 U.S. 260 (1988).

of the Constitution to the public school environment and finding that those principles include the freedom of speech by students.

Bethel and *Hazelwood* seem to me to be distinguishable from *Tinker* by their facts, in that they involve speech by students in school-sponsored forums whereas *Tinker* involves private speech by students that occurs on school property. *Hazelwood* involves the censorship of a school newspaper. Someone must decide what goes into a newspaper, and when a school is the sponsor or publisher, it is the school that decides.

The Supreme Court denied certiorari to review *DeNooyer v. Livonia Public Schools,* a case in which a second-grade public school student was prevented from showing a videotape of her singing a religious song as part of a class show-and-tell. The district court found from the evidence that the class assignment required an oral, not recorded, presentation by the students, that the school feared allowing the presentation would be interpreted by some as a school endorsement of the student's religious views, and that it feared students of other religious faiths might be offended. The district court also found that in the closed school-sponsored forum of the classroom, the school only had to demonstrate that its actions were reasonably related to pedagogical concerns, rather than to meet the heavier material and substantial disruption standard of *Tinker.*[57]

The impact of *Tinker* cannot be measured only by the actions of courts and lawyers. Court decisions report only those instances when students and their school authorities disagree. They do not reflect, of course, incidents when students express themselves freely during their school hours without interference. Students and educators have embraced Justice Fortas' ringing principles often out of sight of courts and litigators. I believe it has become education policy and practice in many schools to encourage and nurture free speech among students as advocated in *Tinker.*

Tinker may have had a more immediate impact. Sam Brown of Council Bluffs, a national leader of the antiwar movement, who later became the secretary of state of Colorado, has observed that *Tinker* may have hastened the end of the Vietnam War by encouraging school officials to allow antiwar organizers better access to high school and college students, who were, after all, those most interested in the war because they were the ones drafted to fight it.

If the views of John Tinker, Mary Beth Tinker, and Christopher Eckhardt had prevailed sooner, the geopolitical world would look just as it does now, and hundreds of thousands of young men and women would be alive or living without disabling injuries. If Sam Brown is right, then *Tinker*'s impact on hastening the end of the war is a benefit that cannot be eroded.

---

[57]Tinker v. Des Moines Independent Community School Dist., 258 F. Supp. 971 (1986).

   Twenty-five years after the Supreme Court decision, the Tinkers and
Eckhardts were invited to a discussion of their case at Roosevelt High School in
Des Moines. Thirty years later a daylong symposium was sponsored by the constitutional law center at Drake University, the same institution that forced Professor Sawyer out of the case. Both of these events were devoted to celebrating
the decision.

Chapter 4

THE "MIRACLE" of BURSTYN V. WILSON

Marjorie Heins[*]

EDITOR'S INTRODUCTION

Public discontent with motion pictures with religious themes at their core did not begin with 2004's The Passion of the Christ. Mel Gibson's graphic account of the final hours of Christ attracted criticism, including accusations of being anti-Semitic. Before that, Martin Scorsese's 1988 film The Last Temptation of Christ portrays Jesus as a tormented, fearful young man confused by sex and uncertain of his path in life. The film was condemned by virtually every Christian denomination, domestically and internationally. Showings of the film were protested, picketed, subject to boycotts and bomb threats, and excluded from the titles carried by the Blockbuster Video chain.

But both of these motion pictures and the controversy that surrounded them were preceded by a history of control, led in part by the Catholic Church in the United States. "Film censorship is almost as old as film itself," writes Marjorie Heins in chapter 4, "and from the beginning, religion played a major role." This came to head in 1950 when Roberto Rossellini's The Miracle *debuted in the United States. The film ignited a firestorm that pitted censorship efforts against the First Amendment rights of the filmmaker, distributors,*

*Founding Director, Free Expression Policy Project; Democracy Program Fellow, Brennan Center for Justice at N.Y.U. School of Law; Author, Not in Front of the Children: "Indecency," Censorship, and the Innocence of Youth (Hill & Wang, 2001). © Marjorie Heins; all rights reserved. An early version of this article was presented at the University of Virginia Forum for Contemporary Thought on October 28, 2002. A condensed version was published in Conscience: The Magazine of Catholics for a Free Choice, Spring 2003. Thanks to William Barnett for research assistance.

and exhibitors. The U.S. Supreme Court ultimately settled the matter. As illustrated in chapter 4, the issues rooted in this clash surrounding the film and the attempts to censor are not merely historical, but also reach to the present day. Artistic freedom and church–state separation, for example, are matters debated then and now.

From 1991 to 1998, Ms. Heins directed the American Civil Liberties Union's (ACLU) Arts Censorship Project, where she was co-counsel in a number of U.S. Supreme Court cases, including National Endowment for the Arts v. Finley *and* Reno v. ACLU *(the challenge to the 1996 Communications Decency Act). She is the founding director of the Free Expression Policy Project and is a Democracy Program Fellow at the Brennan Center for Justice at New York University's School of Law.*

*   *   *

INTRODUCTION: FOREIGN FILM MEETS THE FIRST AMENDMENT

Late in December 1950, an obscure foreign movie called *The Miracle* opened at the Paris Theater in Manhattan. Directed by the pioneer of Italian neorealism, Roberto Rossellini, *The Miracle* is a religious parable featuring a dim-witted peasant woman who is plied with drink and then seduced by a vagabond whom she mistakes in her stupor for St. Joseph. It is not clear whether she's awake for the actual sex act, but she soon discovers she is pregnant. Her fellow villagers mock and torment her; she escapes to a hilltop church and experiences a beatific moment of religious ecstasy after giving birth.

When first released in Italy in 1948, *The Miracle* was condemned by the Catholic Cinematographic Center, an arm of the Vatican devoted to vetting movies for moral propriety. But the film was not banned—indeed, it was shown at the Venice Film Festival, where works that the Vatican considered blasphemous would not have been allowed.[1] The Vatican's semiofficial newspaper, *Osservatore Romano,* published a guardedly appreciative review, noting that "objections from a religious viewpoint are very grave," but also pointing to "scenes of undoubted screen value," and concluding that "we still believe in Rossellini's art."[2]

In New York, however, local officials were not so broad-minded. City License Commissioner Edward McCaffrey, a former state commander of the Catholic War Veterans, announced that he found *The Miracle* "officially and personally blasphemous," and ordered the manager of the Paris Theater to

---

[1]ALAN WESTIN, THE MIRACLE CASE: THE SUPREME COURT AND THE MOVIES 10 (1961).

[2]*Id; Criticism of "The Miracle"* (an excerpt from the *Osservatore Romano* review), 53 COMMONWEAL 592 (Mar. 16, 1951); Camille Cianfarra, *Vatican Views "Miracle" Row,* N.Y. TIMES, Feb. 11, 1951, at §2.

stop showing it. The next day, the Catholic Church's Legion of Decency condemned *The Miracle* as "a sacrilegious and blasphemous mockery of Christian-religious truth," and McCaffrey suspended the theater's license. The New York Film Critics association called the action "dangerous censorship," and the ACLU said it violated the First Amendment. But these protests did little to deter McCaffrey or the Legion, which since the 1930s had been a powerful force in American film censorship, and hence assumed its ability to suppress movies it did not like.[3]

The distributor of the film, Joseph Burstyn, filed suit in state court to challenge McCaffrey. Burstyn was a champion of foreign films; several years earlier, he had introduced Americans to the glories of post–World War II European cinema by exhibiting Rossellini's masterpiece, *Open City*. The film star Ingrid Bergman, bored by performing in formulaic Hollywood vehicles, was entranced by *Open City* when she saw it, and by Rossellini's next feature, *Paisan*. She thereupon sent Rossellini one of the more famous letters in cinema history. "I am ready to come and make a film with you," Bergman wrote, even though she knew only two words in Italian: "*Ti amo*."[4] With this introduction, it was probably only a matter of time before Bergman deserted her husband and ran off with Rossellini. The affair was still good tabloid copy when *The Miracle* opened at the Paris in Manhattan as part of a trilogy of short foreign films called "The Ways of Love."[5]

At a preliminary hearing in Burstyn's case against McCaffrey, the judge questioned the license commissioner's power to suppress films. Official film censorship was well entrenched in New York, but it was vested by law in the state Board of Regents, to which all exhibitors had to apply in advance before showing a movie anywhere in the state. After the preliminary hearing, McCaffrey backed off and lifted his ban.

But now a more powerful figure, Francis Cardinal Spellman, entered the fray. Spellman had not seen *The Miracle*, but he had heard about it. This was enough for him to condemn the film in a passionate attack that he ordered read at every Mass in all 400 parishes of the New York Archdiocese, including St. Patrick's Cathedral.[6] The film was a "diabolical deception at its depths," he said; "a despicable affront to every Christian," and "a vicious insult to Italian womanhood" that should really be named "'Woman Further Defamed,' by Roberto Rossellini" (a reference, of course, to the affair with Bergman). It was, moreover, "a blot upon the escutcheon of the Empire State that no

---

[3]Westin, *supra* note 1, at 5–6; Richard Parke, *Rossellini Film Is Halted by City; "The Miracle" Held "Blasphemous,"* N.Y. TIMES, Dec. 24, 1950, 1; Richard Parke, *"Miracle" Banned Throughout City,* N.Y. TIMES, Dec. 25, 1950, at 21.

[4]INGRID BERGMAN, MY STORY 4 (1972).

[5]Bosley Crowther, *The Strange Case of "The Miracle,"* ATLANTIC MONTHLY, Apr. 1951, at 36. The other two short films were Jean Renoir's *A Day in the Country* and Marcel Pagnol's *Jofroi*.

[6]*McCaffrey, Warned of Injunction, Drops "Miracle" Ban in 5 Minutes,* N.Y. TIMES, Dec. 30, 1950, at 1; *Court, Disallowing "Miracle" Ban, Denies City Has Censorship Powers,* N.Y. TIMES, Jan. 5, 1951, at 1; *Spellman Urges "Miracle" Boycott,* N.Y. TIMES, Jan. 8, 1951, at 1; Westin, *supra* note 1, at 6–9.

means of appeal to the Board of Regents is available," Spellman protested. *The Miracle*'s "blasphemous darts ... divide religion against religion and race against race," and "[d]ivide and conquer is the technique of the greatest enemy of civilization, atheistic Communism."[7]

Picketing began in front of the Paris the same day as Spellman's appeal, and continued daily for several weeks. Sometimes numbering more than 1,000, these representatives of the Catholic War Veterans, Knights of Columbus, and Archdiocesan Union of the Holy Name Society carried signs reading "This Picture is an Insult to Every Decent Woman and Her Mother," "This Picture is Blasphemous," and "Don't be a Communist—all the Communists are inside." They yelled similar affronts: "Don't enter that cesspool!", "Buy American!", and "Don't look at that filth!" A smaller counterdemonstration, organized by two Protestant groups, protested the calls for censorship.[8]

Just 8 days after Cardinal Spellman's lament that there was no way for the state to rectify its error in having licensed *The Miracle*, a way was found. A three-man committee of the Board of Regents convened, viewed the film, and declared it "sacrilegious." Four days later, the full board directed Burstyn to appear and show cause why *The Miracle*'s exhibition license should not be withdrawn. And on February 15, 1951, despite briefs supporting artistic freedom from the Authors League, prominent Protestant clergy, the ACLU, and assorted writers and intellectuals, the Board of Regents ruled that the film was sacrilegious and therefore in violation of New York's 30-year-old film censorship law. The Regents explained that *The Miracle* inexcusably parodied the Immaculate Conception and Virgin Birth and associated them with "drunkenness, seduction, mockery and lewdness." This "mockery or profaning of those beliefs that are sacred to any portion of our citizenship is abhorrent to the laws of this great state."[9]

Burstyn's attorney, the First Amendment expert Ephraim London, filed an appeal, but the New York courts rejected London's arguments that not only the state's sacrilege standard, but the very existence of movie licensing, violated the First Amendment. Indeed, the New York courts said that they were simply accommodating citizens' preferences, and that not to protect believers against sacrilegious expression would amount to discrimination against them. Hence, Rossellini's "public gratuitous insult to recognized re-

---

[7]*Spellman Urges "Miracle" Boycott*, N.Y. TIMES, Jan. 8, 1951, at 1, 14; Westin, *supra* note 1, at 9; Crowther, *supra* note 5, at 37.

[8]*"Miracle" Picketed By 1,000 Catholics*, N.Y. TIMES, Jan. 15, 1951, at 23; Garth Jowett, *A Significant Medium for the Communication of Ideas: The Miracle Decision and the Decline of Motion Picture Censorship, 1952–1968, in* MOVIE CENSORSHIP AND AMERICAN CULTURE 263 (Francis Couvares, ed., 1996); Westin, *supra* note 1, at 11; Crowther, *supra* note 5, at 37.

[9]*Text of Regents' Report Banning "Miracle*," N.Y. TIMES, Feb. 17, 1951, 9; also *quoted in* Burstyn v. Wilson, 303 N.Y. 242, 257 (1951). *See also* Douglas Dales, *"Miracle" Banned by Regents' Board; Court Fight Pends*, N.Y. TIMES, Feb. 17, 1951, 1; Westin, *supra* note 1, at 14–15.

ligious beliefs ... is not only offensive to decency and morals, but constitutes in itself an infringement of the freedom of others to worship and believe as they choose."[10]

The court rejected arguments by both London and the American Jewish Congress (in a friend-of-the-court brief) that the Church-driven censorship of *The Miracle* violated the First Amendment's Establishment Clause, which prohibits Congress from making any law "respecting an Establishment of Religion" and is the constitutional basis for the separation of church and state. The benefits to religion from state suppression of sacrilegious films were only "incidental" to a legitimate state purpose, the court said; and in any event, "we are essentially a religious nation, ... of which it is well to be reminded now and then."[11]

London appealed to the Supreme Court, and in a unanimous decision in May 1952, the Court declared "sacrilege" far too vague a censorship standard to be permissible under the First Amendment. Weaving an elaborate metaphor, Justice Tom Clark wrote for the Court in *Burstyn v. Wilson* that trying to decide what qualifies as sacrilege sets the censor "adrift upon a boundless sea amid a myriad of conflicting currents of religious views, with no charts but those provided by the most vocal and powerful orthodoxies." Clark added: "It is not the business of government ... to suppress real or imagined attacks upon a particular religious doctrine."[12]

Clark noted in passing that banning films because of sacrilege might also "raise substantial questions under the First Amendment's guaranty of separate church and state." Indeed, the sacrilege test would inevitably be applied to favor vocal and powerful religions such as Catholicism. "Under such a standard, the most careful and tolerant censor would find it virtually impossible to avoid favoring one religion over another."[13]

But Clark stopped short of deciding the case on Establishment Clause grounds—with consequences that reverberate today. With government vouchers funding religious schools, an official White House Office of Faith-Based Initiatives under the administration of President George W. Bush, and widespread condemnation of a federal court decision recognizing the seemingly obvious fact that "under God" in the Pledge of Allegiance is a direct endorsement of religion,[14] we are still wrestling with the issues in *The Miracle* case.

---

[10]Burstyn v. Wilson, 303 N.Y. at 260–61.

[11]*Id*. at 258–59. Briefs supporting Burstyn were also filed by the New York Civil Liberties Committee, Artists' Equity, and the Metropolitan Committee for Religious Liberty. The New York State Catholic Welfare Committee filed a brief supporting the state.

[12]Burstyn v. Wilson, 343 U.S. 495, 504–05 (1952).

[13]*Id*. at 505.

[14]Newdow v. U.S. Congress, 292 F.3d 597 (9th Cir. 2002), *rev'd on other grounds*; Elk Grove School Dist. v. Newdow, 124 S. Ct. 2301 (2004).

FILM CENSORSHIP AND THE CATHOLIC CHURCH

When Cardinal Spellman pressured New York authorities to revoke the exhibition license for *The Miracle,* he was exercising a power that the Catholic Church had come to take for granted. How the Church came to control the content of movies is one of the more remarkable chapters in American censorship history.

Film censorship is almost as old as film itself, and from the beginning, religion played a major role. In the early 1900s, Progressive Era Protestant reformers joined with more conservative clergy in alarm over the new, cheap "nickelodeon" theaters that were popular with urban adolescents, immigrants, and working people of all ages. The nickelodeons were an outgrowth of vaudeville, a genre in which film travelogues, news clips, comedies, and dramas were interspersed with live acts.[15]

The early movies shown in the nickelodeons included vaudeville-inspired melodrama and burlesque, bawdy street scenes (e.g., breezes exposing women's underclothes), "slumming" comedies, and crime stories like *The Great Train Robbery* of 1903, America's first cinematic hit. (Another popular crime film reenacted a sensational 1908 murder trial and led to prosecution of the film's exhibitor for imperiling the morals of young boys.[16]) Early filmmakers also "turned to popular literature, drama, and contemporary issues," writes the historian Gregory Black; they explored "'the corruption of city politics, the scandal of white slave rackets, the exploitation of immigrants' …; [they] 'championed the cause of labor, lobbied against political "bosses," and often gave dignity to the struggles of the urban poor.'"[17]

But neither the social concerns nor the artistry of early American cinema mitigated the anxieties of the Progressive Era's anti-vice crusaders. The movies' "carnival of vulgarity" caused grave harm to audiences, according to a 1908 report, *Cheap Amusement in Manhattan,* that was produced by two civic groups.[18] The historian Garth Jowett explains that reformers accused the nickelodeons of causing "every conceivable social ill, from sexual license to demonstrating the arts of pickpocketing to fomenting social revolution."[19]

Municipalities and states soon responded with censorship laws. Chicago led the way in 1907, with an ordinance that required exhibitors to secure a permit from the police superintendent before showing any film. New York reformers established a nongovernmental Board of Motion Picture Censor-

---

[15]Daniel Czitrom, *The Politics of Performance: Theater Licensing and the Origins of Movie Censorship in New York,* in Couvares, *supra* note 8, at 20.

[16]*Id.* at 22, 31.

[17]GREGORY BLACK, HOLLYWOOD CENSORED: MORALITY CODES, CATHOLICS, AND THE MOVIES 7 (1994), *quoting* KEVIN BROWNLOW, BEHIND THE MASK OF INNOCENCE xv (1990), and KAY SOLAN, THE LOUD SILENTS: ORIGINS OF THE SOCIAL PROBLEM FILM 3 (1988).

[18]*Id.* at 28.

[19]Jowett, *supra* note 8, at 259. *See also* GREGORY BLACK, THE CATHOLIC CRUSADE AGAINST THE MOVIES, 1940–1975 6–7 (1998).

ship to which the industry agreed to submit films for review; but the board was unsure of its standards and, according to Black, "reluctant to censor."[20] Its failure to suppress films dealing with prostitution, corruption, and other gritty aspects of life disappointed the pro-censorship lobby,[21] and resulted in more licensing laws: Pennsylvania passed one in 1911, Kansas and Ohio in 1913, Maryland in 1916.[22] New York State established a motion picture commission in 1921, and directed it to deny exhibition licenses to any film considered "obscene, indecent, immoral, inhuman, sacrilegious, or ... of such character that its exhibition would tend to corrupt morals or incite to crime."[23] With little change, this was the law used in *The Miracle* case. Black summarizes: the common goal of film licensing was

> to eliminat[e] depictions of changing moral standards, limit[] scenes of crime ..., and avoid[] as much as possible any screen portrayal of civil strife, labor–management discord, or government corruption and injustice. The screen, these moral guardians held, was not a proper forum for discussion of delicate sexual issues or for social or political commentary.[24]

It did not take the industry long to challenge the government censorship schemes. A lawsuit begun in Ohio reached the Supreme Court in 1915. The Mutual Film Company's argument against Ohio's censorship law was squarely based on the First Amendment and a similar free-speech provision in the Ohio Constitution. Film licensing, the company said, was an unconstitutional "prior restraint" on artistic expression: No film could be shown until approved by the authorities. But the Supreme Court, in a decision that shocked the nascent industry, ruled that Ohio's licensing scheme was constitutional because cinema was not protected by the First Amendment.

The exhibition of movies "is a business, pure and simple," wrote Justice Joseph McKenna for a unanimous Court. Movies are "originated and conducted for profit, like other spectacles [such as circuses, and are] not to be regarded ... as part of the press of the country, or as organs of public opinion." Certainly, movies communicate ideas, McKenna acknowledged. But censorship is justified because of the nature of movie audiences—"not of women alone nor of men alone, but together, not of adults only, but of children"—and because of the medium's capacity for "evil" and potential appeal to "prurient interest."[25]

---

[20]BLACK, *supra* note 19, at 7. *See also* Francis Couvares, *Hollywood, Main Street, and the Church: Trying to Censor the Movies Before the Production Code*, in Couvares, *supra* note 8, at 131. One scholar asserts that New York City enacted a municipal censorship law in 1906; Black states that Chicago was the first, in 1907. Charlene Regester, *Black Films, White Censors*, in Couvares, *supra* note 8, at 167, *citing* GARTH JOWETT, FILM: THE DEMOCRATIC ART 108–38 (1976).

[21]BLACK, *supra* note 17, at 15.

[22]BLACK, *supra* note 19, at 7; Regester, *supra* note 20, at 167, *citing* JOWETT, *supra* note 20, at 108–38.

[23]Burstyn v. Wilson, 278 A.D. 253, 258 (N.Y. S.Ct. 3rd Dept.); 343 U.S. at 497.

[24]BLACK, *supra* note 19, at 7.

[25]Mutual Film Corp. v. Industrial Comm'n of Ohio, 236 U.S. 230, 244, 242 (1915).

The subtext here was difficult to miss. As Jowett writes, movies were not conceptually different from books and newspapers, which also were sold for profit but were not subject to prior-restraint licensing. The assertion that cinema had greater "capacity for evil" was based on the presumed susceptibility of "the primary audience for the movies—largely the immigrant working class."[26]

Indeed, much the same dynamic had been at work in the development of obscenity laws half a century earlier. Fears that the newly literate working class—especially its youth—would be corrupted by sexually arousing art and literature formed the basis for literary and artistic censorship in England and America.[27] The difference was that obscenity law operated for the most part after the fact of publication; state and local governments in America did not generally establish prior-restraint licensing boards for books, magazines, or art exhibits.

The Supreme Court decision in the *Mutual Film* case gave the green light to official film censorship, and in the 50 years that followed, thousands of movies were cut, bowdlerized, or simply banned by state and local censors. Chicago banned newsreels of policemen shooting at labor pickets; ordered deletion of a scene in which a buffalo gives birth in a Walt Disney film; refused a license for *Anatomy of a Murder*, "because it found the use of the words 'rape' and 'contraceptive' to be objectionable"; and banned Charlie Chaplin's *The Great Dictator*, "apparently out of deference to its large German population." Atlanta banned *Lost Boundaries*, the story of "a Negro doctor's attempt to pass as white," on the ground that it would "adversely affect the peace, morals, and good order" of the city. Memphis suppressed another social conscience film, *Curley*, "because it contained scenes of white and Negro children in school together," and *The Southerner*, a film about poor tenant farmers, because it reflected badly on the South. A film version of *Carmen* was condemned in Ohio "because cigarette-girls smoked cigarettes in public," and in Pennsylvania because of "the duration of a kiss."[28] In 1928 alone, writes Black, "the New York State censorship board cut over 4,000 scenes from the more than 600 films submitted, and Chicago censors sliced more than 600 scenes."[29]

This highly decentralized censorship system left much to be desired from the viewpoint of both Catholic and Protestant activists, as well as antivice crusaders such as the Women's Christian Temperance Union (the

---

[26] Jowett, *supra* note 8, at 260.

[27] *See* MARJORIE HEINS, NOT IN FRONT OF THE CHILDREN: "INDECENCY," CENSORSHIP, AND THE INNOCENCE OF YOUTH 23–36 (2001).

[28] Times Film Corp. v. Chicago, 365 U.S. 43, 69–72 (1961) (Warren, C.J., with Black, Douglas, & Brennan, JJ., dissenting); Jane & Allen Otten, *Hour of Decision? Supreme Court Petitioned on Film Censorship*, N.Y. TIMES, Oct. 15, 1950, at §2, 5; Jowett, *supra* note 8, at 261; Regester, *supra* note 20, at 173–75.

[29] BLACK, *supra* note 17, at 34.

WCTU), and indeed, the industry itself. For one thing, not all states and localities had censorship boards. (By 1922, seven states and about 100 localities did.) For another, their ideological, moral, and religious criteria varied widely. Whereas Protestant clergy and moral reformers expressed continuing outrage at sexual content (Cecil B. DeMille's orgiastic biblical epics were a particular target), southern cities banned anything even remotely provocative on the subject of race. The film industry thus found itself not only under escalating attack but subjected to varying, uncertain standards.

As more licensing bills were introduced in state legislatures (100 were considered in 1921 alone),[30] reformers like the WCTU and Protestant Canon William Chase's Federal Motion Picture Council pushed for a uniform national censorship system. In response, Hollywood undertook its first concerted effort to improve its image and stop the legislative juggernaut. In 1922, the major studios formed the Motion Picture Producers & Distributors of America (MPPDA) and hired Will Hays, former Postmaster General and head of the Republican National Committee, as its director. "Teetotaler, elder in the Presbyterian Church, Elk, Moose, Rotarian, and Mason," as Black writes, "Hays brought the respectability of mainstream middle America to a Jewish-dominated film industry."[31]

Hays introduced a list of "Don'ts and Be Carefuls" for movies that banned, among other things, profanity, nudity, or any mention of "illegal traffic in drugs," white slavery, miscegenation, "sex hygiene and venereal diseases," scenes of childbirth, and "ridicule of the clergy," and urged caution in dealing with sedition, crime, marriage, and seduction.[32] But the studios interpreted this pre-Code as they chose, and bridled at the efforts of Hays' Studio Relations Department to control them. Dissatisfied, Protestant clergy continued to press for a national censorship law. Canon Chase wrote in 1921, for example, that the industry's "Hebrew" owners were "vile corrupters of American morals," and told the House Committee on Education that the movies were a "threat to world civilization."[33]

Catholic activists now began to organize a campaign more focused and ambitious than the critiques that their various magazines, radio stations, and movie review committees had thus far contributed to the censorship debate. The major strategist was Martin Quigley, a Chicago publisher of an industry trade journal who favored censorship but not by municipal licensing authorities, which had shown themselves all too amenable to payoffs and bribes.

---

[30]*Id.* at 30.
[31]*Id.* at 31. *See also* Stephen Vaughn, *Morality and Entertainment: The Origins of the Motion Picture Code*, 77 J. AMER. HISTORY 39–65 (1990); Jowett, *supra* note 8, at 260–61; Alison Parker, *Mothering the Movies: Women Reformers and Popular Culture*, in Couvares, *supra* note 8, at 73–90; Richard Maltby, *To Prevent the Prevalent Type of Book: Censorship and Adaptation in Hollywood, 1924–34*," in Couvares, *supra* note 8, at 97–121.
[32]Vaughn, *supra* note 31, at 44.
[33]BLACK, *supra* note 17, at 33–34.

Quigley saw that far more effective control of movie content could be achieved through vetting and editing at the preproduction stage. He persuaded Chicago's Cardinal George Mundelein and a Jesuit priest, FitzGeorge Dinneen, to develop a Catholic code for movies. In 1929, they invited a young Jesuit theologian named Daniel Lord to help them draft such a code.[34]

Lord's draft not only contained specific prohibitions but also announced sweeping moral prescriptions. It began with the "general principle" that "no picture shall be produced which will lower the moral standards of those who see it. Hence the sympathy of the audience should never be thrown to the side of crime, wrongdoing, evil or sin." "Impure love"—that is, any sex outside marriage—could not be presented as attractive or "in such a way as to arouse passion"; nudity and seminudity were forbidden, along with "lustful kissing." Law and government could not be disparaged; nor could organized religion: Ministers could not be comic characters or villains.[35] The Hays Office later fleshed out the Code provisions governing religion, to specify that "no film or episode may throw ridicule on any religious faith," and "ceremonies of any definite religion should be carefully and respectfully handled."[36]

Lord's code was just what the Hays Office needed. With the industry in jitters after the recent stock market crash (one producer, Fox, would soon be in bankruptcy), with the Church's threat of 20 million Catholics boycotting immoral movies, and perhaps most important, with investment bankers—on whom the new, expensive "talkies" depended for financing—sounding the alarm to studio boards, Hays persuaded the producers to accept Father Lord's draft, and in 1930, with only minor changes, it became the Hollywood Production Code.

Between 1930 and 1934, Hays and his censorship staff struggled with Hollywood's producers to enforce the Code. Quigley and his allies in the Church were far from satisfied: If anything, movies got saltier in the early 1930s, as studios labored to bring in customers despite the privations of the Depression. Mae West's *She Done Him Wrong*, with its sexy banter and hip-rolling heroine, was a big hit in 1932; her *I'm No Angel* the following year was equally bawdy, and popular with both women and men throughout America. The great gangster films—*Little Caesar, Scarface, Public Enemy*—were all produced in the early 1930s when Lord's Code was supposedly in effect. Cecil B. DeMille's Roman orgies continued to succeed at the box office and outrage the Church.

In 1934, Quigley and several prominent American bishops persuaded Monsignor Amleto Cicognani, visiting from the Vatican to address a meet-

---

[34]Vaughn, *supra* note 31, at 49–51; Black, *supra* note 17, at 37.

[35]*Working Draft of the Lord–Quigley Code Proposal*, in BLACK, *supra* note 17, at 302 (Appendix A); *The 1930 Production Code*, in Jon Lewis, *Hollywood v. Hard Core* 302–07 (2000).

[36]LEONARD LEFF & JERROLD SIMMONS, The DAME IN THE KIMONO: HOLLYWOOD, CENSORSHIP, AND THE PRODUCTION CODE FROM THE 1920s TO THE 1960s 283 (1990) (describing various minor changes made by Hays in 1934 and by the MPAA in subsequent years, including the addition of "major sections on crime (1939), profanity (1939), and cruelty to animals (1940)").

ing of Catholic Charities in New York, to urge more vigorous action against Hollywood. Cicognani's subsequent speech mourned the movies' "massacre of innocence of youth" and urged Catholics to unite in a campaign "for the purification of the cinema."[37] With this seeming imperative from Rome, the Conference of Catholic bishops, meeting in Washington, DC, several weeks later, vowed to create a "Legion of Decency," which would not only review movies and decide which ones should be forbidden to Catholics, but would organize boycotts of theaters that showed any film thus condemned.

However potent the studios might have found the Church's boycott threat, its influence with some of the bankers on whom Hollywood depended was even more persuasive. A. H. Giannini, head of the Bank of America and a loyal Catholic, made it clear to producers at a meeting in late 1933 that continued financing depended on serious enforcement of the Code. Chicago's Cardinal Mundelein and New York's Cardinal Patrick Hayes made use of their Wall Street connections to apply similar pressure. Mundelein's longtime friend and golfing partner, Harold Stuart, was a principal in the firm of Halsey, Stuart, a major underwriter for Fox. As the historian Stephen Vaughn writes, Cardinal Mundelein "knew exactly where to go to get the Church's message to the producers."[38]

The Hays Office welcomed the pressure. Hays agreed with the Church in preferring industry self-regulation to government censorship. Bolstered by the bankers' threats and the fear of boycotts, Hays now established the Production Code Administration (PCA) specifically to enforce the Code, announced that all scripts would have to be vetted by the PCA, and hired Joseph Breen, a brash PR man and unrepentant anti-Semite who had worked with Martin Quigley in Chicago, to head the new censorship office.

Breen had already expressed frustration at the producers' independence. In 1932, he wrote to Father Wilfred Parsons, a fellow censorship activist and a Jesuit professor, that Hays was wrong to think "these lousy Jews out here [in Hollywood] would abide by the Code's provisions." Hays lacked "proper knowledge of the breed," Breen continued. "They are simply a rotten bunch of vile people with no respect for anything beyond the making of money.... They are, probably, the scum of the earth."[39] There is no record of Parsons or other church officials taking Breen to task for these and similar comments.

By the late 1930s, between the Legion of Decency in New York and Breen, the Church's delegate at the PCA in Hollywood, the Catholic Church controlled the content of American movies. Every script was submitted in advance. (In 1936, Breen's office reviewed over 1,200 of them, and had more than 1,400 conferences with producers and directors to dis-

---

[37]BLACK, *supra* note 19, at 20.

[38]Stephen Vaughn, *Financiers, Movie Producers, and the Church: Economic Origins of the Production Code*, in 4 CURRENT RESEARCH IN FILM: AUDIENCES, ECONOMICS, AND LAW 213 (Bruce Austin ed., 1988). *See also* BLACK, *supra* note 19, at 24; BLACK, *supra* note 17, at 158–59; Francis Couvares, *Hollywood and the Culture Wars*, 50 AMER. Q. 192, 197 (1998).

[39]BLACK, *supra* note 19, at 20; BLACK, *supra* note 17, at 70; LEFF & SIMMONS, *supra* note 36, at 33–34.

cuss rewrites.[40]) Any script the PCA rejected was rewritten to conform to its requirements. And if, after this laborious process, Legion of Decency headquarters in New York still objected to certain dialogue or scenes, Breen would force further changes. Thus, in 1941 when the Legion disapproved a Greta Garbo comedy, *Two-Faced Woman,* because of its "un-Christian attitude toward marriage," and Cardinal Spellman, already entrenched at the Archdiocese of New York, pronounced the film "dangerous to public morality," MGM withdrew it, then added scenes to negate any hint of adultery.[41]

This is not to say, of course, that Hollywood's output from 1934 until the gradual weakening of the Code in the 1950s consisted only of mom and apple pie. Producers were adept at suggesting events that could not be shown directly. Crime, evil, and fallen women were timeless themes; and as long as sin was punished in the end, a moralizing voice-over penned by Breen would usually suffice to qualify the film for PCA approval. In addition, rebel producers occasionally won small victories, such as David O. Selznick's famous refusal in 1939 to delete Rhett Butler's "frankly, my dear, I don't give a damn" from *Gone With the Wind.* But overall, the system was tightly controlled by the Hays Office, with the Legion often forcing even more changes after Breen had finished tinkering.

The historian Francis Couvares summarizes the role of the Catholic Church in American film censorship:

> The Church knew that the higher the level of government, the more marginal its influence. With blatant anti-Catholic and anti-immigrant feeling welling up regularly in local and national election campaigns, the Church declined repeatedly to endorse any call for national regulation of thought and expression, fearing with reason that the result could not fail but reflect Protestant theological and moral hegemony.[42]

The ironic result was that a nonmajority religion, Catholicism, controlled the content of American movies for more than 20 years. "From the mid-1930s until Otto Preminger's release of *The Moon is Blue* in 1953," Gregory Black writes, "no Hollywood studio seriously challenged the right of the priests to censor their films."[43]

THE THREAT TO CHURCH CONTROL: *BURSTYN* AND ITS AFTERMATH

In 1950, the Legion of Decency's annual report noted with dismay that an increasing number of foreign films were gaining popularity in America. The problem, of course, was that these films were not subject to PCA and Legion

---

[40]BLACK, *supra* note 17, at 238–39.
[41]LEFF & SIMMONS, *supra* note 36, at 120–21.
[42]Couvares, *supra* note 38, at 194.
[43]BLACK, *supra* note 19, at 5.

censorship. In the preceding year, the report said, 53% of foreign films had been judged objectionable by the Legion either "wholly or in part."[44]

If one work can be identified as triggering this post–World War II American enthusiasm for foreign films, it was Roberto Rossellini's *Open City*. The 1945 neorealist classic dramatizes the Nazi occupation of Rome during the last months of the war. With its gritty realism, clear suggestions of lesbianism, horrifying scenes of Nazi torture, and powerful performance by Anna Magnani as Pina, a working-class woman pregnant without benefit of marriage, who is savagely shot down in the film's most famous scene, *Open City* was certainly a change from sanitized Hollywood fare. Joseph Burstyn had purchased the American rights to the film from an enterprising GI who reportedly brought home a print in his duffel bag.[45]

Based on the true story of an Italian priest who had been executed for helping the Resistance, *Open City* was lauded by the Catholic Church. But it contained a hint of things to come when the film's evil Nazi commander asks the priest, Don Pietro, why he aids subversives and atheists. The good father responds: "I am a Catholic priest and I believe that a man who fights for justice and liberty walks in the pathways of the Lord—and the pathways of the Lord are infinite."[46] This expression of Rossellini's unconventional, egalitarian religiosity would be developed more fully 3 years later in *The Miracle*.

Open City grossed an amazing (for a foreign film) $3 million at the U.S. box office and was chosen Best Film of 1946 by the New York Film Critics.[47] Audiences in New York and Los Angeles loved it. (We already know how Ingrid Bergman reacted.) But with the U.S. Catholic Church still angry at the adulterous pair, Rossellini could expect little mercy from Cardinal Spellman when *The Miracle* opened in New York in December 1950.

The year 1950 was not a relaxed time for the American film community. The House Committee on Un-American Activities (HUAC) had been investigating "communist subversion" in the movie industry ever since its famous 1947 hearings, which ended with 10 directors and screenwriters in prison for refusing, on First Amendment grounds, to answer HUAC's questions about their politics. Eric Johnston, who had succeeded Will Hays at the helm of the Motion Picture Association of America (MPAA—the name having been changed from the more unwieldy MPPDA), responded to the HUAC hearings by initiating a blacklist that drove politically suspect directors, producers, screenwriters, and actors out of the industry. Cardinal Spellman, a personal friend of FBI director J. Edgar Hoover, was an avid supporter of the anticommunist crusade. He was also an aggressive advocate of government funding for parochial schools, and an important force

---

[44]*Legion of Decency Lauds U.S. Movies*, N.Y. TIMES, Nov. 17, 1950, at 33.
[45]PETER BONDANELLA, THE FILMS OF ROBERTO ROSSELLINI 47–48 (1993).
[46]*Quoted in* PETER BRUNETTE, ROBERTO ROSSELLINI 47 (1987).
[47]BLACK, *supra* note 19, at 74. *See also* BRUNETTE, *supra* note 46, at 41–60.

in pressuring city and state officials to suppress "immoral," "subversive," or "sacrilegious" entertainments.[48]

Spellman had little tolerance for Rossellini's maverick spirituality as represented in *The Miracle*. The film's protagonist (again played by Anna Magnani) is ignorant and demented—hardly the model for a modern Virgin Mary. Yet her implicit seduction by the bearded vagabond whom she mistakes for St. Joseph (played by a young Federico Fellini) is accompanied by a voice-over reciting Bible passages. This lazy, thieving heroine refuses to do any work after her "immaculate conception," and steals an apple from a woman in church. Yet when she is tormented by the villagers, who crown her with a basin, the scenes obviously recall Christ's passion. Finally, she struggles toward a church high on a hill, to give birth. The last scene is bathed in light. As Don Pietro says in *Open City*, "the pathways of the Lord are infinite."

The campaign against this unusual retelling of the biblical passion soon went beyond New York City's Commissioner McCaffrey and Cardinal Spellman. Picketing at the Paris Theater in January 1951 escalated to bomb threats. The fire commissioner issued summonses for alleged overcrowding. Performances were interrupted. Martin Quigley threatened Radio City Music Hall with a Catholic boycott if an award that the New York Film Critics planned to present to *The Miracle* were given there as planned. Church officials supported Quigley by informing the Music Hall's management that Spellman would be gravely offended if the ceremony went forward. The critics moved it to another location.[49]

Not all Catholics, however, agreed with the Legion and Spellman. In addition to the more nuanced appreciation of the film noted 3 years earlier in the Vatican's *Osservatore Romano*, a group of American Catholic intellectuals protested the Church's condemnation of the film. Their reaction was summarized by Otto Spaeth, Director of the American Federation of Arts, who wrote: "There was indeed 'blasphemy'" in *The Miracle*, "but it was the blasphemy of the villagers, who stopped at nothing, not even the mock singing of a hymn to the Virgin, in their brutal badgering of the tragic woman."[50] *Commonweal* magazine likewise editorialized: "Sometimes it seems as if we American Catholics reduce the struggle for the hearts and minds of men to a contest between picket lines and pressure groups and in doing so slight the emphasis Catholic doctrine puts on free consent and reasoned morality."[51] Two weeks later, an article by Notre Dame professor William Clancy

---

[48]See JOHN COONEY, THE AMERICAN POPE: THE LIFE AND TIMES OF FRANCIS CARDINAL SPELLMAN xv, 104, 116, 145, 180 (1984).

[49]*"Miracle" Theatre Charges Bias*, N.Y. TIMES, Feb. 6, 1951, 29; *"Miracle" Theatre Accused of Bribes*, N.Y. Times, Feb. 10, 1951, 15; Westin, *supra* note 1, at 11–12; Crowther, *supra* note 5, at 37–38.

[50]Otto Spaeth, *Fogged Screen*, MAGAZINE OF ART, Feb. 1951, at 44, *quoted in* Burstyn v. Wilson, 343 U.S. at 514–15 (Frankfurter, J., concurring).

[51]*"The Miracle" and Related Matters*, 53 COMMONWEAL 507 (1951).

in *Commonweal* reported that many prominent Catholics had found *The Miracle* "deeply moving" and "profoundly religious." Clancy essayed that Catholic campaigns against movies shocked "many loyal Catholics," who were "profoundly disturbed to see certain of our co-religionists embarked upon crusades which we feel can result only in great harm to the cause of religion, of art, and of intelligence."[52]

Even the idiosyncratic Rossellini tried to persuade Cardinal Spellman of his religious intentions. "In *The Miracle*, men are still without pity because they have not gone back to God," the director explained.

> But God is already present in the faith, however confused, of the poor persecuted woman and since God is forever, a human being suffers and is misunderstood. "The Miracle" occurs when, with the birth of the child, the poor demented woman regains sanity in her maternal love. They were my intentions and I hope that your Eminence will deign to consider them with paternal benevolence.[53]

As the case made its way through the courts, dissent within the Catholic Church intensified. The legal historian Alan Westin recounts that a group of Catholic writers, teachers, editors, and lawyers, "some of whom had voiced individual disagreement publicly over *The Miracle* ban, decided that more than individual statements would be necessary if the American public were to understand the division of Catholic opinion." They decided to file a brief in the Supreme Court, "as Catholics, taking the opposite side." The resulting Committee of Catholics for Cultural Action circulated a draft friend-of-the-court brief to like-minded coreligionists, inviting them to join in this effort to demonstrate the nonmonolithic character of American Catholicism and their opposition to "a narrowly short-sighted sectarianism, and an anti-Communism which is too frequently uncritical, sterile, and negative."[54]

The Archdiocese did not take this lying down. It summoned the rebels to a meeting where Monsignor John Middleton of the Chancery office assured them that he was deeply concerned about recent "extremist actions" by Catholic lay groups such as the "picketing of the Metropolitan Opera House for the portrayal of the Church in Verdi's *Don Carlo*." Middleton "went on to suggest that a better result might be achieved for both the Church and cultural freedom if the Committee did not file a brief in the Supreme Court.... If the Committee withdrew, Monsignor Middleton suggested, the views of the Committee would be solicited by the Chancery in future censorship issues."[55] So the Committee of Catholics for Cultural Ac-

---

[52]William Clancy, *The Catholic as Philistine*, 53 COMMONWEAL 567 (1951). Clancy was fired, later became a priest, and for years "regaled listeners with his tale of colliding with Spellman." Cooney, *supra* note 48, at 45.

[53]*Rossellini Appeals to Spellman on Film*, N.Y. TIMES, Jan. 13, 1951, at 10.

[54]WESTIN, *supra* note 1, at 23.

[55]*Id.* at 25.

tion folded its tents—"out of consideration," it said, "for the larger ambiguities in the situation and out of filial deference" to Cardinal Spellman.[56]

The result was that, greatly to Ephraim London's chagrin, the only brief to the Supreme Court representing Christianity came from New York's State Catholic Committee, in support of banning *The Miracle*. (Protestant groups did not get organized in time to file a brief in opposition to the ban.) The motion picture industry stayed out of the Supreme Court case, as it had kept silent during the entire course of the controversy. As Spellman's biographer John Cooney writes, "The business, plagued with federal investigators scouring Hollywood for Communists, was running scared. Movie moguls didn't need to be singled out by anti-Communist Catholics. They bent over backward to appease modern inquisitors such as Spellman and the Legion of Decency."[57] Cooney might have added that Hollywood had long ago made its peace with the Catholic hierarchy, and in fact used it to standardize film content and appease local censorship boards. Now, with Church and state combining to suppress a work that would plainly not have passed muster under the Production Code, the industry was stuck in a dilemma of its own creation.

Burstyn and London faced many hurdles in *The Miracle* case, not least of which was the 1915 Supreme Court decision announcing that movies are not a form of expression protected by the First Amendment. In a 1948 antitrust case, Justice William O. Douglas, writing for the Court, had taken note of this anomaly, and even seemed embarrassed by it. Douglas opined that "moving pictures, like newspapers and radio, are included in the press whose freedom is guaranteed by the First Amendment."[58]

But the New York Court of Appeals, in its decision in *The Miracle* case, dismissed Douglas' assertion as merely "dictum," and insisted that movies are constitutionally unprotected entertainment spectacles, "and not such vehicles for thought as to bring them within the press of the country."[59] Two of the New York judges dissented, arguing that the *Mutual Film* decision was no longer good law and "should be relegated to its place on the history shelf."[60] Obviously, the Supreme Court would have to resolve this issue in the *Burstyn* case.

The Supreme Court's agreement to accept review in *Burstyn* was in itself a hopeful development, for the Court had, in the preceding few years, turned down two invitations to check the wide-ranging power of film licensing boards. The films in these cases had both involved race discrimination (Atlanta's ban on *Lost Boundaries* and Memphis's ban on *Curley*).[61] Hot-button issue though it was, sacrilege in 1951 was evidently a safer subject than racism.

---

[56]*Id.*

[57]COONEY, *supra* note 48, at 200.

[58]United States v. Paramount Pictures, 334 U.S. 131, 166 (1948).

[59]Burstyn v. Wilson, 303 N.Y. at 260–61.

[60]*Id.*. at 264–68 (Fuld & Dye, JJ., dissenting).

[61]Otten, *supra* note 28.

At oral argument in *Burstyn v. Wilson* on April 24, 1952, Charles Brind, counsel to the Board of Regents, argued that in enforcing the New York law, the board did not refer to its own religious opinions or those of the Catholic Church. Justice Felix Frankfurter found this astonishing. "Do you mean that whether or not a film is sacrilegious can be mechanically determined?" Frankfurter asked. "How do you find out that it profanes a religious doctrine? To what authority to you refer?" Brind said the Regents concluded that *The Miracle* was "of such a nature as to be offensive to the American public." "The Regents didn't profess to go on any proclaimed doctrine of any religion?" Frankfurter pressed. Unbelievably, Brind answered: "That's right."[62]

Wendell Brown, the New York Solicitor General, addressed the church–state issue. He denied that banning "sacrilegious" expression violated the exhibitor's freedom of speech or religion. "On the contrary," he averred, "it is a violation of the public's freedom of religion…. It is wholly within the guarantee of religious freedom that the State prohibits that which seeks to destroy religion."[63]

The justices queried Brown on the First Amendment question, and he eventually acknowledged that despite the 1915 *Mutual Film* case, movies do have constitutional protection.[64] But this did not mean that prior-restraint licensing was unconstitutional. Ephraim London, arguing that "a movie cannot ever be censored in advance," got into an argument with Justice Sherman Minton on this point. "Not even for obscenity?" Minton asked. London said: "That's right."[65] It was a position the Supreme Court would reject in its *Burstyn* decision the following month.

That decision, as we have seen, did away with sacrilege as a censorship standard, and with the archaic ruling in *Mutual Film* that cinema is only a business. On the contrary, as Justice Clark wrote for the Court, it is undoubtedly "a significant medium for the communication of ideas." It did not follow, however, that all prior-restraint licensing was unconstitutional. Clark left open the question whether states could impose prior censorship "under a clearly drawn statute designed and applied to prevent the showing of obscene films."[66]

Frankfurter was clearly the justice most interested in the church–state issue. His separate concurring opinion in *Burstyn*, counting its encyclopedic appendix, was three times as long as Clark's opinion for the Court. In it, Frankfurter not only detailed the course of events—Commissioner McCaffrey's ban, Cardinal Spellman's lament, and the dissenting views of Catholic intellectuals like the poet Allen Tate and Notre Dame's William Clancy—but he explored the history of sacrilege and blasphemy (two differ-

---

[62]Westin, *supra* note 1, at 27.
[63]*Id.* at 29.
[64]*Id.*
[65]*Id.* at 25–29.
[66]Burstyn v. Wilson, 343 U.S. at 505–06.

ent concepts that had been used interchangeably throughout the controversy by both the Church and the Board of Regents), and he asserted the total impossibility of applying an evenhanded "sacrilege" test.

"A motion picture portraying Christ as divine, for example," Frankfurter said, "… would offend the religious opinions of the members of several Protestant denominations who do not believe in the Trinity, … Conversely, one showing Christ as merely an ethical teacher could not but offend millions of Christians … Which is sacrilegious?" And so on, for transubstantiation, veneration of relics, and other beliefs sacred to one or another of America's 300 religious sects.[67]

THE DEMISE OF CHURCH CONTROL

Although the Supreme Court's decision in *Burstyn v. Wilson* was narrowly limited to the impropriety of "sacrilege" as a censorship criterion, its repercussions were broader. The Court's comments about the vagueness of "sacrilege"—setting the censor "adrift upon a boundless sea, … with no charts but those provided by the most vocal and powerful orthodoxies"—could obviously be applied to other open-ended censorship standards such as "immoral" or "harmful." And over the next 6 years, the Supreme Court, relying on *Burstyn*, overturned bans on *Pinky*, a Hollywood film about a light-skinned African American girl who passes as White; a film version of Richard Wright's *Native Son;* a remake of Fritz Lang's expressionist classic, *M;* French director Max Ophuls's *La Ronde;* and Otto Preminger's *The Moon Is Blue*, a Hollywood farce that is often credited with breaking the Production Code.[68] *Moon* played successfully without a Code seal—and despite the Legion's and Spellman's condemnation—after Preminger refused to eliminate the sexual banter from its script. Preminger's defiance came just a year after the *Burstyn* decision, and theater owners' willingness to show *Moon* was no doubt influenced by the Church's loss in *The Miracle* case.

Bosley Crowther, the film critic for *The New York Times*, later suggested that the Catholic Church made a such a fuss over a limited-audience art film like *The Miracle* precisely because it represented a new breed of postwar foreign movies that were not subject to the Production Code, and therefore to the Church's control. Even though *Burstyn* as a legal matter involved only official government censorship, it weakened the industry's privately enforced Code by opening the U.S. market to foreign films that, as Crowther said, looked at

---

[67]*Id.* at 530 (Frankfurter, Jackson, & Burton, JJ., concurring).

[68]Gelling v. Texas, 383 U.S. 960 (1952) (*Pinky*); Superior Pictures v. Department of Education, 346 U.S. 587 (1954) (*Native Son* and *M*); Commercial Pictures v. Department of Education, 346 U.S. 587 (1954) (*La Ronde*); Holmby v. Vaughn, 350 U.S. 870 (1955) (*The Moon Is Blue*). On *The Moon* and breaking the Code, *see* LEFF & SIMMONS, *supra* note 36, at 185–203; BLACK, *supra* note 19, at 119–28.

life in all its "rawness and reality."[69] Hollywood could no longer get away with Code-approved formulas and sanitized versions of the human condition.

As Quigley, Breen, and others had perceived years before, a private industry code, strictly enforced, is far more effective than government censorship as a means of imposing religious dogma. It is secret, for one thing, working at the preproduction stage. The audience never knows what has been trimmed, cut, revised, or never written. Even more significant, private censorship can be far more sweeping in its demands, because it is not bound by constitutional due process or free-expression rules (in general, these apply only to government), or by the constitutional command of church–state separation.

But neither film licensing nor Production Code enforcement ended with *The Miracle* case. The New York Board of Regents continued banning films, and in 1959, the Supreme Court again chastised it, this time over its denial of a license to a tame film version of D. H. Lawrence's scandalous novel, *Lady Chatterley's Lover*. The ban was based on the film's apparent approval of adultery. Justice Potter Stewart wrote for the Court that the First Amendment "is not confined to the expression of ideas that are conventional or shared by a majority. It protects advocacy of the opinion that adultery may sometimes be proper, no less than advocacy of socialism or the single tax."[70]

The Supreme Court never did rule that banning films unless their exhibitors first seek and obtain a license from the state is per se unconstitutional. In 1961, in fact, it squarely rejected the argument. Tom Clark wrote the opinion, over an impassioned dissent by Chief Justice Earl Warren, that enumerated many examples of absurd and bigoted censorship decisions still being perpetrated by various state and local licensing boards.[71] Four years later, though, the Court crippled prior-restraint censorship by invalidating Maryland's licensing scheme because it did not provide for prompt judicial review of determinations that a film was obscene.[72] Stripped of their freewheeling power to ban films *without* first going to court, the licensing boards faded away. (The Dallas, Texas board was a holdout, lasting until the 1990s.)

Hollywood finally got rid of the Production Code in the 1960s. In its place, the MPAA's new head, Jack Valenti, created the secretive rating system that we know today. Movie ratings are not without censorial effects—producers negotiate with the ratings board and cut scenes or dialogue in order to achieve a desired classification—but there is no question that American cinema today is far freer than in the heyday of the Code, when Joe Breen's heavy blue pencil and the Legion of Decency's ever-present boycott threat combined to assure that films adhered to Catholic Church doctrine.

[69]Crowther, *supra* note 5, at 35.
[70]Kingsley Int'l Pictures Corp. v. Regents of the Univ. of the State of New York, 360 U.S. 684, 689 (1959).
[71]Times Film Corp. v. City of Chicago, 365 U.S. 43 (1961); *Id.* at 69–72 (Warren, C.J., with Black, Douglas, & Brennan, JJ., dissenting).
[72]Freedman v. Maryland, 380 U.S. 51 (1965).

Ironically, the boycott threat was probably never as potent as the Church pretended. As with birth control and other issues on which large numbers of Catholics follow their own consciences, Gregory Black and other film historians have shown that millions of American Catholics "ignored the Legion's ratings and flocked to see films that were condemned."[73] Had the producers held out against the Church's pressure in the 1930s, it is likely that many boycotts would not have materialized, and those that did would have been less impressive than the studios feared. On the other hand, the producers may have known this, but financial pressure from their bankers proved decisive in establishing Father Lord's Code as the rule of law in Hollywood for more than 20 years.

THE CONTINUING PROBLEM
OF CHURCH–STATE SEPARATION

What does *The Miracle* case and the history of film censorship teach us about religion, artistic freedom, and church–state separation in America? As many scholars have noted, the Establishment Clause is not unrelated to the other freedoms enumerated in the First Amendment. Freedom of speech and religion are intrinsically connected to, and dependent on, church–state separation. When one church or one religion exercises political power, as Christianity clearly does in America, the freedoms of religious minorities—among them Jews, Muslims, Hindus, Wiccans, Buddhists, secular humanists, and nonbelievers—are threatened. Indeed, the freedoms of Christians are threatened as well. The Establishment Clause was designed *both* to keep religion out of government affairs and to keep government out of religion.

This dual goal is compromised by church–state entanglements that have intensified in America since the early 1990s. Government-sponsored prayer breakfasts obviously promote the dominant religion. Government funding, through vouchers, for predominantly Catholic parochial schools supports the religious indoctrination that is a fundamental aim of such schools, and diverts funds from secular public education. "Charitable choice" provisions in federal and state law permit religious organizations to receive government funds even while discriminating in employment against those of other faiths, and while denying services that violate their religious beliefs—most dramatically, denying emergency contraception and other reproductive health services, even where they are the only hospitals in the area serving low-income citizens, and where a woman's life or health is in danger.[74]

---

[73]BLACK, *supra* note 19, at 241.

[74]The Personal Responsibility and Work Opportunity Reconciliation Act of 1996, §104, 42 U.S. Code §604a (the welfare reform law), allows religious organizations to receive state funds for social services while maintaining discriminatory employment practices pursuant to a religious exemption in the federal employment discrimination law.   (*continued*)

President George W. Bush's 2001 Executive Order establishing the Office of Faith-Based Initiatives instructed federal agencies to "eliminate regulatory, contracting, and other programmatic obstacles" to the funding of religious organizations to provide social services.[75] Jewish, atheist, and church–state separation groups protested that the Executive Order opened the door to religious proselytizing with government funds.[76] The Catholic Church, however, welcomed the new policy, noting that it was important to assure that religious groups are "empowered" without being "bound by excessive regulations."[77]

The administration's next step was to press for legislation that would go beyond the terms of existing law (primarily, the 1996 welfare reform act) in providing favors to religion. When Congress failed to pass this proposed "Charitable Choice Act of 2001," the administration went forward anyway, enacting regulations and additional Executive Orders that: allow religious groups to have sectarian symbols and scriptures in their publicly funded programs, allow government grants for the renovation of houses of worship, and establish "training vouchers" for those pursuing careers in ministry.[78] *The New York Times* commented: "The president's unilateral order, which wrongly cuts Congress out of the loop, lets faith-based organizations use tax dollars to win converts and gives them a green light to discriminate in employment. It should be struck down by the courts."[79]

---

[74](*continued*) On the public-health effects of charitable choice, see Amy Nunn *et al.*, *Contraceptive Emergency: Catholic Hospitals Overwhelmingly Refuse to Provide Emergency Contraception*, CONSCIENCE (Summer 2003), at 38; Katha Pollitt, *Special Rights for the Godly?* THE NATION, June 24, 2002, at 10 (describing a California case in which a court found a Christian born-again nurse who was fired after refusing to provide emergency contraception at a public clinic had suffered a violation of her religious freedom); George Gund Foundation, Pro-Choice Resource Center, & Reproductive Freedom Project, ACLU, *Conscientious Exemptions and Reproductive Rights* (Aug. 2000).

[75]"Executive Order—Establishment of White House Office of Faith-Based and Community Initiatives," White House Press Release, Jan. 29, 2001, usgovinfo.about.com/library/weekly/aa012901c.htm (accessed Nov. 13, 2001).

[76]*See, e.g.*, Elisabeth Bumiller, *Talk of Religion Provokes Amens as Well as Anxiety; Faith Has Become a Central Part of the Administration*, N.Y. TIMES, Apr. 22, 2002, at A19; Americans United for Separation of Church & State, *President Bush and "Faith-Based" Initiatives*, www.au.org/press/pr12601.htm (accessed Nov. 13, 2001); Thomas Edsall, *Jewish Leaders Criticize "Faith-Based" Initiative*, WASH. POST, Feb. 27, 2001, at A4; *More Media Stories Raise Questions About "Faith Based" Partnerships*, Amer. Atheist, Oct. 24, 2000, www.atheists.org/flash.line/church26.htm (accessed Nov. 13, 2001).

[77]U.S. Conference of Catholic Bishops, *Catholic Bishops Welcome Faith-Based Initiatives, Seek Specifics*, National Conference of Catholic Bishops Office of Communications, www.nccbuscc.org/comm/archives/2001/01-019.htm (accessed Nov. 13, 2001).

[78]Executive Orders 13,279 and 13,280 (Dec. 12, 2002); 42 Code of Federal Regulations §54a.5 (funded religious organizations "may use space in their facilities to provide services supported by applicable programs, without removing religious art, icons, scriptures, or other symbols"); 42 Code of Federal Regulations §54a.6 (funded religious organization may discriminate in employment on the basis of religion); Jennifer Bernstein, *On a Wing and a Prayer*, CONSCIENCE (Autumn 2003), at 23; Joseph Conn, *Faith-Based Fiat*, CHURCH & STATE, Jan. 2003, at 4.

[79]*Using Tax Dollars for Churches*, N.Y. TIMES, Dec. 30, 2002, at A20. The magazine of Catholics for a Free Choice likewise noted that charitable choice provisions "will undermine the traditional role of religion as a prophetic critic of government.... Like every other government-subsidized group, religion will be less likely to bite the hand that feeds it." Bernstein, *supra* note 78, at 24–25.

Government support for parochial schools has probably been the most contentious Establishment Clause issue in American politics and in the courts. In the 1960s, the Supreme Court decided a series of cases that limited state aid to religious education. The assistance had to be finite, secular in nature, and not supportive of the parochial school's overall religious program.[80] By the 1990s, though, with changes in American politics and the makeup of the Court, these principles began to bend. Asserting the need to accommodate—to help parents whose religious beliefs compel them to send their children to parochial schools—the Court first approved public school teachers' giving remedial instruction on church school premises; then allowed state funding for interpreters and other aids to enable pupils to pursue religious education; and finally in 2002 reversed course entirely and upheld state-funded vouchers for parochial school tuition.[81]

That voucher decision came at the end of the Supreme Court's 2001–2002 term, only days after a federal appeals court in California ruled that the words "under God," added by Congress to the Pledge of Allegiance in 1954, at the height of anticommunist fervor, constituted a government endorsement of religion, and therefore a violation of the Establishment Clause. The widespread shock and indignation that greeted this ruling—including assumptions that it would be swiftly overruled—were a measure of how far America had moved beyond the concept of accommodation and toward direct government support for religion.[82]

---

[80]Committee for Public Education v. Nyquist, 463 U.S. 388 (1983); Lemon v. Kurtzman, 403 U.S. 602 (1971); Tilton v. Richardson, 403 U.S. 673 (1971); Meek v. Pettinger, 421 U.S. 349 (1975).

[81]Zobrest v. Catalina Foothills School Dist., 509 U.S. 1 (1993); Mueller v. Allen, 463 U.S. 388 (1983); Agostini v. Felton, 521 U.S. 203 (1997); Zelman v. Simmons-Harris, 536 U.S. 639 (2002). Relying on this string of victories, advocates of government support for religion brought a challenge in 1999 to a Washington State constitutional provision that prohibits funding of religion education, including ministerial training. They argued that denying government funds discriminates on the basis of "viewpoint" and thus burdens the free exercise of religion. A federal appeals court agreed, but in 2004, the Supreme Court reversed, ruling that even though state funding of religious education is not prohibited by the Establishment Clause, neither is it required by the Free Exercise Clause. Locke v. Davey, 540 U.S. 712 (2004). As Justice Stephen Breyer recognized at oral argument, if the rule were otherwise, then every government program, "not just educational programs but nursing programs, hospital programs, [and] social welfare programs" would have to fund religious along with secular service providers. Linda Greenhouse, *Justices Resist Religious Study Using Subsidies*, N.Y. TIMES, Dec. 3, 2003, at A1.

[82]Newdow v. U.S. Congress, *supra* note 14. The Supreme Court reversed, but not on the merits of the case. Five justices voted to reverse on the ground that Newdow, a noncustodial parent, did not have standing to sue on behalf of his daughter. (The girl's mother had filed a brief supporting the use of "under God" in the Pledge.) Three justices—Rehnquist, O'Connor, and Thomas—would have reached the merits and upheld the use of "under God"—though for different reasons. Justice O'Connor called it a permissible example of "ceremonial deism." *Elk Grove School Dist. v. Newdow*, 124 S.Ct. 2301 (2004); *see* Arthur Schlesinger, Jr., *When Patriotism Wasn't Religious*, N.Y. TIMES, Jul. 7, 2002, Week in Review section, at 9 (adding "under God" to Pledge in 1954 "came about in order to emphasize the antagonism between God-fearing Americans and godless Communists"); David Rosenbaum, *With Little Ado, Congress Put God in Pledge in 1954*, N.Y. TIMES, June 28, 2002, at A14.

On the art scene, too, religion has continued to drive attempts at censorship. Then-New York City Mayor Rudolph Giuliani's effort in 1999 to defund the Brooklyn Museum and oust it from its headquarters because of a painting titled "Holy Virgin Mary," which he thought blasphemous, was one well-publicized instance of a government official applying religious tests to art. Ten years earlier, Senator Jesse Helms and other members of Congress excoriated the National Endowment for the Arts (NEA) for allowing a museum that received an NEA grant to include Andres Serrano's large luminous photograph, "Piss Christ," in a show of contemporary work. Their efforts were more successful than Giuliani's: Congressional threats to defund the NEA combined with new legislation requiring the agency to consider "respect for the diverse beliefs ... of the American people" in awarding grants,[83] forced changes making it unlikely that any work, artist, or show that uses religious imagery in ways offensive to dominant religious authorities will receive support.

Of course, the argument is made that this is not really censorship, only a prudent use of public funds. But, as the Supreme Court said in *Burstyn*, government "has no legitimate interest in protecting any or all religions from views distasteful to them." Arts funding decisions that are driven by fear of offending the "beliefs" of the American people not only violate this principle but inevitably squelch expression offensive to the hierarchies of Christianity, America's dominant religion.

Outside the funding context as well, some Catholic groups continue to press for censorship of art they consider sacrilegious. As in 1951, they argue that any art they find offensive, and indeed any failure to suppress it, is an act of anti-Catholic bigotry. In 1988, for example, a number of Catholic and Protestant groups launched protests—often violent and anti-Semitic—against Martin Scorsese's *The Last Temptation of Christ* (Jews were prominent among the producers); Hollywood responded by limiting the film's distribution.[84] Ten years later, the Catholic League for Religious and Civil Rights picketed and denounced Terrence McNally's play, *Corpus Christi*, when it opened in New York City, temporarily causing the theater to cancel the production. Like Rossellini, who had used ignorant villagers and a demented suffering woman to illustrate his understanding of the gospels, McNally attempted in his play to show the sufferings of gay men in the homophobic Texas town where he grew up.[85]

---

[83]National Endowment for the Arts v. Finley, 524 U.S. 569 (1998), upheld the legislation but noted that likely First Amendment problems would arise if the clause were applied to discriminate against particular political or religious views. *Id.* at 587. Giuliani's attempt to retaliate against the Brooklyn Museum was squelched by a federal court in *Brooklyn Institute of Arts & Sciences v. City of New York*, 64 F. Supp.2d 184 (E.D.N.Y 1999); *see generally Free Expression in Arts Funding: A Public Policy Report* (2003), www.fepproject.org/policyreports/ artsfunding.html (accessed Mar. 4, 2004).

[84]*See* Charles Lyons, *The Paradox of Protest: American Film, 1980–1992*, in Couvares, *supra* note 8, at 300–09; Lewis, *supra* note 35, at 280.

[85]*New York Audiences Get A Choice ... Will San Antonio and Anchorage Be So Lucky?* 70 CENSORSHIP NEWS (Summer 1998), www.ncac.org/cen_news/cn70corpuschristi.html (accessed 9/23/02); *Terrence McNally's Corpus Christi Under Attack in Indiana*, www.ncac.org/issues/corpuschristi.html (accessed 9/23/02).

In early 2002, the Catholic League protested an exhibit at a California museum because it included figurines by the Spanish artist Antoni Miralda in postures of defecation. Among the persons represented were the pope and several nuns. These "caganers," as the figurines are called, are "a part of Catholic Catalonian tradition that dates back to the 1800s," as the museum explained, and symbolize the cycle of eating and fertilization. "They're included in nativity scenes to ensure good luck for farmers in the following year."[86]

"'I know that American society is more strict with its religious ideas than we are in Catalonia,'" the Associated Press quoted one elderly collector of the figurines during this controversy. But what the caganer does "is natural. Even the king has to do it every day, or at least every other day."[87]

As the history of *The Miracle* shows, our constitutional mandates of religious freedom and church–state separation have not necessarily led to toleration. Officials of the Catholic Church, and of some Protestant denominations, have propounded a narrow and reductive approach to art, thereby missing the nuance, ambiguity, or spiritual but unconventional explorations of religious experience in such works as *The Miracle* or *Piss Christ*. Yet their views do not always represent the range of opinion, and tolerance for artistic freedom, that exists among the members of their congregations.

Censorship history shows that powerful organized religious institutions—in America, inevitably Christian—can compromise artistic and intellectual freedom even without state involvement. It also shows that government officials are easily swayed by powerful religions: It happened in 1951 with *The Miracle*, and it continues with parochial school vouchers, "charitable choice," and "faith-based initiatives." The Hollywood Production Code and the New York film licensing board may seem amusing relics of a distant past, but their legacy is powerfully present in today's church–state dilemmas.

---

[86]John Glionna, *Catholics Slam Napa Art Exhibit*, L.A. TIMES, Jan. 5, 2002, www.latimes.com/news/local/la-000001083jan05.story (accessed Jan. 7, 2002).

[87]*Catholic League Objects to Traditional Figures in Art Installation*, Jan. 7, 2002, www.ncac.org/issues/antonimiralda.html (accessed Nov. 11, 2002).

Chapter 5

Suppressing Hateful Ideas
by Force of Law

Reflections on *R.A.V. v. St. Paul*
and *Virginia v. Black*

Hon. Edward J. Cleary*

EDITOR'S INTRODUCTION

Each generation must reaffirm the guarantee of the First Amendment with the hard cases. The framers understood the dangers of orthodoxy and standardized thought and chose liberty. We are once again faced with a case that will demonstrate whether or not there is room for the freedom for the thought that we hate, whether there is room for the eternal vigilance necessary for the opinions that we loathe. The conduct in this case is reprehensible, is abhorrent, and is well known by now. I'm not here to defend the alleged conduct, but as Justice Frankfurter said forty years ago, history has shown that the safeguards of liberty are generally forged in cases involving not very nice people. He might as well have said, involving cases involving very ugly fact situations.

Ed Cleary began his presentation to the U.S. Supreme Court in 1991 with those words. The case was R.A.V. v. St. Paul. *He represented a cross burner. More than a decade later, he would be at the Court again, this time to witness the argument in a case with similar circumstances,* Virginia v. Black.

Cleary's first journey to the Supreme Court began when he was assigned the R.A.V. *case. He examined the circumstances and the St. Paul ordinance with which*

*Ramsey County (Minn.) District Court Judge; lead counsel in *R.A.V. v. St. Paul;* author, BEYOND THE BURNING CROSS (1994).

*his client was charged with violating. "Am I crazy, or is this law unconstitutional?"
he asked a colleague. Ultimately, he viewed the case as being about the right to dissent.
And by playing a role in protecting that right, he realized he was walking in the foot-
prints of those who preceded him in that fight.*

> When I'd go to Washington, I'd start to feel a certain pride in what I was do-
> ing that would outlive me—simply that I was fighting for a good cause. I re-
> member buying Jefferson's and Madison's correspondence and reading a lot
> of those letters—seeing how the Federalists and anti-Federalists really went
> at it over some of these issues, and how to this day all of it ties in. I see it as a
> kind of giant tree with all these different branches coming from the same
> trunk of issues that Madison and Jefferson dealt with. You do see the tie-in if
> you give yourself the time and permission to do it. You start to feel the histor-
> ical context. Frankly, it's exciting and something to be proud of.

*In the following chapter, Mr. Cleary provides a one-of-a-kind perspective with a
comparative analysis of the Court's rulings in* R.A.V. v. St. Paul *and* Virginia v.
Black. *It is a perspective uniquely his, acquired through his work as* R.A.V.'s *lead
counsel and as a consultant to Black's attorney, Rodney Smolla (author of chap. 6).*

*   *   *

> I received my elementary education in a public school in a very small town in
> Nazi Germany. There I was subjected to vehement anti-Semitic remarks
> from my teacher, classmates and others.... I can assure you that they hurt.
> More generally, I lived in a country where ideological orthodoxy reigned
> and where the opportunity for dissent was severely limited. The lesson I have
> drawn from my childhood in Nazi Germany and my happier adult life in this
> country is the need to walk the sometimes difficult path of denouncing the
> bigot's hateful ideas with all my power, yet at the same time challenge any
> community's attempt to suppress hateful ideas by force of law.[1]

In authoring the U.S. Supreme Court's majority opinion in *Virginia v.
Black,*[2] Justice Sandra Day O'Connor included part of the preceding quotation from the late Gerald Gunther. She did so in support of the Court's ruling that the provision of a Virginia statute that provided that the burning of
a cross in public view constitutes prima facie evidence of an intent to intimidate was unconstitutional under the First Amendment. Although the Court
was undoubtedly correct in striking down this provision in the Virginia law,
a persuasive argument can be made that Gunther's comments (originally
given in response to a student conduct legislative council consideration of a

---

[1]Gerhard Casper, *Tribute to Professor Gerald Gunther,* 55 STAN. L. REV. 647, 649 (2002).
[2]538 U.S. 343 (2003).

speech code at Stanford University) would also support the striking down of the entire Virginia cross-burning statute, for the remaining provisions also serve as a "community's attempt to suppress hateful ideas by force of law."

Having briefed and argued the case of *R.A.V. v. St. Paul*[3] in 1991, a case that also involved a burning cross, I had followed the *Virginia v. Black* case with great interest and attended the oral argument in December of 2002. Though I was disappointed in the Court's decision, I was greatly relieved that it did not go further in undermining the *R.A.V.* doctrine outlined years before. Initially, I was surprised at how poorly the media reported the *Virginia v. Black* decision, with few exceptions. Yet when I went back to review the media's response to the *R.A.V. v. St. Paul* case, I quickly recalled how poorly the media had reported that case, as well. There are several factors that influence the accuracy of reporting of cases of this type. First, the media representative must put aside his or her personal, and often visceral, reaction to the facts of the case involved. Once the reporter successfully approaches the case neutrally, he or she then must have the legal acumen to properly evaluate and report what the decision means in light of previous First Amendment cases. Few media members were successful in analyzing the issues in the *R.A.V. v. St. Paul* both before and after the decision, and fewer still were successful in their analysis of *Virginia v. Black*, to-wit: *R.A.V. v. St. Paul* does not stand for the proposition that cross-burning is legal. In a number of instances, it is illegal and can be addressed by a content-neutral criminal code provision. *Virginia v. Black* does not stand for the proposition that cross burning is illegal. In a number of settings, without a showing of the requisite intent to intimidate, cross burning is legal. Any analysis of these cases must begin there. Few observers, who have not been legally trained, grasp this starting point.

It is my position in the pages that follow that: (a) The *Black* decision was an unfortunate retreat from the broad protection given freedom of expression in the *R.A.V.* decision; (b) that, even with this setback, the *R.A.V.* doctrine is alive and well; and finally, (c) that an analysis of the voting patterns and reasoning of the seven justices who sat on both the *R.A.V.* and *Black* Courts reveals a great deal about their motivations and attitudes toward the First Amendment.

BACK TO THE FUTURE

1992

President George H. W. Bush is in the White House. The economy is in the doldrums, soon to cost the incumbent commander-in-chief his office. The

[3]505 U.S. 377 (1992).

nation is at peace, having prevailed in the abbreviated Gulf War known as "Operation Desert Storm." Domestic terrorism has not yet erupted; citizens travel freely throughout the country and airline clerks don't require identification from passengers nor question them in any manner.

Chief Justice William Rehnquist leads the nation's highest court. Though the Court is demonstrably conservative in its collective outlook, in the area of First Amendment jurisprudence, specifically as it pertains to unpopular symbolic expression, the Court has been mostly speech protective. Some years earlier in the case of *Texas v. Johnson*,[4] the Court struck down a Texas law criminalizing flag desecration. The World War II veterans on the Court, Stevens, Rehnquist, and White, had protested vigorously in dissent, suggesting that the American flag was "a unique" symbol deserving of constitutional protection. In response, Congress passed the Flag Protection Act of 1990 in an effort to protect the flag without violating First Amendment principles. Congress failed in its attempt, and the court struck down the legislation in June of 1990 in *United States v. Eichman*.[5]

Cases involving burning flags had arrived before the court, in some form or another, for more than 20 years prior to these decisions.[6] A cross-burning case had not arrived before the Court until the spring of 1991 when the Court agreed to hear *R.A.V. v. St. Paul*. The incendiary displays of cross burning and flag burning are somewhat unique in form, if not content. It is the destruction of the symbols themselves that are expressions of hate—hate for certain groups in the American body politic or hate for what our nation represents. Unlike other symbols of hate, such as the Nazi swastika, these symbols draw power from the destruction of the symbol, rather than the display of one. Individual reactions to the sight of such hateful expression depend on an observer's ethnic background, beliefs, and value system. Few of those who witness the display of either of these hateful symbols welcome their appearance; most feel pain, shock, or outrage. Some military veterans may feel indifference to the sight of a burning cross and overwhelming outrage upon observing the burning of an American flag. Many Black Americans might well register the opposite reaction, and feel fear as well at the sight of a burning cross. The problem with the dissent in *Texas v. Johnson* labeling the American flag "a unique" symbol is that such a label simply reflects an individual value system, which may not be shared by others. Furthermore, whereas outrage might well be the reaction to the sight of a burning flag, terror might be the reaction of some members of our society to the sight of a burning cross. Can two symbols be "unique"? What then of the Nazi swastika?

---

[4]491 U.S. 397 (1989).
[5]496 U.S. 310 (1990).
[6]*See* Street v. New York, 394 U.S. 576 (1969); Spence v. Washington, 418 U.S. 405 (1974); and Smith v. Goguen, 415 U.S. 566 (1974).

As the end of the October 1991 term approached, the Court struggled with an opinion addressing a law that was used to prosecute an alleged cross burning in Minnesota. It had been more than 6 months since the Court heard the oral argument. Recently appointed Justice Clarence Thomas had remained silent on that occasion. Finally, on June 22, 1992, the Court issued its opinion in *R.A.V. v. St. Paul.*

2003

President George W. Bush is in the White House, the son of the man who held the position in 1992. The economy is in the doldrums, after a heady period of expansion. The nation is at war, a not-so-abbreviated Gulf War, this one labeled "Operation Iraqi Freedom." The war will remain controversial among many American citizens and those abroad. It has been less than 2 years since the American way of life changed irrevocably with the first significant attack on the civilian population by foreign enemies on American soil in September 2001. The war on terrorism has claimed not only the victims of the air attacks in New York City and Washington, DC, and the combatants on both sides of the struggle in Afghanistan, but further threatens a number of freedoms heretofore taken for granted by many American citizens. American airports begin to resemble their counterparts in nations across the seas, nations that have struggled with terrorist acts and have reacted with greatly heightened security measures. An uneasiness among some American citizens remains; for many others, a climate of fear has lead to a willingness to silently accept the loss of personal freedoms that comes with the expansion of police power.

Now, as the October 2002 term of the U.S. Supreme Court runs its course, the members of the Court prepare to address the law that was used to prosecute and convict several defendants who had burned crosses in the Commonwealth of Virginia. Oral arguments take place on December 11, 2002. In contrast with his demeanor of 11 years earlier at the *R.A.V.* oral arguments, Justice Clarence Thomas no longer remains reticent. Instead he uses the opportunity to take issue with the argument that a burning cross could ever be used in a manner not intended to intimidate or threaten. The Justices look closely at their colleague as he speaks; he is, after all, the only minority member on the Court. A number seem surprised, if not stunned, at either the content or the vehemence of his remarks or both. Those who observed both oral arguments could only marvel at the contrast in demeanor exhibited by Justice Thomas. He had had the opportunity to express this outrage 11 years earlier at the only other oral argument directly involving a cross burning and the First Amendment, when his earlier years in the segregated South were more recent in his memory, but he had not chosen to do so. Now his colleagues listen closely as he argues for a virtual ban on this form of hateful symbolic expression.

On April 7, 2003 the Court issued its opinion in *Virginia v. Black.*

THE *R.A.V.* LEGACY

In the closing days of the Supreme Court's 2001 October term, the Court surprised a number of observers by agreeing to decide the constitutionality of a law legislated by the Commonwealth of Virginia half a century earlier. The law, among other things, made it a crime to burn a cross with "the intent to intimidate any person or group of persons."[7] Virginia had enacted the law in 1952 in a legislative response to a series of cross-burnings.[8]

Three decades after the passage of Virginia's cross-burning law, the city of St. Paul, Minnesota, enacted an ordinance that made it a crime to engage in symbolic speech, knowing or having reasonable grounds to know that others would find such displays offensive or alarming based on the subject matter (race, color, creed, religion, or gender); specifically banned were the display of a burning cross or a Nazi swastika. The city of St. Paul had put the law in place in response to "episodes of vandalism."[9] Unlike the South of the early 1950s, the Midwest of the early 1980s had not experienced any wave of cross burnings in advance of the legislation. Virginia at the time of the passage of the virtual ban on cross-burning, was attempting, inartfully, to address a perceived attempt by some of its citizens to threaten and/or intimidate primarily Black Americans in a pre–civil rights era. St. Paul, at the time it passed cross-burning legislation, even more inartfully, did so primarily to make a political statement to mollify a number of groups, not only Black Americans.[10]

Perhaps it was inevitable in 2002 that the U.S. Supreme Court would feel the need to revisit the 1992 *R.A.V.* decision. Confusion over the parameters of the holding commenced almost immediately. In 1993, in *Wisconsin v. Mitchell,*[11] the Court reviewed, and ultimately reversed, a decision by the Wisconsin Supreme Court striking down a hate crime "enhancement" law. As the attorney for *R.A.V.,* I had found the Wisconsin Supreme Court decision puzzling, or perhaps to a First Amendment purist, wishful thinking. The St. Paul ordinance involved "hate speech"—that is, the expression it-

---

[7]O'Mara v. Commonwealth, 262 Va. 764, 767, 553 S.E.2d 738, 741 (2001).

[8]Va. Code Ann. § 18.2-423. "It shall be unlawful for any person or persons, with the intent of intimidating any person or group of persons, to burn, or cause to be burned, a cross on the property of another, a highway or other public place. Any person who shall violate any provision of this section shall be guilty of a Class 6 felony. Any such burning of a cross shall be prima facie evidence of an intent to intimidate a person or group of persons."

[9]EDWARD J. CLEARY, BEYOND THE BURNING CROSS 14 (1994).

[10]*Id.* at 15.

[11]508 U.S. 464 (1993).

self provided the basis for the alleged crime. The Wisconsin law, and laws similar to it nationwide, required a precipitate crime (assault, trespass, etc.) and then punished the criminal act more severely if it was "motivated" by "bias." A number of First Amendment advocates felt that the enhancement provision rendered the entire law unconstitutional. However, *R.A.V.* had been charged with just such a provision and we had not challenged the constitutionality of the law because we believed that the language was probably constitutional given that it required a criminal act before the impact of the enhancement provision would be felt. The U.S. Supreme Court in *R.A.V.* had noted that we had not challenged that provision in the second footnote in the majority opinion. I believed then, and I believe now, that such provisions are ill-conceived, that there are less onerous alternatives available, and that the passage of such provisions is not wise public policy. As I opined in 1994, "the issue was never one of public safety; a severe sentence for one convicted of criminal conduct is not necessarily objectionable. The same sentence becomes dangerous only when it is attributed in part to the actor's beliefs, opinions, and even hatreds."[12] We have always punished criminal conduct; these laws singled out motive for additional punishment as well.

However dangerous these provisions may be, I believed that the Court would find them constitutional and they did so in *Wisconsin v. Mitchell*, giving the green light to lawmakers to pass this type of legislation. One can only surmise that at least some members of the unanimous Court, though holding such provisions constitutional, had concerns surrounding the likely proliferation of such laws, making it a greater crime to have a motive based on the group identity of the victim, thus equating group identity with vulnerability. The Court did not address the various potential applications of such laws; it seemed enough to the Justices to draw a bright line between hate speech laws (*R.A.V.*) and hate crime laws (*Mitchell*).

The confusion did not end with the Court's decision in *Wisconsin v. Mitchell*. Across the nation, lower courts seemed confused about the parameters of *R.A.V.* Was it an extension of *Texas v. Johnson* and *U.S. v. Eichman*, decisions that resulted in the striking down of flag-burning prohibitions? Was the decision related to *Collin v. Smith*,[13] the Seventh Circuit case that had protected the right of the Nazis to march in Skokie, Illinois? More specifically, was it simply the latest in a line of cases protecting hateful and disturbing symbolic speech, or was it something else?

R.A.V. undeniably addressed symbolic speech, but it went much further. The decision led to a new type of First Amendment analysis. In reviewing suspect laws, it was no longer sufficient to separate speech into protected and unprotected categories, for now speech within unprotected

---

[12]CLEARY, *supra* note 9, at 220.
[13]578 F.2nd 1197 (7th Cir.); cert denied; 439 U.S. 916 (1978).

categories might be protected if viewpoint discrimination occurred. Consequently, the basic "categorical" approach to free speech, which had resulted in such unprotected categories of expression as "fighting words," libel, and obscenity, was modified significantly. Line drawing would be more difficult now; simply classifying expression as "unprotected" was only a first step in the analysis. Government would no longer be allowed to regulate speech based on hostility or favoritism toward the underlining message, even if the message fell into the "fighting words" doctrine or some other unprotected category. "The Court found that the statute was impermissible discrimination based on the point of view of the speaker—something the Court had long suggested is typically not permitted in the case of presumptively protected speech."[14]

The impact was far reaching. As one observer noted, *R.A.V.* implicitly overruled *Beauharnais v. Illinois.*[15] The Beauharnais decision had been issued by the Court in 1952, the same year that Virginia had passed the cross-burning law. In *Beauharnais,* the Court had held that a state legislature could make a group libel a crime. This had been a dramatic extension of the unprotected category of libel, suggesting that group libel, like libel against an individual, was without constitutional protection. However, in *New York Times v. Sullivan,*[16] the Court gave protection to statements made against public officials that some might have found libelous, and this became the first nail in the coffin for the group libel doctrine found in *Beauharnais.* The threat posed to the First Amendment had been considerable. *R.A.V.* implicitly confirmed the *Sullivan* holding that free expression and group libel could not coexist; the groups listed in the St. Paul ordinance could not use the threat of libel to silence offensive expression.

The same commentator also noted that the *R.A.V.* decision reached back two centuries to provide a basis for making the Sedition Act of 1798 "unconstitutional, since it banned seditious libel used against the Federalist President but not if used against the Republican Vice President. More broadly, the Sedition Act protected incumbents but not challengers."[17] Libel remains an unprotected category of speech. However, the libel must be aimed at an individual and not a group, and speech restrictions must be neutral and not viewpoint specific.

In the years following the *R.A.V.* decision, then, it became clear that the decision did not extend to enhancement hate crime laws, that it had fundamentally changed First Amendment analysis in amending the categorical approach, and that it had ended any attempt to resurrect the doctrine of group libel. Furthermore, the decision had reached back two centuries, to

---

[14]MICHAEL KENT CURTIS, "FREE SPEECH," THE PEOPLE'S DARLING PRIVILEGE 410 (2000).
[15]343 U.S. 250 (1952), noted in Curtis, *supra* note 14.
[16]376 U.S. 254 (1964).
[17]CURTIS, *supra* note 14, at 410.

the early days of constitutional interpretation, and confirmed that not only was the Sedition Act of 1798 dangerous and a bad idea, but, in hindsight, unconstitutional as well.

THE 2002 OCTOBER TERM

What impact, if any, did the events of September 11, 2001, have on the decisions issued by the Supreme Court in the October 2002 term? Did the events lead not only to legislation aimed at the national security that curbed civil liberties but also to a newfound reluctance to recognize and condone an expansive view of free expression? What accounted for the "new hesitation" on the part of a Court that had been viewed as libertarian on the First Amendment? Why did the Court pick this term to focus on government and law enforcement interests in turning away all those who sought protection under the First Amendment in cases on its docket?

Perhaps it is a mistake to view the *Black* decision in isolation, apart from the other First Amendment cases decided in the same term. A Court that had been classified by some as "speech-protective,"[18] turned back First Amendment–based constitutional claims in cases ranging from anti-pornography filters on library computers to bans on direct corporate contributions to candidates in federal elections to access to public housing projects. When the dust had settled, all parties seeking First Amendment protection during the October 2002 term came up empty-handed. Whatever the reason, the majority of the Court did not seem willing to extend First Amendment protections in this term, and, in a number of decisions, including *Black*, the Court arguably reined in, or at least modified, established First Amendment principles.[19]

Telemarketers, minors seeking access to pornography on the Internet, and cross burners, do not constitute the most sympathetic of parties. The Court, in decisions from previous terms, had given First Amendment protection to charities paying professional fund-raisers, libraries reluctant to use filtering software to block access to pornographic sites, and those who defended the most unpopular forms of symbolic speech.

Not this term. This term the Court seemed to be finding reasons to stem the tide and find limits to First Amendment protection. In the telemarketing case, the Court gave the green light to the prosecution for fraud of a charity and the fund-raising entity for the charity, based on the size of the fund-rais-

---

[18]*See* Linda Greenhouse, *In a Momentous Term, Justices Remake the Law, and the Court*, N.Y. TIMES, Jul. 1, 2003, at 1.

[19]*See* Tony Mauro, *High Court Hands Government Sweep in Free-Speech Cases*. First Amendment Center Online, Jul. 7, 2003. The Court extended this deference to government in the October 2003 term in the area of campaign finance regulation in *McConnell v. Federal Election Commission*, decided December 10, 2003, with Justice O'Connor once again writing the majority decision turning back a First Amendment challenge.

ing fees.[20] Previously the Court had said these fees could not be dictated by the government, but this time the Court said the First Amendment did not shield fraud.

In the Internet case, the Court resorted to the "strings attached" approach[21] to curbs on free speech, ruling that because the government was providing the funds for access to the Internet as provided by the libraries, the required blocking software was not prohibited by the First Amendment.[22]

The other First Amendment challenges met with the same results.[23] However, it was the *Virginia v. Black* decision that surprised some and confused others, given that seven of the nine justices signing on to it had also been on the Court in 1992 when *R.A.V.* was decided. It appeared the members of the Court were amending the doctrine they had put in place, but to what extent?

FROM 1991 MINNESOTA TO 2002 VIRGINIA

The best protection against the threat such symbols imply is a citizenry united against their message.

—*Christian Science Monitor* (June 4, 2002)

In 1991, the attorneys general in eight states—Arizona, Connecticut, Maryland, Massachusetts, Michigan, New Jersey, Oklahoma, and Utah—urged the U.S. Supreme Court, along with nine other states, to uphold the St. Paul hate speech ordinance.[24] They argued that the state had a compelling interest in prohibiting bias-motivated "activity" and that this activity could be prohibited without infringing on First Amendment rights. Specifically they argued that "to the extent state laws [including the St. Paul ordinance] reach pure speech, they tend to address only genuine threats, which are not protected under the First Amendment."[25] No explanation was offered as to why a "threats" statute, which addresses a threat in a content-neutral manner, without the unconstitutional baggage, was not sufficient for law enforcement purposes.

---

[20]Illinois ex.rel Madigan v. Telemarketing Associates, Inc. 538 U.S. 600 (2003). *Compare with* Schaumburg v. Citizens for a Better Environment, 444 U.S. 620 (1980).

[21]*See* Rust v. Sullivan, 500 U.S. 173 (1991).

[22]U.S. v. American Library Assn, Inc., 539 U.S. 194 (2003). *Compare with* Reno v. ACLU, 512 U.S. 844 (1997).

[23]*See* Virginia v. Hicks, 539 U.S. 113 (2003); Federal Election Commission v. Beaumont, 539 U.S. 146 (2003); and Nike v. Kasky 539 U.S. 654 (2003).

[24]The other states: Minnesota, Alabama, Idaho, Illinois, Kansas, Ohio, South Carolina, Tennessee, and Virginia. Eleven years later, of these states, only Virginia sought review of the lower Court decision.

[25]RAV v. St. Paul, 1990 U.S. Briefs 7675.

Prior to 1991, the Court had made it clear that incitement to violence and true threats were among categories of unprotected speech. However, the danger continued to exist that offensive speech about a sensitive topic could become a "threat" in the eyes of law enforcement. Consequently, specific proof of an intent to threaten, implied in the *Brandenburg v. Ohio*[26] case, appeared to be required before a defendant could be held criminally liable for such expression. The St. Paul ordinance had no such requirement. The Court in *R.A.V.* had specifically addressed "fighting words"[27] in ruling that expression included within that categorical exception could not be proscribed based on viewpoint. Observers appeared to be on solid ground in assuming that the same logic applied to what appeared to be another categorical exception, true threats.[28] Such directed threats are not worthy of First Amendment protection, and *R.A.V.* noted the necessity of protecting individuals from the fear of violence, "from the disruption that fear engenders, and from the possibility that the threatened violence will occur."[29] Even so, *R.A.V.* seemed to suggest that threats could not be proscribed based on the viewpoint expressed. Indeed, how, under *R.A.V.*, can the use of a categorical exception—in this case true threats—be utilized to save a cross-burning law that proscribes not all threats, but threats backed by a hateful but recognizable viewpoint?

One could argue that the answer is that the Court viewed "true threats" less as a categorical exception to protected speech and more as an underlying crime as found in *Wisconsin v. Mitchell*. More specifically, it seems likely that the Court's decision in *R.A.V.* was related to the collective abhorrence of the majority to political correctness and, as the Florida Supreme Court was to put it several years later, to the "playing of favorites" under the St. Paul ordinance.[30] The *R.A.V.* decision appeared more directed to this issue than it was to a proscription against cross-burning laws. The petition for a writ of certiorari, filed by the petitioner *R.A.V.* in April of 1991, examined the impact of the St. Paul ordinance, in light of other laws silencing offensive speech nationwide, particularly on college campuses. Though it seems clear in retrospect that all nine justices were offended by the St. Paul ordinance, it seems likely they were offended for different reasons, as evidenced by the concurring opinions in the Court's decision. The majority's interest in the *R.A.V.* case, it appears, was less about adding to the list of nonproscribable, protected symbolic speech (i.e., burning flags, etc.) than it was in addressing the proliferation of speech codes, designed to stifle offensive expression often

---

[26]395 U.S. 444 (1969).

[27]*See* Chaplinsky v. New Hampshire, 315 U.S. 568 (1942).

[28]*See* G. Robert Blakely and Brian J. Murray, *Threats, Free Speech and the Jurisprudence of the Federal Criminal Law*, 2002 B.Y.U. L. REV. 829, 851.

[29]505 U.S. 377, 388 (1992).

[30]*See* State v. T.B.D., 656 So.2d 479 (1995).

within the university environment. Justice Blackmun's concurrence in *R.A.V.* notwithstanding,[31] the movement to silence offensive expression based on disfavored topics or group identity had gained rapid momentum at the time the Court agreed to hear *R.A.V.*, and continued at the time the Court issued its decision. This movement directly threatened free expression, particular in a forum designed to be free of such censorship—the university campus. Furthermore, contrary to the allegation made by Justice Blackmun, the Court was not "manipulating doctrine" in abandoning the categorical approach to First Amendment analysis. In reining in lawmakers who wrote provisions aimed at unpopular expression and who then hid behind categories of heretofore unprotected speech, the Court sent a message that government could not betray sympathy for one viewpoint over another, directly or indirectly favoring one and censoring the other. The ideological rift between the justices should not be allowed to shade the importance of this holding.

Before *Black,* as a Florida jurist noted in dissenting in a case that upheld a cross-burning provision, it was "not just the subjects to which protection is afforded that must be neutral it also is the expressive activity itself that must be prohibited in a neutral fashion."[32] With *Black,* as we see later, the Court amended the latter and left the former protection in place, allowing one form of expression, cross burning, to be proscribed as a threat.

Eleven years after having unsuccessfully intervened in the *R.A.V.* case, the attorneys general in the same eight states (Arizona, Connecticut, Maryland, Massachusetts, Michigan, New Jersey, Oklahoma, and Utah) now joined with six other states (Iowa, Nebraska, Nevada, North Carolina, Oregon, and Vermont) in asking the Court to hear the Commonwealth of Virginia's appeal. Virginia's brief sought a ban on cross burning, suggesting it was "an especially, virulent, even unique, form of intimidation in American society." Virulent, unquestionably, but the "unique" label has been applied to other symbols as well, usually as a suggestion that censorship should be permissible because it need not be extended beyond the "unique" symbol.

The following events provided the factual background for *Black:*

1. On or about May 2, 1998, several individuals criminally trespassed and burned a cross aimed at an African American man, a neighbor who had inquired about their use of firearms on an earlier occasion.
2. On or about August 22, 1998, the Ku Klux Klan held a rally and a cross burning on private property with the permission of the landowner, and this cross burning was visible from the state highway.
3. Virginia code 18.2-423, enacted in 1952, stated the following:

---

[31]505 U.S. 377, 414 (Blackmun, J. Concurring).
[32]State v. T.B.D. 656 So. 2d, 479, 483 (Overton, J. dissenting).

It shall be unlawful for any person or persons, with the intent of intimidating any person or group of persons, to burn, or cause to be burned, a cross on the property of another, a highway or other public place.... Any such burning of a cross shall be prima facie evidence of an intent to intimidate a person or group of persons.

Virginia argued strenuously that the provision was content-neutral, and that it was not limited to disfavored subjects or particular victims, and was aimed at anyone who burns a cross with the intent to intimidate for any reason.[33] Perhaps accepting the disingenuous nature of the content-neutral argument, given Virginia's history of race relations, the state went on to the crux of its argument: "Since it is constitutionally permissible to ban all forms of intimidation, it is constitutional to ban its most virulent forms."[34] This, in so many words, was the argument made by the city of St. Paul 11 years earlier (because it is constitutionally permissible to ban all forms of "fighting words," it is constitutional to single out the most hurtful forms). Undeniably, true threats are distinguishable from "fighting words" even though both constitute categories of unprotected expression. Furthermore, the Virginia law required a different *mens rea* or *intent* on the part of the actor than the St. Paul ordinance. It is one thing to hold people responsible for expressing themselves in a way that they should "know or have reasonable grounds to know" would upset others; it is quite another to hold them responsible for expressing themselves with the intent of intimidating others. The question remained as to how targeted and immediate a threat would have to be before intent could be inferred.

VIRGINIA V. BLACK

So what is one to make of the *Black* decision? One could easily conclude that the Commonwealth of Virginia succeeded in banning cross burning, if one relied on the media reports in the wake of the decision.[35] Once again it is important to remember that nowhere in the *R.A.V.* decision did the Court indicate that cross-burning could not be treated as a crime. In fact, the Court went to great lengths to state the opposite, that content-neutral laws existed to address the crime of cross burning when it was used to threaten or intimidate another.[36] *R.A.V.* did not hold that cross burning was protected expression in

---

[33]*See* George Will, *Burning to Regulate Expression*, JEWISH WORLD REV., Apr. 14, 2003. "Oh, please. And the St. Paul law prevented both Jews and anti-Semites from painting swastikas on synagogues."

[34]Brief of Petitioner, Commonwealth of Virginia, 10.

[35]*See, e.g.*, Alan Cooper, *Cross Burning Limits Upheld*, RICHMOND TIMES DISPATCH, Apr. 8, 2003, at A1; Laurence Hammack, *Supreme Court Upholds Cross Burning Ban*, ROANOKE TIMES & WORLD NEWS, Apr. 8, 2003, at A1; Jon Frank, *Supreme Court Upholds Va. Ban On Cross Burning; Justices Rule Horror of the Act Outweighs Free Speech Concerns*, THE VIRGINIAN PILOT, Apr. 8, 2003, at A1.

[36]538 U.S. 343, 386 (2003).

all instances; *Black* did not hold that cross burning was unprotected speech in all instances. The *Washington Post* noted in an editorial that news stories had inaccurately reported the case, helped in part by the confusing comments made by Virginia Attorney General Jerry Kilgore. It noted the opinion of the Court "looks rather different from the victory Mr. Kilgore sought" and noted that "Mr. Kilgore was not alone in his confusion; news stories also declared that the Court upheld the ban."[37] Still, the *Washington Post* saw little danger in the decision. "A state that chooses to isolate in its laws particularly egregious or threatening forms of intimidation is, the Court rightly ruled, free to do so ... provided that the law obliges the prosecution to prove to a jury that the expression was intended as intimidation."[38]

But did the majority in *Black* "rightly rule"? One cannot escape perhaps a more accurate conclusion, noted in the dissent of Justices Souter, Kennedy, and Ginsburg: "The Virginia statute in issue ... selects a symbol with particular content from the field of all proscribable expression meant to intimidate."[39] Unlike the "brandishing of an automatic weapon" used by analogy by Justice Scalia at oral argument,[40] "the burning cross can broadcast threat and ideology together, ideology alone, or threat alone...."[41]

Justice Souter was undoubtedly correct when he noted that the Virginia law did not comfortably fit into a "special virulence" exception to the *R.A.V.* doctrine, given that the examples in the *R.A.V.* did not involve communication generally associated with a particular message.[42] As he notes, to the extent the Court relied on that *R.A.V.* exception, it was clearly treating the exception in a more "flexible" manner than originally outlined in that decision.[43] This "flexibility" could conceivably be the exception that someday swallows the rule. It is too soon to tell, but the Court's willingness in the future to resort to this exception warrants close scrutiny.

The *Black* dissent also accurately points out that contrary to another *R.A.V.* observation, here there was not only a "realistic possibility that official suppression of ideas" was "afoot," there was concrete evidence of such attempted suppression with the existence of a prima facie provision presuming intent to intimidate.[44] Finally, Justices Souter, Kennedy, and Ginsburg returned to the undeniable conclusion of those who accept the *R.A.V.* doctrine, undiluted:

[37]*See Cross-Burning in Court*, WASH. POST, Apr. 8, 2003, at A32.
[38]*Id.*
[39]538 U.S. 343, 381 (2003).
[40]Virginia v. Black, 2002 U.S. Trans. Lexis 74 at 25.
[41]538 U.S. 343, 381 (2003) (Souter, J. dissenting).
[42]*Id.* at 382.
[43]*Id.*
[44]*Id.*

Since no *R.A.V.* exception can save the statute as content based, it can only survive if narrowly tailored to serve a compelling state interest ... a stringent test the statute cannot pass; a content-neutral statute banning intimidation would achieve the same object without singling out particular content.[45]

The *Virginia v. Black* decision seemed to confuse commentators. Many did not understand it; some felt vaguely threatened by it from a free expression standpoint, but conceded that if there ever was a time to make an exception for prohibited and unpopular symbolic speech, this was the time.[46] Most recognized that, at a minimum, the finding of the majority that the portion of Virginia law that provided that burning a cross in public view was "prima facie" evidence of an intent to intimidate was unconstitutional, was correct and that the "per se" banning of the burning cross went well beyond the constitutional exercise of police power.[47]

Others were left to wonder how this decision fit into the *R.A.V.* doctrine, which had struck down a hate speech ordinance that engaged in viewpoint discrimination based on topics addressed, and had cited specific examples of unpopular symbolic speech, that is, a burning cross and the Nazi swastika.

R.A.V.: ALIVE AND WELL

For those who welcomed and embraced the *R.A.V.* decision and recognized the significance of the move away from the categorical approach to free expression and the need for viewpoint neutrality, even within formerly unprotected categories of speech, the *Black* decision is undoubtedly a disappointment. If, as the Court appeared to hold in *R.A.V.*, proscribable expression cannot be regulated based on viewpoint, how did the Court arrive at the *Black* decision?

As we have seen, at least at this point, *Black* should be viewed as an aberration, this Court's attempt to draw a line, suggesting that when a symbol is used to broadcast "threat and ideology together,"[48] the law may treat the display of the symbol as "threat alone" and proscribe it, *specifically*. It is the Court's willingness to allow government to specify the symbols, rather than instruct the state to use content-neutral criminal code provisions, that is the problematic outcome of the *Black* decision. *R.A.V.* supporters would argue that this is not only unnecessary to effectively prosecute those who intend to

---

[45]*Id.*

[46]*See, e.g.,* James J. Kilpatrick, *Good Opinion on Cross-Burning, Probably,* AUGUSTA CHRONICLE, Apr. 20, 2003, at AO4. *See also Cross Burning In Court,* WASH. POST, Apr. 8, 2003 at A32 (quoting Virginia attorney general Jerry Kilgore claiming complete victory in spite of the Court ruling that the Virginia law in question was unconstitutional).

[47]*See, e.g.,* George F. Will, *Burning To Regulate Expression,* WASH. POST, Apr. 13, 2003, at BO7; *Limits on Cross Burning,* CHRISTIAN SCIENCE MONITOR, Apr. 9, 2003, at A10.

[48]538 U.S. 343, 381 (2003) (Souter, J., concurring in part and dissenting in part).

threaten when using the burning cross, but dangerous to the right of free expression to allow government to do so.

Support for these content-based laws should not be seen as a racial litmus test. Many who support civil rights worry equally about civil liberties in our country. One wonders if the anger and emotion displayed by Justice Thomas at oral argument had an impact on his brethren. Perhaps even the members of the Court did not wish to be seen minimizing displays of racial hatred.[49] More likely, however, is that the "law and order" side of the Court trumped its concerns over free expression once, in the majority's opinion, adequate safeguards were in place, removing the presumption and requiring the intent to threaten.

A CATEGORY OF ONE

Still, the likely legacy of *Black*, is the creation of "a category of one, that converts cross-burning into a special form of speech that, like obscenity, can be banned."[50] With the requirement of an intent to intimidate, the remaining provisions of the Virginia law would appear to be quite different than the St. Paul hate speech ordinance and more similar to an enhancement hate crime law. As long as the Court continues to require that the law requires an intent to intimidate without a presumption, and as long as the focus is on what the speaker intended rather than how a recipient reacted, limits are placed on overzealous advocates of such provisions and lawmakers seeking to add additional symbols to such laws. Nevertheless, the *Black* decision was not a certainty, given the language of *R.A.V.* One could be excused for believing that the singling out of a symbol that carriers ideological meaning, warped or not, would result in the nullification of such a law.

How did the seven justices who were on both the *R.A.V.* and *Black* Courts rationalize the two, apparently conflicting, opinions? Where did the two new Justices, Ginsburg and Breyer, who replaced Justices Blackmun and White, fit in?

THE MEMBERS OF THE UNITED STATES SUPREME COURT (1992, 2003)

Justices Souter, Kennedy, and Ginsburg

At the *R.A.V.* oral argument, Justice Souter focused on the "fighting words" doctrine from *Chaplinsky v. New Hampshire*,[51] which had originated in his na-

---

[49]*See* Tony Mauro, *U.S. Supreme Court Hears Dramatic Debate over Cross-Burning*, LAW. COMM., Dec. 12 2002, ("... other justices appeared deeply affected by Thomas' comments, some placing cross-burning from that point on in a different category of expression.")

[50]*See* Tony Mauro, *Too Early to Know Full Effect of Cross-Burning Ruling*, First Amendment Center, Apr. 8, 2003, at 1.

[51]315 U.S. 568 (1942).

tive state. He appeared to have concerns at that argument about the elasticity of the portion of that decision referring to words that "inflict injury" or harm. At the same argument Justice Kennedy inquired about "threats" and the element of immediacy of such threats, apparently weighing First Amendment concerns against the need to protect targeted parties. Neither appeared at that time to be as directly interested in the fact that the St. Paul ordinance punished some "fighting words" and not others, as Chief Justice Rehnquist and Justice Scalia were.

At the time of the *R.A.V.* oral argument, Justice Souter had completed only one term as a Justice, and during that term he had voted with Justice O'Connor 90% of the time.[52] He had seldom voted with Justice Stevens, a pattern that would reverse itself in the coming years. However, with his vote joining with the majority in *R.A.V.* and his dissent in *Black,* Justice Souter has made his position clear with regard to symbolic speech. He is a strong First Amendment jurist in this area who, along with Justices Kennedy and Ginsburg, fully embraces the *R.A.V.* doctrine. With only narrow exceptions, he views any attempt at banning symbolic speech based on its content with skepticism, if not outright hostility.

Justice Kennedy had more of a track record at the time of the *R.A.V.* oral argument. In both *Texas v. Johnson* and *U.S. v. Eichman,* he had shown a willingness to strike down laws aimed at unpopular symbolic speech. In the years since the *R.A.V.* decision, Justice Kennedy has carved out a niche as a consistent supporter of the First Amendment position.[53] His comments at the *Black* oral argument reflected a continued interest in threats and the need for "immediacy" of such threats before proscription. By joining in Justice Souter's dissent in *Black,* he maintained his position in *R.A.V.*

Justice Ginsburg's position in the *R.A.V.* doctrine was unknown at the time *Black* was heard, because she was not on the Court during the October 1991 Term when *R.A.V.* was decided. Perhaps, from a First Amendment standpoint, Justice Ginsburg's concurrence with Justice Souter's dissent in *Black* is a ray of sunlight in a dark cloud. Having replaced Justice Harry Blackmun, who in his concurrence had furiously rejected the *R.A.V.* doctrine as it pertained to the protection of subcategories of heretofore unprotected expression, Justice Ginsburg has apparently taken the opposite position and that is welcome news to First Amendment advocates concerned about the future path of the Court.

---

[52]CLEARY, *supra* note 9, at 169.

[53]*See, e.g.,* David G. Savage, *Figures of Speech,* 87 A.B.A. J. 30 (2001) (citing the work of UCLA law professor Eugene Volokh, who has tracked the Supreme Court's voting patterns since 1994. In 40 cases, Justice Kennedy emerges as the most protective justice of free speech, voting in favor of First Amendment interests 75% of the time).

Chief Justice Rehnquist, Justices Scalia and Thomas

In the *Black* decision, Chief Justice Rehnquist and Justice Scalia did not
back away from their position on the *R.A.V.* doctrine, at least as it pertains
to the recognition that viewpoint discrimination results when some
disfavored topics are singled out within a class of unprotected expression.
What they did do in *Black* is make an exception for the outlawing of symbolic speech based on content, agreeing with the majority that a state may,
without infringing on the First Amendment, prohibit cross burning carried out with the intent to intimidate.[54] Scalia went further, and disagreed
with the majority decision to find facially invalid the portion of the Virginia statute that provided that the burning of a cross in public view was
"prima facie evidence of an intent to intimidate."[55] In doing so, both Justices arguably revealed their reasoning for supporting the *R.A.V.* doctrine
in that majority decision.

Prior to *R.A.V.*, Chief Justice Rehnquist seldom sided with the defendant
making a First Amendment challenge to a penal provision that was being
defended by the government. Indeed, he reacted furiously to the majority's
decision in *Texas v. Johnson,*[56] which had resulted in the invalidation of a
provision outlawing flag burning, several years before *R.A.V.* It came as a
surprise to some, then, that he appeared so welcoming of my oral argument
in *R.A.V.*, specifically questioning me regarding what came to be the main
thrust of the decision:

> *Chief Justice Rehnquist*: Mr. Cleary, isn't one of your complaints that the Min-
> nesota statute as construed by the Supreme Court of Minnesota punishes
> only some "fighting words" and not others?
> *Mr. Cleary*: It is, your Honor. That is one of my positions that in doing so, even
> though it is a subcategory, technically of unprotected conduct, [the govern-
> ment] is still picking out an opinion, a disfavored message, and making that
> clear through the State. It's a paternalistic idea, and the problem that we have
> is the government must not betray neutrality, and I believe it does, even when
> it picks out a subcategory. With the First Amendment, it does not necessarily
> follow that if you punish the greater you can punish the lesser.[57]

One could go back further to the filing of the petition for a writ of certiorari in April of 1991 to see how we had succeeded in getting the Court's
attention:

---

[54]538 U.S. 343, 368 (2003) (Scalia, J., concurring in part, concurring in the judgment in
part, and dissenting in part).
[55]*Id.*
[56]491 U.S. 397, 421 (1989) (Rehnquist, C.J., dissenting).
[57]CLEARY, *supra* note 9, at 163–64.

It is no secret that the Rehnquist Court has been known for its conservative stance on constitutional interpretation. It was within the context of student speech codes specifically, and politically correctness generally, that we saw our chance.... we concentrated on censorship of conservatives on campus, reasoning that a majority of the Court might find such efforts offensive, in both a constitutional and personal sense.[58]

We needed four votes to get the case heard, and five or more votes to succeed in our First Amendment challenge. We had aimed our petition at the conservatives on the Court, hoping to pick up the few left-of-center votes later, as we eventually did.

How did the justice (Scalia) who wrote the majority opinion in *R.A.V.* evolve into the man who joined the majority to uphold the Virginia's cross-burning provision and who went so far as to suggest that, "I believe the prima facie evidence provision in the Virginia cross-burning statute is constitutionally unproblematic"?[59] Again, the answer is most likely to be found in an examination of the apparent reason for his support for the *R.A.V.* doctrine initially. Scalia's focus, like those of Chief Justice Rehnquist and Justice Thomas, was not on the cross-burning language found in the St. Paul ordinance (though, given later comments, it is hard to understand how Justice Thomas was able to look beyond the burning cross) but in the listing of subjects or topics that were off limits in the ordinance. At the oral argument of *R.A.V.*, Justice Scalia had bristled when I had accepted, only for purposes of argument, that the inclusion of "a burning cross or a Nazi swastika" in the ordinance, were "mere examples" of outlawed expression. Scalia at the time would have none of it. These are more than mere examples, he stated, they were evidence of blatant viewpoint discrimination. He was undoubtedly correct, as I noted at the time. Yet, now 11 years and 1 week later at the *Black* oral argument, he suggested to Rod Smolla, arguing counsel on behalf of the respondents, that a burning cross could be analogized to the brandishing of an automatic weapon when used in an intimidating manner, suggesting that there wasn't any difference in the two. Furthermore, he had cited content-neutral attempts to address cross-burning in the first footnote in *R.A.V.*[60] Now it was left to Justice Souter in his dissent to point out that content-neutral alternatives "banning intimidation would achieve the same object without singling out particular content."[61] It appears that Justice

---

[58]*Id.*

[59]538 U.S. 343, 385 (2003) (Scalia, J., dissenting in part).

[60]505 U.S. 377, 381, n.1 (1992) ("The conduct might have violated Minnesota statutes carrying significant penalties. *See, e. g.*, Minn. Stat. § 609.713(1) (1987) (providing for up to five years in prison for terroristic threats); § 609.563 (arson) (providing for up to five years and a $ 10,000 fine, depending on the value of the property intended to be damaged); § 609.595 (Supp. 1992) (criminal damage to property) (providing for up to one year and a $3,000 fine, depending upon the extent of the damage to the property.")

[61]538 U.S. 343, 387 (2003) (Souter, J., dissenting).

Scalia viewed the *R.A.V.* decision primarily in terms of the ban on some "fighting words" and not others. It was the limitation on subject matter that apparently offended him, not the ban on offensive symbolic speech.

Perhaps the clearest example of *R.A.V.* "disconnect" is in the vitriolic dissent in *Black* written by Justice Clarence Thomas. Thomas had been on the Court for only a few months at the time of the *R.A.V.* oral argument in December of 1991. Only a short time earlier, he had suggested at his Senate confirmation hearings that he was a victim of an attempted "high-tech lynching,"[62] thereby evoking the specter of racial hatred while under attack for alleged sexual harassment.

At the *R.A.V.* oral arguments, Thomas sat silently, never making a comment or asking a question of either counsel. A number of observers thought he would use that occasion to become actively involved in the questioning of the opposing sides. It was, after all, a case with a factual setting involving racial hatred, and Thomas was the only minority member of the Court and had come of age in the deep South. He must have held strong feelings on the subject. However, he remained silent, and though he joined the majority opinion of *R.A.V.*, he did not issue a concurrence.

Three years later, in 1995, in another First Amendment case with another majority opinion written by Justice Scalia, Thomas began to reveal his feelings on the sight of a burning cross. The case, *Capital Square Review and Advisory Board v. Pinette*,[63] involved a Klan request for the issuance of a permit for the erection of a cross in a plaza next to the state capitol in Columbus, Ohio. The board had been ordered by a federal judge to issue the permit to the Klan but the board had refused to do so. The Supreme Court held that the state did not violate the establishment clause of the First Amendment by permitting a private party to display an unattended cross on the grounds of the state capitol. Thomas concurred, but used the occasion to sound off on the Ku Klux Klan, noting that the Klan's "erection of such a cross is a political act, not a Christian one."[64] He continued, "The cross is associated with the Klan not because of religious worship, but because of the Klan's practice of cross-burning ... the Klan simply has appropriated one of the most sacred of religious symbols as a symbol of hate."[65] Nevertheless, Thomas conceded that the cross was "a religious symbol of Christianity for some Klan members" and noted that a Christian hymn was "sometimes played during cross-burnings."[66] He further observed that the

---

[62]*See, e.g.,* Ruth Marcus, *Hill Describes Details of Alleged Harassment; Thomas Categorically Denies All Her Charges,* WASH. POST, Oct. 12, 1991, at A1.

[63]515 U.S. 753 (1995).

[64]*Id.*

[65]*Id.*

[66]*Id.* at 771.

display of the cross by the Klan was "primarily a political one"[67] and the message "was both political and religious in nature."[68]

Seven years later at the *Black* oral argument, Thomas unleashed his fury, surprising onlookers and even apparently surprising his colleagues, who turned to watch him question the petitioners' co-counsel, the deputy solicitor general appearing on behalf of the Department of Justice. The attorney had just stated, under questioning by Justice Kennedy, that the threat and violence signaled by a cross burning left a pervasive fear that hung like a "sword of Damocles" over the threatened party. He did not appear in any way to be minimizing the impact of the sight of a burning cross on those targeted. He nevertheless incurred the wrath of Justice Thomas, who had apparently been looking for an opening to express his feelings, and now his voice and manner became inpatient and insistent:

Justice Thomas:	Mr. Dreeben aren't you understating the—the effects of—of the burning cross? This statute was passed in what year?
Mr. Dreeben:	1952 originally.
Justice Thomas:	Now it's my understanding that we had almost 100 years of lynching and activity in the South by the Knights of Camellia and—and the Ku Klux Klan, and this was a reign of terror and the cross was a symbol of that reign of terror. Was—isn't that significantly greater than intimidation or threat?
Mr. Dreeben:	Well I think they're co-extensive, Justice Thomas, because it is—
Justice Thomas (interrupting):	Well, my fear is, Mr. Dreeben, that you are actually understating the symbolism on—of and the effect of the cross, the burning cross. I—I indicated, I think, in the Ohio case that the cross was not a religious symbol and that it has—it was intended to have a virulent effect. And I—I think that what you are attempting to do is to fit this into our jurisprudence rather than stating more clearly what the cross was intended to accomplish and, indeed, that it is unlike any symbol in our society.

---

[67]*Id.* at 770.
[68]*Id.* at 771.

Mr. Dreeben:	Well, I don't mean to understate it, and I entirely agree with Your Honor's description of how the cross has been used as an instrument of intimidation against minorities in this country. That has justified 14 states in treating it as a distinctive—
Justice Thomas (interrupting):	Well it's—it's actually more than minorities. There's certain groups. And I—I just—my fear is that the—there was no other purpose to the cross. There was no communication of a particular message. It was intended to cause fear ...
Mr. Dreeben:	It—
Justice Thomas:	and to terrorize a population.[69]

Four months later when the Court issued the *Black* decision, Thomas went beyond all of the members of the Court in arguing that a ban on cross burning was permissible and that "the majority errs in imputing an expressive component to the activity in question."[70] Justice Thomas apparently failed to see the irony in the fact that the depth of his feelings on the topic, completely understandable to be sure, were a response to the "expressive component" of the burning cross. Surely Justice Thomas would have been upset if someone "brandished an automatic weapon" at him (Justice Scalia's content-neutral example), but would the depth of his reaction have been the same? It seems unlikely because there would not have been the underlying hateful message of racial hatred and superiority. It was this very message, from the sight of a burning cross, that he had noted in 1995 was "political."[71] One can sympathize with the depth of feeling displayed by Justice Thomas on the topic of cross burning and still take issue with his analysis of such hateful expression under the First Amendment.

Thomas began his dissent with an attempt to tie the burning flag and burning cross together. "In every culture certain things acquire meaning, well beyond what outsiders can comprehend," he wrote. "That goes for both the sacred [i.e., flag burning] and the profane. I believe that cross-burning is the paradigmatic example of the latter."[72]

All the members of the *R.A.V.* Court were "outsiders," too, at least as it pertained to cross burning. In addition, it is not clear which "outsiders" Thomas is referring to as it relates to flag burning (non-Americans? non-veterans?) but it does not appear that Thomas considers the Catholic

[69]Transcript of Oral Argument: Virginia v. Black (Dec. 11, 2002), 22–24.
[70]538 U.S. 343, 388 (2003) (Thomas, J., dissenting).
[71]515 U.S. at 770.
[72]538 U.S. 343, 388 (2003) (Thomas, J., dissenting).

members of the Court to be "insiders" given that his argument is clearly aimed at the racial animus behind the burning cross. Again, this appears to contradict his point at oral argument that the burning cross is aimed at "more than minorities."[73] He seems to be intentionally isolating himself from other members of the Court, none of whom joined in his dissent.

Thomas went even further noting, that "even assuming that the statute implicates the First Amendment, in my view, the fact that the statute permits a jury to draw an inference of intent to intimidate from the cross-burning itself presents no constitutional problems."[74]

So what changed Justice Thomas in the 11 years between *R.A.V.* and *Black*? No one other than close friends and family can know the personal experiences he may have had in the intervening years between the decisions. In putting that possibility aside, it remains a fair assumption that Justice Thomas had been exposed to racial bias, anger, and even hatred leading up to the *R.A.V.* oral argument. Indeed, he had chosen to characterize his Senate hearings, noted earlier, in racial terms, only weeks before the argument and months before the *R.A.V.* decision. The answer, I believe then, lies instead in his motive for joining in the *R.A.V.* majority opinion. Thomas agreed with the majority and looked beyond the cross burning that occurred on the east side of St. Paul, to focus on what the St. Paul hate speech ordinance symbolized, namely what was then an ongoing nationwide attempt to stifle conservative opinion, particularly on college campuses, a subject he also felt strongly about. One could say that his conservative identity and his belief in the First Amendment took precedence in *R.A.V.*. Once that portion of the equation was removed, his identity as a black man in America overcame any First Amendment allegiance; indeed one could argue that with his inference to the "sacred" in his dissent, flag-burning restriction advocates may have found a new vote.

Justices O'Connor, Stevens, and Breyer

Justice O'Connor has shown very little patience with the argument that the First Amendment protects offensive and unpopular symbolic speech. She joined with the dissenters in *Texas v. Johnson,* suggesting that flag-burning restrictions were constitutional and she wrote the majority opinion in *Black*, finding that cross-burning laws could be constitutional as well, provided there existed an "intent to intimidate" prerequisite, and providing that there was not a presumption in the law that treated cross burning as evidence of such an intent. In *R.A.V.,* she had joined with Justices White,

---

[73]Virginia v. Black, 2002 U.S. TRANS LEXIS 74, 21.
[74]538 U.S. 343, 395 (2003) (Thomas, J., dissenting).

Blackmun, and Stevens in arguing that the St. Paul hate speech ordinance was defective because it was overbroad, and because it criminalized not only unprotected expression, but expression protected by the First Amendment. She did not join with the majority's finding in *R.A.V.* that the ordinance regulated expression based on hostility aimed a viewpoint, found within a subcategory of heretofore unprotected expression. O'Connor noted in the *Black* majority opinion, that the First Amendment affords protection "to symbolic or expressive conduct as well as to actual speech," citing *R.A.V.*, among other cases.[75] Perhaps this is a hopeful sign that *stare decisis* is at work at least to that extent, even though it failed, at least in part, in this instance. Furthermore, her focus in the *Black* majority decision on the intent of the speaker rather than the reaction of the observer in analyzing when speech constitutes "a true threat" is a form of speech-protective analysis that will hopefully limit the impact of *Black*.

Justice Stevens also has had little patience for offensive and/or unpopular symbolic expression. He alone in *R.A.V.* objected to the categorical approach to the First Amendment in its entirety, suggesting that "the history of the categorical approach is largely the history of narrowing the categories of unprotected speech"[76] (noting how libel and the "fighting words" doctrine had been construed to allow more expression, rather than less). He concluded that if the St. Paul ordinance had not been overbroad, he would have voted to uphold it, finding it "evenhanded."[77] He did, however, stop short of endorsing a ban on cross burning. His concurrence with the majority in *Black* referenced his concurrence in *R.A.V.*

Justice Breyer agreed with the majority in *Black* that the Virginia law permissibly outlawed cross-burning carried out with the intent to intimidate. However, his position on the constitutionality of laws that single out disfavored subjects or topics for proscription, even within unprotected categories of speech, is unknown.

CONCLUSION

It seems likely that the case of *R.A.V. v. St. Paul* was granted review by the U.S. Supreme Court in June of 1991 primarily because the ordinance punished expression discriminately, based on the viewpoint of the speaker and the group identity of those protected. Not all "fighting words" were proscribed, only those on disfavored subjects. The decision in June of 1992 confirmed that a majority of the Court found the ordinance problematic on those grounds. At the time review was granted, it seems possible, if not likely, that several Justices saw the ordinance as unconstitutional for other

---

[75]538 U.S. 343, 358 (2003).
[76]505 U.S. 377, 428 (Stevens, J., concurring).
[77]*Id.* at 435.

reasons, namely, that the ordinance was overbroad and singled out symbolic speech based on content. The anger displayed in the concurring opinions, particularly the opinions of Justices White and Blackmun, seems to indicate that they felt blind-sided by the majority's rationale, even though the petition for a writ of certiorari analogized the ordinance to speech codes that were proliferating on college campuses, and that seldom specified types of symbolic speech. The die had been cast early on, briefed (not adequately enough for Justice White), and confirmed at oral argument.

Though both *R.A.V.* and *Black* involved factual settings that included cross burnings, the comparison is superficial. For *Black*, the burning cross was front and center both at the oral argument and in the decision. For *R.A.V.,* the burning cross, though always present, remained in the background and did not play a large part in the case, either at oral argument or in the decision. It was not the focus of the Court.

As a result, the majority rationale found in the *R.A.V.* decision, though amended, remains intact, and perhaps has even been strengthened with the departures of Justices White and Blackmun. Singling out one form of unacceptable symbolic expression in a law, expression that can, and should, be addressed by content-neutral felony terroristic threats provisions is dangerous. Let us hope that this "foot-in-the-door" curbing of free expression that the *Black* decision represents remains just that. Let us also hope that the *R.A.V.* decision and the resulting doctrine as amended remains intact.

There will always be those who threaten the right of free expression in our nation, often with the best of intentions. We owe it to those who come after us to do what we can to preserve the right to dissent, even when we find the expressed opinion hateful or offensive. We can prosecute and incarcerate those who threaten or terrorize others, and denounce the bigoted opinion, but we must find room for those who disagree with us and wish to be heard. It is this difficult path that Gerald Gunther referenced at the beginning of this chapter that we must walk in challenging attempts to suppress hateful ideas by force of law.

APPENDIX A

THE U.S. SUPREME COURT (2003)

R.A.V. DOCTRINE (1992)

	Oppose Laws That Single Out Disfavored Topics (Viewpoint Discrimination)	*Oppose All Laws That Single Out Symbolic Speech Based on Content*
SOUTER	Yes	Yes
KENNEDY	Yes	Yes
GINSBURG	Yes	Yes
REHNQUIST	Yes	Exception (with intent and no presumption)
SCALIA	Yes	Exception
THOMAS	Yes	Ban permissible
O'CONNOR	No	Exception (with intent and no presumption)
STEVENS	No	Exception (with intent and no presumption)
BREYER	?	Exception (with intent and no presumption)

ANATOMY OF AN ORAL ARGUMENT

Rodney A. Smolla*

EDITOR'S INTRODUCTION

While the previous chapter compares two U.S. Supreme Court cases that had cross burning at the heart of their circumstances, chapter 6 primarily examines one element of the most recent of those two cases.

Oral arguments remain perhaps the most public aspect of Supreme Court litigation. Most clearly, they embody the spirit of judicial confrontation and debate. Two sides face off not only against one another, but—and perhaps more so—against the Court's nine justices. Even many of those who have not personally witnessed this verbal sparring are familiar with what transpires through audio recordings that have been made available. How attorneys maintain their wits and composure amidst the ebbs and flows of emotion and momentum, not to mention the peppering of questioning from members of the Court, is an issue for the ages.

In addition, there exists a very basic question about oral arguments: Do they matter? In the chapter that follows, prolific First Amendment scholar Rodney Smolla examines that question, and does so through the lens of first-hand experience. As he details, Mr. Smolla represented the First Amendment interests of three cross burners at the Supreme Court in December 2002. What he experienced in the hour the case was argued is what he shares in the pages that follow.

*Dean, University of Richmond School of Law, author of DELIBERATE INTENT (1999), FREE SPEECH IN AN OPEN SOCIETY (1992), SUING THE PRESS, *JERRY FALWELL V. LARRY FLYNT*: THE FIRST AMENDMENT ON TRIAL (1988), LAW OF DEFAMATION (1986), and many other works.

It was a noteworthy oral argument on several levels. Only eight justices attended. Chief Justice Rehnquist was ill that day, although he did take part in the discussion and opinion process. Most notable, however, was the role played by Justice Thomas, the Court's only African American member. He spoke. Veteran Court observers will tell you that is a rarity. Newspaper headlines and articles the next day overwhelmingly emphasized Justice Thomas' oration. But more than the uncommonness of his words were their meaning and passion. They changed the dynamic of the arguments. And perhaps the nature of the Court's opinion.

As a historical footnote, this event was concurrent with another race-infused debate in Washington. A whirlwind of controversy existed regarding then Senate majority leader Trent Lott. Senator Lott was defending his recent praise of Senator Strom Thurmond, a onetime segregationist. Lott had said the country would have been better off if Thurmond had won the 1948 presidential election. Lott resigned as Senate majority leader 9 days later.

*   *   *

Do oral arguments matter? One hears different things. I've heard judges say they simply do not. To these judges, oral arguments are ceremonial courtesies granted to placate the collective instinct that somehow a literal "opportunity to be heard" is a core element of due process—but the unfortunate truth is cases are decided on the briefs and records and not on what lawyers say or do not say in court. I've heard judges say oral argument matters enormously, and good judges approach oral argument with open minds (though not empty ones) and pay a great deal of attention to the push and pull of the jurists and the advocates, often deciding a case based on those interchanges.

What I most often hear, however, is that it just depends on various factors such as the case, the jurist, and the advocate. I've heard judges say that a lawyer can't *win* a case on oral argument, but he or she can sure as hell *lose* one. I've heard judges say that they come into an oral argument with a working hypothesis as to how they will decide the case, or least as to how they will decide certain issues, and then use the argument to explore and test that working judgment.

I've argued a fair number of cases, including a fair number of First Amendment cases. My take is this: Whether or not oral arguments "matter" in the ultimate sense of directly influencing outcomes, they certainly matter in some larger sense of helping to make sense of outcomes. They are not merely cathartic; they are revealing, and often to all involved. An oral argument is the golden moment of mediation between all the past that leads up to a presentation of a case and all the future that determines its resolution and future meaning. The deconstruction of an oral argument can be enormously illuminating in the deconstruction of a final written opinion.

It is with this spirit that I present the following review of an oral argument in which I participated as an advocate, in *Virginia v. Black*.[1] This is a controversial and difficult First Amendment case about which much has been written, and will be written. Here I am not so much interested in dense legal analysis, however, as I am interested in the dynamic of oral argument itself and the interplay of argument with the evolution of legal doctrine in an especially emotional and analytically difficult First Amendment conflict.

Virginia v. Black was actually a consolidation of three separate convictions for cross-burning, the conviction of Barry Elton Black, Richard Elliott, and Jonathan O'Mara. Black organized and led a Ku Klux Klan rally on private property in Cana, Virginia on August 22, 1998. During the rally, which was conducted with the permission of the landowner (who was present during the rally), Klan members set fire to a cross, approximately 25 to 30 feet in height. Following a Klan custom, the Klan members played the sacred hymn *Amazing Grace* over a loudspeaker as they marched around the cross, shouting and chanting. Their statements included diatribes against Blacks and Mexicans, and Bill and Hillary Clinton. The burning cross was visible from a nearby public highway. The County Sheriff and a Deputy Sheriff, upon learning of the rally, parked on the highway and walked up to the Klan members, letting them know they would be watching the rally from the road, keeping an eye on things. Several cars drove by the scene while the cross was lit, including one car with an African American family inside. Other than the two officers and these itinerant highway travelers, only one outsider observed the rally.

The cases of Richard Elliott and Jonathan O'Mara involved an entirely separate incident that took place at the opposite end of the state. After consuming alcohol, Elliott and O'Mara sought to "get back" at a neighbor, James Jubilee, by burning a crudely constructed cross in Jubilee's back yard. Jubilee was African American, and while there was some evidence in the record that racism may have been a factor in the incident, the defendants did not appear to have any large ideological agenda in their assault on Jubilee, but were rather acting out their mean prank in retaliation for Jubilee's disquiet over the fact that Elliott liked to discharge firearms in his backyard, a practice that worried Jubilee.

The defendants in both of these cross-burning incidents were convicted under a Virginia cross-burning law first passed in 1952, and subsequently modified a number of times to broaden its sweep and increase its potency. Virginia passed its first law targeting certain expressive activities of the Klan

---

[1] Virginia v. Black, 538 U.S. 343, 123 S.Ct. 1536, 155 L.Ed.2d 535 (2003).

in 1952. The law arose against the backdrop of cross-burnings in front of businesses and residences owned and occupied by African Americans. Responding to these racist episodes, Virginia's Governor proposed statutory restrictions on the cross-burning activities of the Klan. The state's first anti-cross-burning statute only prohibited cross-burning on the property of another person, and was indisputably enacted to target the cross-burning activities of the Klan. The law as it had evolved at the time of the prosecutions against Black, O'Mara, and Elliott was quite sweeping:

> It shall be unlawful for any person or persons, with the intent of intimidating any person or group of persons, to burn, or cause to be burned, a cross on the property of another, a highway or other public place. Any person who shall violate any provision of this section shall be guilty of a Class 6 felony. Any such burning of a cross shall be prima facie evidence of an intent to intimidate a person or group of persons.[2]

In an opinion by Virginia Supreme Court Justice Donald Lemons, the Supreme Court of Virginia struck down all three convictions under the statute, holding that the statute's singling out of a specific symbolic ritual, the burning cross, was a form of content and viewpoint discrimination that violated the First Amendment. The Virginia Supreme Court also held that "prima facie evidence"[3] provision of the law rendered it overbroad. Virginia sought review in the United States Supreme Court, and review was granted. I represented all three cross-burners.

William Hurd, Solicitor General for the Commonwealth of Virginia, began his oral argument before the United States Supreme Court with a rhetorical flourish: "Our Virginia cross-burning statute protects a very important freedom," he began confidently, "freedom from fear, and it does so without compromising freedom of speech. Our statute does not ban all cross-burning, only cross-burning used to threaten bodily harm. And unlike the ordinance in *R.A.V.*, our statute does not play favorites. It bans cross-burning as a tool of intimidation by anyone, against anyone, and for any reason. Surely, for all the reasons why we can ban threats of bodily harm, one hundred times over we can ban this exceedingly virulent weapon of fear."

This was a confident and efficient start. Hurd's assertion that the law was designed to secure "freedom from fear" struck a strong and emotionally resonant chord. At the same time, he immediately engaged the principal precedent that stood against the cross-burning law, *R.A.V. v. City of St. Paul.*[4] In *R.A.V.*, several youths entered an African American family's yard at night

---

[2]Va. Code Ann. §18.2-423 (Michie 1996).

[3]*Prima facie* refers to evidence that, on its face, requires no further support to establish its existence, validity, and credibility.

[4]505 U.S. 377, 112 S.Ct. 2538, 120 L.Ed.2d 305 (1992).

and lit a small cross. The perpetrators were charged with violating an ordinance of St. Paul Minnesota that provided:

> Whoever places on public or private property a symbol, object, appellation, characterization or graffiti, including, but not limited to, a burning cross or Nazi swastika, which one knows or has reasonable grounds to know arouses anger, alarm or resentment in others on the basis of race, color, creed, religion or gender commits disorderly conduct and shall be guilty of a misdemeanor.[5]

The Court held that "the ordinance goes even beyond mere content discrimination, to actual viewpoint discrimination,"[6] striking down the ordinance. Justice Scalia had written the opinion of the Court in *R.A.V.*, and Justice Thomas had been among the Justices who joined in that opinion. I checked their faces to see if they reacted at all to the mention of this precedent, but could read nothing.

Justice O'Connor jumped in with the first question to Hurd, stating that:

> There's one part of the statute that may be troublesome, and that is the prima facie evidence provision. I suppose you could have a cross-burning, for instance, in a play, in a theater, something like that, which in theory shouldn't violate the statute, but here's the prima facie evidence provision. Would you like to comment about that, and in the process, would you tell me if you think it's severable?

At the time, I heard this as a good question for my side. Justice O'Connor obviously had difficulties with the law's prima facie evidence provision, and seemed to be hinting that it rendered the law overly broad, so broad that it might bring within its compass even a cross-burning shown in a play or a movie. What I failed to see was the negative pregnant suggested by her remark—the suggestion that there was only *one* part of the law that was troublesome, the prima facie evidence provision—which might mean that the main body of the law, the basic prohibition on cross-burning for the purpose of intimidation, was fine. This would ultimately be precisely what she wrote in her plurality opinion in *Black* announcing the judgment of the Court. The outcome of the case was thus presaged in the very first question asked by the very first Justice to speak, less than 1 minute's time into the argument.

If I did not at the time see where Justice O'Connor was coming from or going, however, neither, it seemed, did Hurd. His response to Justice O'Connor struck me as a bit tentative. All the prima facie evidence provision did, he claimed, was restate a "common sense rule of evidence." The jury was

---

[5]*Id.* at 380, 112 S.Ct. at 2541, 120 L.Ed.2d at 2541 (quoting St. Paul, Minn. Legis. Code § 292.02 (1990)).

[6]*Id.* at 391, 112 S.Ct. at 2547, 120 L.Ed.2d at 323.

not bound by the prima facie evidence presumption. Justice O'Connor's face was skeptical. I could read also doubt on the faces of several other Justices. Justice O'Connor pressed Hurd, asking whether the jurors were instructed that it was free to disregard the presumption. Hurd seemed to fumble for an answer. Justice Ginsburg now joined the attack. She wanted to know the exact instruction the jury was given by the trial court in Black's case. Hurd hesitated. There was an awkward silence. Justice Ginsburg asked for the citation to the page in the appendix where the instruction was printed.

Page one hundred forty-six, I said to myself. *Page one hundred forty-six*. William Hurd did not know where in the appendix the instruction was. More awkward silence as he reached for the bound appendix and began, nervously now, flipping through pages. He told the Justices it was "instruction number nine," but he could not find it. "I apologize for the delay," he stated awkwardly.

I felt terrible for Hurd, a lawyer I very much liked. I also felt, foolishly, at that early moment, that we were going to win the case. I knew the page—*one hundred forty-six*. It was the only citation in the entire record before the Supreme Court that I *did* know. Out of all the pages in the appendix, out of all the briefs and documents that had existed in the *Black*, *Elliott*, and *O'Mara* cases through multiple levels of trial and appeals, this was the one page number I had memorized. This was the one page in the entire appendix to which I had appended a sticky note to mark the spot for fast reference. It had come to me the day before, in an eerie premonition. When I argue a case I like to have my hands and eyes free. I often do not bring any documents or papers to the podium at all. I look the judges or justices in the eyes the entire time. At most, I try to limit myself to one sheet of paper with a few key phrases or memory-jogging words. I am not the kind of lawyer who has cites to the record memorized. Yet the afternoon before the argument, while sitting around with others on our legal team brainstorming, the question of the jury instructions popped into my mind. I wanted to know exactly what page in the appendix the key instructions on the prima facie evidence provision appeared in each of the three cases, *Black*, *O'Mara*, and *Elliott*. This turned out to be easy for *O'Mara* and *Elliott*. Because Elliott had pled guilty, subject to his constitutional attack on the statute, there was no jury instruction in his case, because there was no jury. In *O'Mara*, as it turned out, no jury instruction regarding the prima facie evidence provision had ever been given. So *Black* stood alone. Hurd finally found the right spot and read from page one hundred forty-six. The trial judge had instructed the jury in the Black trial that: "The burning of a cross by itself is sufficient evidence from which you may infer the required intent."

Bingo, I thought. This must be fate—a sign, a portent. How else could it be that the one page I would commit to memory would be the page that the Justices would instantly zero in upon in the argument? The Justices clearly saw that the prima facie evidence provision, as interpreted in the *Black* jury instruction, essentially meant that a person could be convicted in Virginia for burning a cross—period. Although the statute required an intent to intimidate, this was a now-you-see-it-now-you-don't requirement. Under the prima facie evidence provision the government could skip providing any real proof of intimidation.

Hurd stuck to his guns, defending the provision, but he was getting battered. There was no direct evidence that anyone who passed the sight of the burning cross on the highway was intimidated. The best that Hurd could do was note that one car that drove by contained a Black family, which paused for a moment to watch the burning cross, and then sped away. Justice Kennedy noted that surely nobody in the car could have felt fear of immediate violence. He followed with the observation that "our *Brandenburg* line of cases says there must be an element of immediacy."

Brandenburg was more music to my ears. The facts in *Brandenburg v. Ohio*[7] were almost identical to the facts in the *Black* case. *Brandenburg* involved a Ku Klux Klan rally on a private farm near Cincinnati. The Supreme Court in *Brandenburg* struck down a conviction against Brandenburg, an Ohio Klan leader, holding that "the constitutional guarantees of free speech and free press do not permit a State to forbid or proscribe advocacy of the use of force or of law violation except where such advocacy is directed to inciting or producing imminent lawless action and is likely to incite or produce such action."[8]

Hurd had an answer to *Brandenburg*. That was an *incitement* case, he argued. But the Virginia law did not purport to punish incitements, it purported to punish intimidation, or threats. A statement could constitute a threat even if the harm being threatened was not immediate.

From my perspective, this was one of Virginia's best arguments. It indeed made sense to me that incitement law was different, at least to some degree, from threat law. When a speaker engages in incitement, the words themselves do not cause *instant* harm. The evil is not really "complete" until the lawless action being urged actually takes place. One may plausibly argue, however, that a threat is different. The evil inures *in the menace of the threat itself*, whether or not the threat is ever carried out. The mere making of the threat may cause disruption, as when a building is evacuated due to a bomb threat, or a object of the threat suffers emotional distress from the fear of future violent reprisal.

I had a counter to Hurd's position, and made a mental note to raise it in my argument. But there was no need, as several Justices did it for me. Why couldn't Virginia simply rely on general threat laws to handle this problem, Hurd was asked. Why did the state need a cross-burning statute when a broad law banning all threats or intimidation would seem to work just as well?

---

[7]Brandenburg v. Ohio, 395 U.S. 444, 89 S.Ct. 1827, 23 L.Ed.2d 430 (1969).
[8]*Id.* at 447, 89 S.Ct. at 1830, 23 L.Ed.2d at 434.

Hurd had an answer: "Your honor, there's a downside to having a broad statute, and it is this. That whenever you prohibit a proscribable category of speech, there will be a zone of protected speech that looks a lot like the proscribed category and in which people must be somewhat careful or they may be arrested mistakenly, as happened with Mr. Watts in the *Watts* case."

I didn't think much of this response. He seemed to be arguing that a broad statute—a statute that simply made it a crime to engage in a threat—was actually more damaging to freedom of speech than the cross-burning law, because of its very broadness. People might be swept into its ambit even when engaging in action protected by the First Amendment. This was, he seemed to be claiming, what had happened in *Watts v. United States*,[9] a case in which the Supreme Court had struck down a prosecution against a Vietnam protestor for saying that he'd like to shoot President Lyndon Johnson, ruling that in context it was plain that the protester was simply using graphic and colorful language to express a political statement, not engaging in a serious or "true threat" meant literally as an expression of intent to place the President in harm's way.

I felt advocate's anger welling up—that rise that all advocates know that comes when you think your opponent is trying to pull an argumentative fast one. There were multiple flaws in Hurd's argument, as I saw it. First and foremost, the beauty of a general threat law, as I saw it, was that it was entirely viewpoint-neutral. By definition all threat laws do penalize "expression," in the narrow sterile sense that the whole concept of a "threat" connotes communication. The notion of "threat" is otherwise incoherent. Thus "threat laws" are always "speech laws," as we cannot imagine a threat without imagining speech of some kind as the medium through which the threat is communicated, as we cannot imagine electricity without electrons. Threat laws are in this sense like other laws, such as libel or copyright infringement statutes, in that their nature always involves the content of expression. A general threat law, however, looks merely to those aspects of the communication that express an intention to cause someone harm. Beyond that, a general threat law is content- and viewpoint-neutral. It is thus misleading to think of threat laws as *broader* than the cross-burning statute. I would instead argue they are narrower. For threat laws look only to those bare-bones elements of the communication that communicate the serious intention to do harm—no other content or viewpoint is relevant. This was, indeed, precisely what I had always thought *R.A.V.* had largely stood for. One could have a "fighting words" law, but not a "racist fighting words" law, or a "fighting words through flag-burning law," or a "fighting words through cross-burning law." One could have a threat law, but not a threat law that singled out the burning cross.

I was also at once puzzled and frustrated by Hurd's invocation of *Watts*. The *Watts* precedent was a tricky one for me to handle. Although the Court

---

[9]394 U.S. 705, 89 S.Ct. 1399, 22 L. Ed. 2d 664 (1969).

in *Watts* had struck down the convictions, it had not held that the federal law banning threats against the President was itself unconstitutional. If society could have a law that specially singled out threats against the President, on the theory that such threats were especially harmful, why could it not have a law that specially singled out threats carried out through cross-burning, on the theory that such threats were also especially harmful?

My view was that the two were not on par. The law banning threats against the President did not punish threats attacking the President or the presidency as a *symbol*. It would violate the First Amendment, for example, to make it a crime to burn the *image of the President* in effigy. The presidential threat law did not operate on any symbol, or on any viewpoint, but rather on the identity of a specific victim. It was like a law that might operate uniquely to punish threats against a school teacher or a cop.

My advocate's anger, however, was soon redirected by alarm. Justice Scalia was joining in. I had counted on Justice Scalia as my single safest vote. He was, after all, the author of my single best precedent, *R.A.V.* "I thought the key here is that this is not just speech," Justice Scalia said, insistently. "It is not just speech. It's action that is intended to convey a message."

This remark was not in itself entirely frightening to me. I think I was more disturbed by the tone in which it was delivered, a tone entirely benevolent. I'd hoped for Justice Scalia to be bulldogging Hurd from the start. "Surely," Scalia continued, "surely your State could make it unlawful to brandish with the intent of intimidating somebody, couldn't it?"

Now I was really worried. Was Scalia seriously equating a burning cross with an automatic weapon? Naww, I thought. He's setting a trap for Hurd.

Hurd jumped right into the steel jaws. "Justice Scalia, we have statutes that prohibit brandishing of firearms."

Sure you do, I thought. *Go get him, Justice!*

Continuing to roll, Hurd explained: "In fact, a burning cross is very much like a brandishing of a firearm."

Gotcha! Get him Justice!

But he did not. Scalia instead nodded with appreciation and approval. "That's your point!" he said, with emphasis.

That's his point? I was flabbergasted. *No, wait a minute—that can't be his point. If it is, it's an absolutely lousy one.*

Hurd, a strong advocate, knew an ally when he saw one, and knew how to run with a ball handed to him with an open field. A burning cross is virtually "a present offer of force," he said, which "makes it an especially virulent form of intimidation."

Justice Kennedy entered the debate, bringing Hurd back to the prima facie evidence provision. For several minutes he questioned Hurd on exactly how the provision operated. Any time a person burned a cross, even on his own property, the statute gave rise to an inference of an intent to intimidate. Justice Breyer joined the gathering storm. "So in a case in which there was a cross burned out in the middle of a desert somewhere, and that's all that's proved, that would be enough to sustain the conviction," he observed. Hurd tried to get out an answer about how the jury would still have to find that there was evidence beyond a reasonable doubt, but this did not get far. What if the defendant merely stands mute, Justice Stevens asked. Hurd tried to explain something about jury instructions, but again he could not complete a sentence. Suppose he burned a circle, Justice Stevens hypothesized. He could not be convicted on the same evidence. Hurd invoked the Due Process Clause now, talking about evidentiary inferences. Justice Breyer interrupted, going back to his middle-of-the-desert theme. "In the case of a desert, he's out in the desert, and he's burning the cross for symbolic purposes and nobody else is around. I guess wouldn't the judge have to set aside the conviction on First Amendment grounds?"

Hurd was wise enough not to fight this. "Justice Breyer, absolutely," he agreed, going on to argue that the statute merely used the phrase "prima facie" evidence, which did not preclude a court from setting aside a conviction for lack of sufficient evidence on "post-conviction review."

To me this was a weak and meandering response. Hurd's argument was losing its narrative thread. He was lost in the desert. Justice Scalia chimed in, and this time he seemed more on my side. Perhaps the statute used the term "prima facie," he observed, but the jury instruction in the *Black* case seemed to take it past that, saying that the burning cross was itself sufficient evidence from which the jury could infer the required intent.

The desert hypothetical surfaced yet again, and again Hurd returned to his due process theme. Justice Breyer said, impishly, "In other words, every due process violation in a First Amendment case is a First Amendment violation." The courtroom erupted in laughter. Hurd seemed to be in growing trouble. Justice Ginsburg now spoke up. I sensed she wanted to help Hurd refocus. "May I ask you about a case of more immediate concern?" she said. "You have said that the burning cross is a symbol like no other. And so this is a self-contained category. What about other things that are associated with the Klan? For example, the white robes and the mask? Are they also symbols that the State can ban, or is there something about the burning cross that makes it unique?"

I thought this a brilliant question, naturally. Hurd's answer was lame. There was a historic connection between a burning cross and ensuing violence, he claimed. But there was no similar connection between people wearing white sheets and ensuing violence.

Where did you get that statistic? I thought, sarcastically. The fact is that at least whenever the Klan members burned crosses, they were almost certainly wearing white sheets. Moreover, I was quite certain that in the sad-sack history of the Ku Klux Klan there must have been thousands and thousands of cross-burning ceremonies, with Klansmen in full regalia burning, cursing, hootin' and hollerin'. No doubt *some* of the time these rallies were followed by acts of violence. But no doubt *most* of the time they were not.

Hurd was asked about the nineteenth century federal "Ku Klux Klan Act," a law that still survives in slightly different form as a still-used federal civil rights law. The act, clearly aimed in its day at Klan lynch mobs, speaks in terms of going out "in disguise on the highway."

Hurd tried to turn the example his way, noting that such laws were aimed largely at the element of disguise. On this point I thought he was exactly right, but I also thought that the point weakened his case instead of strengthening it. If cross burning is the quintessential Klan ritual, the hood and robe are the quintessential Klan uniform. Many states have banned the wearing of masks for the purposes of combating Klan activity, much like the federal law speaks of going out in disguise. Anti-mask statutes are deservedly treated more leniently in First Amendment challenges than anti-cross-burning laws, though hooded masks and burning crosses are both signature symbols of the Klan. The difference lies not in form but in function. The cross-burning ritual is purely communicative, but the hood is both communicative and functional—in addition to signifying membership in the Klan, it functions as a disguise.[10]

Hurd kept going. Cross burning was unique, he said, returning to an earlier theme. "Burn anything else. Burn the flag. Burn a sheet. The message is opposition to the thing that the symbol unburned represents. Burning a cross is not opposition to Christianity. The message is a threat of bodily harm, and it is unique. And it's not simply a message of bigotry. It's a message that bodily harm is coming."

Justice Stevens took issue. "It sounds to me like you're defending the statute on the ground that the message that his particular act conveys is particularly obnoxious."

Hurd resisted. We have a lot of obnoxious speech, he rejoined, and it's all perfectly fine. "This is not obnoxious speech. This is a threat of bodily harm."

Well that's the right answer, I thought. *It's just not believable.*

Almost as if Hurd somehow read my mind, he insisted: "And this is not something that we just made up."

---

[10]A more recent illustration of this principle is *Church of the American Knights of the Ku Klux Klan v. Kerik*, holding that such a New York anti-mask statute did not violate the First Amendment. 356 F.3d 197 (2d Cir. 2004). While not formally associated with other organizations bearing the name "Ku Klux Klan," the American Knights group identified itself "'in part with the Ku Klux Klan which existed earlier in American history insofar as both groups believe in racial separation and in the importance of the Ten Commandments and the virtues of religious belief." *Id.* at 199-200. The group "opposes integration, affirmative action, racial intermarriage, immigration and abortion." *Id.* at 200. "Members wear 'the hood and robe,' the garb traditionally associated with the Klan of the Reconstruction era and its early twentieth-century purported successor." *Id.*

Yes you did.

"Cross-burning has that message because for decades the Klan wanted it to have that message because they wanted that tool of intimidation. And so it rings a little hollow when the Klan comes to court and complains that our law treats that message—treats that burning cross—as having exactly the message that they for decades have wanted it to have."

Hurd's time expired. I thought his final point had actually been a good one, after all. For although the Klan had surely burned thousands of crosses over the years, often with no violence ensuing, Hurd had a fair point in claiming that the Klan probably relished its reputation for violence, and through its own history was largely responsible for the dark associations that many had with the burning cross. Hurd, an adversary that I admired and liked personally, had certainly been through some rocky times in his 20 minutes of argument, but had at least ended on a reasonably strong note.

Next to the podium came Michael Dreeben, a very capable Supreme Court advocate from the United States Solicitor General's Office. The United States had filed a brief in support of Virginia, and had been granted 10 minutes for argument.

Quite wisely, Dreeben picked up on the strong point on which Hurd had ended. "History has revealed that cross-burning has been used as a tool to intimidate and put people in fear of bodily violence in a way that no other symbol has been used," Dreeben stated.

Justice O'Connor asked whether the burning cross was a form of "fighting words," or instead fell within some other category of constitutionally proscribable speech. Dreeben replied that it was best to think of it as "akin to a threat to put somebody in bodily harm."

O'Connor then pressed Dreeben on what the Department of Justice thought of Virginia's prima facie evidence provision. His response was highly ambivalent. The United States had not taken a position one way or another on the prima facie evidence provision, he said. The United States merely was arguing that it was permissible to have anti cross-burning laws. The argument then entered the one brief dramatic lull of the hour, as several Justices asked Dreeben, who is a very articulate but low-key advocate, about various nuances of statutory and common-law threat laws.

It was the calm before the storm. Dreeben meticulously lectured for several more minutes on the law of threats until, suddenly, without warning, it happened. Justice Thomas spoke.

Merely to hear Justice Thomas speak was an event in itself. As writer Dahlia Lithwick, describing the moment, put it nicely, it was He-Who-Never-Speaks booming in a rich James Earl Jones baritone like "Luke, I am your father."

In all my years as a lawyer I have never witnessed the mood in a courtroom turn so completely and suddenly. Hurd had been badly beaten up and to this point Dreeben had been toyed with, but on the whole the mode of the Justices had seemed pervasively skeptical of the constitutionality of Virginia's law.

And then Justice Thomas spoke.

"Mr. Dreeben, aren't you understating the effects of the burning cross? This statute was passed in what year?"

"Nineteen fifty-two, originally."

"Now it's my understanding that we had almost one hundred years of lynching and activity in the South by the Knights of Camellia and the Ku Klux Klan, and this was a reign of terror. And the cross was a symbol of that reign of terror. Isn't that significantly greater than intimidation or a threat?"

He's trapping him, I thought. I was absolutely sure Justice Thomas was on my side. I think Dreeben figured it the same way. Warily, Dreeben partially resisted Justice Thomas's characterization.

"Well, I think they're coextensive, Justice Thomas, because it is—"

Justice Thomas broke in, and the room fell absolutely silent, but for his forceful voice:

> Well, my fear is, Mr. Dreeben, that you're actually *understating* the symbolism and the effect of the burning cross. I indicated, I think, in the Ohio case that the cross was not a religious symbol and that it was intended to have a virulent effect. I think that what you're attempting to do is fit this into our jurisprudence rather than stating more clearly what the cross was intended to accomplish. Indeed, it is unlike any symbol in our society.

I was stunned. Dreeben was *understating* his case. He instantly recovered: "Well I don't mean to understate it, and I entirely agree with Your Honor's description of how the cross has been used as an instrument of intimidation against minorities in this country."

I'll bet you do. Like a quarterback using all his powers of feel and experience and peripheral vision to desperately read a defense in the midst of a furious blitz, my every advocate's sense and instinct took in all that was happening in the adrenal rush of the crisis. I watched as the convivial Justice Breyer, who sits next to Justice Thomas on the bench (though he rarely votes next to Justice Thomas in decisions) lean toward his judicial brother and discretely place an arm on his back, a fleeting but quite poignant collegial gesture of human kinship, a certain "I-feel-your-pain moment" that even in the fury of the battle I found genuinely touching. Not so touching was the scowl that I saw come over the visage of Justice Scalia. I had been waiting for that scowl for nearly 30 minutes, waiting for Justice Scalia to unload on Hurd or Dreeben. But his mood had been, if not generous toward the government, at least benign. Justice Scalia glanced down at me, still seated at the counsel table, awaiting my turn. Just a quick second's look, but I could read his eyes. Clarence Thomas was his friend, and I was not.

Dreeben's time expired, and Justice Stevens invited me to the podium.

Justice Scalia allowed me one sentence. "The heart of our argument," I said, "is that when the State targets a particular symbol or a particular symbolic ritual, it engages in content and viewpoint discrimination of the type forbidden by the First Amendment."

"What about he symbol of brandishing an automatic weapon in somebody's face?" Justice Scalia challenged.

"Justice Scalia," I started.

"*You're next!*" Justice Scalia interrupted, presumably meaning that the cross-burner was stating that "You'll be the next to be lynched or bombed."

"There's a fundamental difference between brandishing a cross and brandishing a gun," I argued. "The physical properties of the gun as a weapon add potency to the threat. And so if the State makes a threat committed with a firearm an especially heinous type of threat, it is acting within the confines of what is permissible under *R.A.V.*, because it's creating a subclass of threat and defining that subclass of threat for the same reasons that allow it to define the outer perimeter of threat law, things going to the danger posed by that threat. But the properties of the cross are not physical properties and the burning element of a burning cross is not what communicates the threat."

I was trying to turn Justice Scalia's own opinion in *R.A.V.* against him. It was a theme I had sounded repeatedly in our briefs. Out of all the objects in the world that might be set on fire, Virginia's cross-burning law selected only a burning cross for unique treatment. At the highest level of abstraction a cross is an object or symbol of a particular shape—a vertical pole traversed by a horizontal bar. There certainly is nothing in this geometric configuration of the vertical and horizontal that carries any peculiarly dangerous potency. It is not the fire that burns hotter when flaming sticks are crossed, but the passions that the fire inflames.

Justice Souter picked up on Justice Scalia's theme. The argument I was making, he suggested, may have been persuasive in 1820, but over time the burning cross has now acquired new potency, perhaps equal to that of a gun. In response I drew an analogy to intellectual property, and to the notion of "secondary meaning" in trademark law. But as I had argued in my brief, this case was not trademark law. This was not the invocation of secondary meaning to avoid consumer confusion in the regulation of the sale of goods or services within the marketplace of commerce. This was free speech law. This was the invocation of secondary meaning in the service of censorship, regulating traffic in one discrete expressive symbol within the marketplace of ideas.

Justice Souter came back. "The burning cross is not merely a trademark for the Ku Klux Klan," he stated. "Isn't it also a kind of Pavlovian signal so that when the signal is given, the natural human response is not recognition of a message, but fear?"

I thought this was a brilliant question, exposing a weakness and a strength in our challenge to the Virginia law. Symbols do indeed often communicate in a manner that is almost Pavlovian, at times speaking heart to heart and seeming to skip the mind. But that did not mean that symbols are somehow second-class citizens as carriers of expression. To the contrary, precisely because of their capacity to express not merely the cognitive messages of the mind but the deeper and perhaps more primal permutations of love, hate, rejection, invitation, anger, peace, or identity, they are deserving of full protection under the Constitution. "No, Your Honor," I said, quietly but firmly. "Respectfully I think that overstates what is being communicated. Any symbol in its pristine state that has gathered reverence in our society—the American Flag, the Star of David, the cross, the symbols of government—is a powerful, emotional symbol in its revered state."

Justice Scalia would not let this set. "Can't the state protect people from threats that scare people?" he asked. And, Justice Scalia wondered, if a particular symbol has acquired such a potent meaning as symbol that engenders fear, can't the state ban it. I tried to respond by examining what we mean by words such as "fear" or "scared" or "intimidating." What do we mean when we use such words? "If I see a burning cross," I observed, "my stomach may churn. I may feel a sense of loathing, disgust, a vague sense of being 'intimidated' because of what I associate with it, but not fear of *bodily harm*."

"How about a cross in your lawn," Scalia challenged. "I dare say you would rather see a man with a rifle on your front lawn. If you were a Black man at night, you'd rather see a man with a rifle than see a burning cross on your front lawn."

This was the moment, I knew, when I had to deal with the history that Justice Thomas had recounted. Justice Thomas had struck the powerful blows against my argument and now Justice Scalia was engaged in the mop-up operation. It was now or never.

I began with a concession. "I concede and totally accept the history that Justice Thomas has recounted," I said solemnly. "As powerful as all of those points are, there's not a single interest that society seeks to protect in protecting that victim that cannot be vindicated perfectly as well, with no fall-off at all, by content-neutral alternatives. Not merely run-of-the-mill threat laws, or incitement laws, or intimidation laws, which may have an antiseptic and sterile quality about them. You can go beyond that ..."

If I had been able to finish my sentence, I would have pointed out that hate *crime* laws, as opposed to *hate speech* laws, are fully constitutional. Under the Supreme Court's decision in *Wisconsin v. Mitchell*,[11] the government may punish a threat made with racist intent, for example, more severely than other threats, without violating the First Amendment. But I did not get to finish my sentence.

---

[11]508 U.S. 476, 113 S.Ct. 2194, 124 L. Ed. 2d 436 (1993).

Justice O'Connor asked whether this was not simply a regulation of "a particularly virulent form of intimidation." Her phrasing was critical, for in the *R.A.V.* opinion, the Court had suggested that the government singled out an especially dangerous subcategory of otherwise proscribable speech, such as particularly virulent threats.

I took Justice O'Connor's question head-on: "Your honor, it is *not* a particularly virulent form of intimidation."

Justice O'Connor made it clear enough I had not persuaded her. "Well, it is for the very reasons we've explored this morning. What if I think it is? Why can't the State regulate it?"

If you think it is, then you'll probably be voting against me I thought. But of course I did not say that. I instead replied, "Because, Justice O'Connor, it is also an especially virulent form of *expression of ideas* relating to race, religion, and politics."

Justice Kennedy seemed to want to help me. He invited me to finish the thought I'd not been able to get to concerning *Wisconsin v. Mitchell*, and what followed was a colloquy between us on the meaning of the case. In *Wisconsin v. Mitchell* the Court held that the penalty for an ordinary crime, such as assault, could be increased if it were performed with biased intent.[12] I stated to Justice Kennedy that the same could be true of threats made with biased intent. This led him to ask if you could make the penalty for a threat consummated by the burning of a cross higher than that of an ordinary threat. I said it would not. The difference is that a pure biased-intent law does not penalize expression, but motivation. A cross-burning threat law punishes the use of one symbol. Justice Kennedy then completed the circle: "Because it's content-based discrimination within the category of activity that can be entirely proscribed."

There's nothing better for an advocate than when a Justice completes your answer for you, and it's the one you want. "That is precisely our argument," I stated.

Justice Stevens jumped in, with a beneficent smile. "Now is there any support for that proposition other than the majority opinion in *R.A.V.*?" he asked. I knew Justice Stevens was no fan of *R.A.V.* I also knew there was no reason to fuss over it. I owned up that "*R.A.V.* is the only case that dealt squarely with this puzzle of what happens when you're dealing with a category of speech that you have the right to proscribe, and then you draw gratuitous content- or viewpoint-based distinctions within it." But I could not resist pushing a bit. "However, Justice Stevens, I would say that it isn't alone in this Court's powerful condemnation of viewpoint discrimination, and a key element to this Court's First Amendment history is that we don't want to cut matters too finely."

---

[12]*Id.* at 476, 113 S.Ct. at 2202, 124 L.Ed.2d at 489.

Now Justice Scalia was back, exploring *R.A.V.*, his own masterpiece. He wanted to know what the fact pattern in the case was. I stated that it was identical to the pattern in one of the cases here, the case involving O'Mara and Elliott. Justice Scalia thought, however, that the law in *R.A.V.* was demonstrably different. In *R.A.V.* it was burning a cross with a "particular motivation, wasn't it?" he asked. "It wasn't the mere act."

I took advantage of his challenge to lay out a central tenet of our case. "At the core of our argument, Justice Scalia, is the claim that the concept of viewpoint discrimination is and ought to be broad enough to encompass not only viewpoint discrimination articulated linguistically, the way that it was done in the statute in *R.A.V.*, but also viewpoint discrimination through the singling out of a symbol. Because symbols acquire meaning in precisely the same way that words acquire meaning."

This clearly intrigued Justice Breyer. "But words are even more," he observed. "I mean, your argument applies *a fortiori* to words, right?"

I hate when someone uses *a fortiori* on me. In my entire career as an advocate no judge or justice has ever uttered the phrase *a fortiori* to express good wishes. It is always the prelude to a trap. Justice Breyer then hypothesized that you could draft a statute that would make it a crime to use certain words. His examples were counterfeiting, or impersonating somebody. We went back and forth on this. The normal method of drafting legislation, I said, was for the legislative body to describe the conduct that the legislature desired to prohibit. Various combinations of words might fit within the definition of that conduct. Thus a law might ban threats, or conspiracies to violate the antitrust laws, and a virtually infinite pattern of words might in any set of circumstances constitute a threat, or price-fixing. But Justice Breyer was not satisfied. Certainly there were words or symbols that could in effect be proscribed, such as impersonating the President or the Great Seal of the United States, he suggested. At most, he argued, the law would be tested under the strict scrutiny test, and perhaps even under the "intermediate scrutiny" test of *United States v. O'Brien*.[13]

I claimed it did not matter which test one invoked, for under any test we should prevail, because there were content-neutral alternatives available that would accomplish society's interests without singling out any one symbol. I then took a direct shot a *O'Brien*. The intermediate scrutiny standard of *O'Brien* was appropriate, I said, only when the harm the government seeks to prevent does not flow directly from the *communicative impact* of the expression. *O'Brien* thus upheld a federal statute forbidding alteration of a draft card, because the harm caused was not geared to what was *expressed* by

---

[13]391 U.S. 367, 88 S.Ct. 1673, 20 L.E.2d 672 (1968).

someone burning a draft card, but by the interference with the orderly maintenance of the selective service system caused by destroying the card. In the case of cross-burning, however, it is *only* what is communicated that causes harm, if any exists. "And there is no getting around the fact that the harm the government seeks to prevent here *indubitably* flows only from the formation of this symbol."

As I said this, a little voice in me snickered to myself. *Where the hell did you pull the word "indubitably" from?* Even the most comfortable of advocates will occasionally show fissures from the pressure of a high-powered argument. In my entire life before that moment I don't think I'd ever once used the word "indubitably," which sounds like some stuffed pontification of Sherlock Holmes, and I hope I never use it again.

Justice Breyer now thought he had me. Wasn't the logic of my argument, he insisted, that it would not be permissible to draft a statute that said you may not make it a crime to use the words "I'll kill you" with an intent to kill somebody?

But I wasn't going down easy. Replying to Justice Breyer, I said, "take the words 'I swear I'll kill you.' Those words in a given context might be break-fast banter. Might be a joke." If a law uses language that simply gives examples of words of threat, and if the law is otherwise viewpoint neutral, it would be fine First Amendment purposes. The problem with the Virginia statute, I maintained, was that it was "a fusion of a true threat law and a gratuitous addition to the true threat law, cross-burning."

Now Justice Ginsburg seemed troubled. What about the many federal statutes, she asked, that are used to prosecute acts of cross-burning. It was a question I welcomed. All the federal civil rights statutes, I stated, were content-neutral, providing breathing space for the First Amendment.

Justice O'Connor then chided that the Virginia law incorporated an intent to intimidate feature, which ought to be enough to save it. Again, I insisted this was wrong under the learning of *R.A.V.* "A law can't be half constitutional," I said.

This prompted a question from Justice Souter. Was I seeking to *apply* the ruling in *R.A.V.* or to *extend* it. "It's our submission," I explained, "that in fact the two cases are identical. The reason they don't seem identical, perhaps, is that it is harder to locate the viewpoint and content discrimination in our minds when we think of the burning cross, than we think of the language used in the statute in *R.A.V.*, which talked about anger or resentment on the basis of race, color, or creed." I suggested that this may be caused in part by what Justice Souter had already noted, the "Pavlovian connection" that is triggered by the sight of the burning cross. I then got to an argument that had actually been suggested to me by a law student in class, during a dialogue about the case. "Even if at a given moment in time, you could take some symbol and freeze it, and you could say that at this second this symbol is always associated with violence," I wanted to argue the meaning of that symbol would not stay frozen, not stay static. It would ultimately acquire multiple meanings, get appropriated for humor or parody or politics removed from the original association with violence. I did not quite get all these words out, for Justice Breyer re-entered the questioning, largely completing my thought for me, and then posing a question to test its consequences.

"You have a very interesting point," he said. "And as I've been thinking about it, it seems to me that the difficulty, the possible difficulty with it, is that the First Amendment doesn't protect words. It protects the use of words for certain purposes. And it doesn't protect for example, a symbol. It protects a thing that counts as a symbol when used for symbolic purposes."

I was fine with this. "That's correct," I said.

"So just as it doesn't protect the words, I will kill you, but protects them when used in a play, but not when used as a threat-"

"—that is correct—"

"—so it doesn't protect the burning of the cross when used as a threat and not as a symbol."

"That is correct."

"And now we have a statute that says you can use it as a symbol, but you can't use it as a threat. And therefore, the First Amendment doesn't apply. Now if that's the right analysis, then what's your response."

I could not resist. "Your Honor, that everything you said up until the very end was right."

The courtroom roared with laughter. Justice Breyer laughed hard himself, nodding.

"I have a hunch I have to at least say that much," I added. Again the courtroom erupted in laughter. Now I had to get serious, as Justice Breyer clearly thought he had closed the trap that began with *a fortiori*.

"Justice Breyer, it comes to this. You cannot make the judgment that this law, in actual impact, only penalizes those acts of cross-burning that result in threat. It certainly chills, Justice Breyer, a wide range of expression, as it did *in this case*." I could not shy away from defending the Klan cross-burning ritual, I knew. "Every time the Ku Klux Klan conducts one its rallies," I pointed out, "at the height of its rally, it burns a large cross, and it plays a hymn such as *The Old Rugged Cross* or *Onward Christian Soldiers* or *Amazing Grace*. This is the ritual." It was inconceivable, I insisted, and there was nothing in the record, I argued, "to support the proposition that every time the Klan engages in cross-burning it is engaged in a threat."

This triggered a flurry of questions from a handful of Justices at once. Out of the barrage the question that emerged most forcefully was the observation that a Klan cross-burning would not be a threat if it was done out of sight, rather than within view of a public highway. I tried to turn this around. Certainly the First Amendment could not be understood to mean that freedom of speech was protected only if conducted in private. The whole point of the First Amendment is that those who do not represent mainstream sensibilities have the right to confront the rest of us with speech that is disturbing or offensive to our majority values. Citing Justice Brandeis' views in *Whitney v. California*,[14] I insisted that we do not make the world safer by driving the speech of hate groups such as the Ku Klux Klan underground. In many societies in the world, the Klan could be banned. But in America we cannot ban the Klan. And we should not be permitted to ban the symbols of the Klan, however loathsome.

Justice Breyer came back to me, continuing to press his hypothetical, this time working the prima facie evidence provision. He hypothesized that it would be permissible to enact a statute that penalized the use of the words "I will kill you" with the actual intent to threaten. If the statute went on to say that use of the words "I will kill you" as prima facie evidence of a threat, this too would be permissible. On those premises, he then concluded, there is nothing wrong with a law treating a burning cross as prima facie evidence of intent to intimidate.

"There is a world of difference, your Honor. And the difference is that the words, 'I will kill you' *are* words of threat that have no additional emanations. They have no additional secondary meaning in this society as the symbol of a group or as the symbol of an idea such as bigotry. They partake of the same rationale, the same defining parameters, which allow you to attack threats in the first instance." The burning cross is entirely different, I argued. Whether it is a burning cross in the nineteenth century or today, I insisted, "you must concede that it is one of the most powerful religious symbols in human history. It is the symbol of Christianity, the symbol of the crucifixion of Christ. When a cross is burned, the same way as when the flag is burned, undoubtedly the burner is playing on the underlying positive repository of meaning to make the intense negative point, often a point that strikes us as horrible and as evil and disgusting."

Justice Ginsburg then spoke, quietly. She has the wonderful power of quietude. With the courtroom and her colleagues suddenly soundless, she took the position that cross-burning and flag-burning are not on a par. "The flag is a symbol of our government, and one of the things about free speech is we can criticize the President, the Supreme Court, anybody, and feel totally free about doing that. It's the symbol of government. But the cross is not attacking the government. It's attacking people, threatening their lives and limbs."

It was not a contrast I was willing to concede. I replied respectfully to Justice Ginsburg:

---

[14] 274 U.S. 357, 372, 47 S.Ct. 641, 647, (1927) (Brandeis, J., concurring).

I only partially accept that dichotomy. If in fact, when the Klan engages in cross-burning, as it did in *Brandenburg v. Ohio*, and as it did here, it is a mélange of messages. Yes, to some degree it is a horizontal message of hate speech, the Klan members attacking Jews and Catholics and African Americans and all of the various people that have been the point of its hatred over the years. But it is also engaged in dissent, and in a political message. If you remember, in *Brandenburg v. Ohio*, Brandenburg was saying that if Congress does not change things, some 'revengeance' will have to be taken. In this case, President Clinton was talked about by the Klan members. Hillary Clinton was talked about by the Klan members. Racial preferences and the idea that taxes were used to support minority groups. There was a jumble of messages, including political anger—

"Mr. Smolla, I would like to take exception to your suggestion in response to Justice Breyer that the words 'I will kill you' always have a threatening meaning," Justice Stevens broke in. I was starting to get the idea, finally, that the Justices are pretty much inclined never to let you get on a roll.

"They may not, Justice Stevens," I said, taking a soft line.

"I think they're often used in casual conversation without any such threatening meaning at all."

I accepted this, and returned to my claim that one could fit the words "I will kill you" within the exceptions to *R.A.V.* in a manner that one just never could with specific symbols, such as flags or crosses, which have powerful ideological connotations. Virginia also has a law that makes it a crime to intimidate anyone through use of a swastika, I noted. The state seemed to think it could browse the universe of symbols and ban the ones it does not like. But as I had argued in our brief, government ought not be allowed to single out any one symbol for specially disfavored treatment, whether it is a cross, a flag, or the likeness of Osama bin Laden. This is perilous business. If the government is permitted to select one symbol for banishment from public discourse there are few limiting principles to prevent it from selecting others. And it is but a short step from the banning of offending symbols such as burning crosses or flags to the banning of offending words. A word is, after all, but a symbol itself, "the skin of a living thought."[15]

Justice Breyer again jumped in, and again I gave the same answer—that to single out any one combination of words or symbols tends to chill their use. To which Justice Kennedy objected that this seemed to give people "a free ride" if they choose to use those symbols or words to intimidate.

"Justice Kennedy," I said in disagreement, "there's no free ride if the government employs content-neutral alternatives." My point was that the

---

[15]*See* Towne v. Eisner, 245 U.S. 418, 425, 38 S.Ct. 158, 159, 62 L. Ed. 372, 376 (1918) (Holmes, J.) ("A word is not a crystal, transparent and unchanged, it is the skin of a living thought and may vary greatly in color and content according to the circumstances and the time in which it is used.")

First Amendment does not *immunize from prosecution* the *act* of cross-burning when done to threaten. It merely requires that we focus only on the act and the intent, and not the symbol. A threat may be made with a burning cross. When it is, the perpetrator may be punished through an ordinary threat law, or even through a threat law with a more powerful penalty attached for biased crimes, and the First Amendment will not be violated.

Justice Kennedy was still troubled. "Why can't we say there's no free ride when the government imposes *scienter*?" he asked.

"Your Honor, because the First Amendment requires that we flip the question. It is not 'Why can't the government single out his particular form of expression?' It is 'Why does government need to?'"

This really bothered Justice Scalia, who jumped in impatiently. "Wait, wait, wait. I don't think the cases say you have to use the least restrictive alternative. I'm sure there are other ways of getting at the person who brandishes an automatic weapon, but surely you can make brandishing an automatic weapon a crime."

I thought this just plain off as an analogy. It was true that the Constitution does not require the "least restrictive alternative" when regulating the use of guns. But typically First Amendment jurisprudence *does* require the least restrictive means when regulating the content or viewpoint of speech. I tried to make this point, but Justice Scalia seemed determined to make the cross and the gun the same.

"Brandishing a weapon is a symbol just as a burning cross is a symbol," he insisted.

I fumbled the answer to this one. Mealy-mouthed, I said that under the *O'Brien* test, "the government has functional elements that relate to the weapon that allow it to cite things utterly unrelated to the content of expression that empower it to say you may not brandish a weapon."

"I don't know what you're talking about," said Justice Scalia with a sour scowl. I couldn't blame him. What I should have said is that a gun shoots bullets and a cross does not. I tried again, and this time probably did a bit better. A gun is functional. But a cross is only symbolic.

Justice Scalia made an exaggerated gesture from the bench, pantomiming a person shaking a gun. "It's an unloaded gun!" he exclaimed. "This is an unloaded gun that is being brandished." There was a roll of laughter through the courtroom. "So once it's unloaded, it's nothing but a symbol."

I was actually ready for this; it was a question I'd anticipated before the argument and I had an answer in reserve. "It is still a weapon, Your Honor, and it is gigantically different from a cross." I then proceeded with a pantomime of my own. Using my arms to act out my point, I stated that if I dip two sticks in kerosene, and light them, and hold them out away from my body, I do not violate the Virginia law. The sticks are simply burning torches. It is only when I cross the sticks, forming a cross, that the law is violated. What is the difference, I asked, "between brandishing a torch and brandishing a cross?"

"*One hundred years of history!*" Justice Kennedy quipped, with lightening speed. There was a huge roar of laughter and approval. I let the crowd quiet, not wanting the noise to step on my response.

"And that one hundred years of history is on the side of freedom of speech," I asserted.

There was yet another appreciative response from the audience to this. Folks were obviously enjoying themselves. Justice Souter seemed to sense that the arguments were very much in equipoise, and certainly the Justices on the Court seemed highly divided. He was searching for something to tip the balance one way or another. What, he asked, "is the tie-breaker."

The tie-breaker, I responded, was the plain fact that content-neutral laws would work just as well as the Virginia statute. I hypothesized two rallies being conducted side-by-side in the city of Richmond. One rally is a Klan group, the other a Christian group that wishes to conduct a counter-rally. Both groups erect large crosses as part of their demonstrations. The Klan ignites its cross. The Klan can be prosecuted under the statute, but the Christian group, which did not light the cross, cannot."

Impishly, I was asked, "what if the other group are all brandishing guns, as Justice Scalia said?"

"Then round them up, Your Honor," I joked. The crowd laughed.

Justice Ginsburg pressed me on a more serious note. What was wrong, she asked, returning to the central debate in the case, with a law that is used to prosecute cross-burning when the law targets only cross-burning used as a threat, and not as a mere ritual.

There would be no problem, I conceded, in prosecuting the act of cross-burning under a content-neutral law, or even under a bias-crime law such as that upheld in *Wisconsin v. Mitchell*. I had only seconds left, and I wanted to punctuate this with a much larger point. The fact that the cross was burned, I said to Justice Ginsburg, might be used as *evidence* of the illicit intent. What was critical, however, was that the law used as the vehicle for the prosecution be neutral. I wanted to end with an emphasis that this was not a mere quibble, but a major and fundamental principle. To many the insistence on the use of a content-neutral law may seem little more than a surface technicality, an overly fastidious insistence that government take one route rather than another to reach the same end. But much more was at stake. "It may seem that it is just a way to get to the same result through some other formality," I conceded. "But our position is that it is enormous for First Amendment purposes. It is *the central divide* of modern First

Amendment law, in which the Court insists that content-neutral alternatives be used if the governmental ends can be accomplished equally well through them."

And with that, Justice Stevens indicated that the time for the argument had expired.

The Supreme Court announced its decision in *Virginia v. Black* the following spring. In a plurality opinion written by Justice O'Connor and joined by Chief Justice Rehnquist, Justice Stevens, and Justice Breyer, the Supreme Court struck down the Virginia cross-burning law, but based its ruling solely on the "prima facie evidence" provision of the law.[16] The plurality also held that a state could enact a cross-burning statute that would be consistent with the First Amendment, if it were limited to cross-burning as a threat or act of intimidation, and if it contained no prima-facie evidence provision such as that contained in the Virginia statute.[17] Three other Justices, Justices Souter, Ginsburg, and Kennedy, joined in a concurring opinion written by Justice Souter that essentially tracked all of the arguments that I had made, which would have affirmed the decision of the Virginia Supreme Court as written by Virginia Supreme Court Justice Donald Lemons, holding that the entire Virginia statute was unconstitutionally infected with viewpoint discrimination because it focused on one symbol, the burning cross.[18] The combined votes of the four Justices joining the O'Connor opinion and the three Justices joining the Souter opinion led to striking down the conviction of Barry Black.

The plurality opinion of Justice O'Connor also reasoned, however, that a cross-burning conviction *not* tainted by the prima facie evidence presumption contained in the Virginia statute could be constitutionally permissible.[19] It was uncertain, in the plurality's view, what role, if any, the prima facie evidence provision had played in the convictions of O'Mara and Elliott.[20]

It was apparent the plurality concluded that the provision as so interpreted "would create an unacceptable risk of the suppression of ideas."[21]

---

[16]Virginia v. Black, 538 U.S. 343, 367, 123 S.Ct. 1536, 1552, 155 L.E.2d 535, 557 (2003).

[17]*Id.* at 365-67, 123 S.Ct. at 1551-52, 155 L.E.2d at 556-57.

[18]*Id.* at 380-87, 123 S.Ct. at 1559-1562, 155 L.E.2d at 565-70 (Souter, J., concurring in part and dissenting in part).

[19]*Id.* at 365-67, 123 S.Ct. at 1551-52, 155 L.E.2d at 556-57.

[20]Unlike the *Black* case, in which the trial court instructed the jury pointedly that the mere burning of a cross was evidence from which the jury could presume an intent to intimidate, no jury instruction at all regarding the prima facie evidence provision had been given by the trial court in Elliot's case, and O'Mara pled guilty to violating the statute, while preserving his right to challenge it. *Id.* at 364, 123 S.Ct. at 1550, 155 L.E.2d at 555.

[21]*Id.* at 365, 123 S.Ct. at 1551, 155 L.E.2d at 556-56 (quoting Secretary of State of Md. v. Joseph H. Munson Co., 467 U.S. 947, 965 n.13, 104 S.Ct. 2839, 2851, 81 L.Ed.2d 786, 801 (1984), quoting in turn, Members of City Council of Los Angeles v. Taxpayers for Vincent, 466 U.S. 789, 797, 104 S.Ct. 2118, 2124-25, 80 L.Ed.2d 772, 782 (1984)).

"The act of burning a cross may mean that a person is engaging in constitutionally proscribable intimidation. But that same act may mean only that
the person is engaged in core political speech," the plurality held.[22] "The
prima facie evidence provision in this statute blurs the line between these
two meanings of a burning cross. As interpreted by the jury instruction, the
provision chills constitutionally protected political speech because of the
possibility that a State will prosecute—and potentially convict—somebody
engaging only in lawful political speech at the core of what the First Amendment is designed to protect."[23]

As the history of cross burning indicates, the plurality elaborated, "a
burning cross is not always intended to intimidate. Rather, sometimes the
cross burning is a statement of ideology, a symbol of group solidarity. It is a
ritual used at Klan gatherings, and it is used to represent the Klan itself."[24]
Among other contexts, cross burnings have appeared in movies such as *Mississippi Burning*, and in plays such as the stage adaptation of Sir Walter
Scott's *The Lady of the Lake*.[25]

Because the prima facie provision of the Virginia law made no effort to
distinguish among these different types of cross burnings, the plurality
held, because it did not distinguish between a cross burning done with the
purpose of creating anger or resentment and a cross burning done with the
purpose of threatening or intimidating a victim, or distinguish between a
cross burning at a public rally or a cross burning on a neighbor's lawn, it violated the First Amendment.[26] The Virginia statute did "not treat the cross
burning directed at an individual differently from the cross burning directed at a group of like-minded believers."[27] The Virginia law, the plurality
observed, allows a jury to treat "a cross burning on the property of another
with the owner's acquiescence in the same manner as a cross burning on the
property of another without the owner's permission."[28]

---

[22] 123 S.Ct. at 365, 123 S.Ct. at 1551, 155 L.E.2d at 556.

[23] *Id.*

[24] *Id.* at 365-66, 123 S.Ct. at 1551, 155 L.E.2d at 556.

[25] *Id.* at 366, 123 S.Ct. at 1551, 155 L.E.2d at 556.

[26] *Id.*

[27] *Id.*

[28] *Id.* On this score the plurality joined with the opinion of Justice Souter, joined by Justices
Kennedy and Ginsburg, stating that "the prima facie provision can 'skew jury deliberations toward conviction in cases where the evidence of intent to intimidate is relatively weak and arguably consistent with a solely ideological reason for burning.'" *Id.* The constitutional defect in the
prim Justices Kennedy and Ginsburg, stating that "the prima facie evidence proa facie evidence
provision is further illuminated by one of the earliest symbolic speech cases decided by this Court,
Stromberg v. California, 283 U.S. 359, 51 S.Ct. 532, 75 L.Ed. 1117 (1931), striking down a conviction under a California statute that made it a crime to display a red flag as an emblem of opposition to organized government or as an invitation to anarchy or sedition. The Court in *Stromberg*
assumed that the First Amendment does permit "the punishment of those who indulge in utter-
ances which incite to violence and crime and threaten the overthrow of organized government by
unlawful means." *Id.* at 369, 51 S.Ct. at 535, 75 L.Ed. at 1123.   *(continued)*

In an important victory for freedom of speech, the plurality admonished that:

> It may be true that a cross burning, even at a political rally, arouses a sense of anger or hatred among the vast majority of citizens who see a burning cross. But this sense of anger or hatred is not sufficient to ban all cross burnings. As Gerald Gunther has stated, 'The lesson I have drawn from my childhood in Nazi Germany and my happier adult life in this country is the need to walk the sometimes difficult path of denouncing the bigot's hateful ideas with all my power, yet at the same time challenging any community's attempt to suppress hateful ideas by force of law.' ... The prima facie evidence provision in this case ignores all of the contextual factors that are necessary to decide whether a particular cross burning is intended to intimidate. The First Amendment does not permit such a shortcut.[29]

When all of this was put together, the conviction of Barry Black could not stand, but the convictions of Elliott and O'Mara required additional proceedings from the Supreme Court of Virginia.[30] On remand, the Supreme Court of Virginia affirmed the convictions of both Elliott and O'Mara.[31]

Justices Scalia and Thomas, apparently defecting from their positions in *R.A.V.*, would have gone well beyond the plurality. Justice Thomas would have been willing to allow a state to attack all cross-burnings, and to permit a state to employ a prima facie evidence provision, and would have affirmed all three convictions.[32] Justice Scalia wrote primarily to express the view that the prima facie evidence provision is probably a mere permissible inference of the sort that in his view would not violate the First Amendment.[33]

---

[28](*continued*) The jury in the case, however, had been instructed that they could convict the defendant Yetta Stromberg not merely for having engaged in such unprotected activity, but also for display of her red flag "as a sign, symbol, or emblem of opposition to organized government.... *Id.* at 363, 51 S.Ct. at 533, 75 L.Ed. 1120. The Court found this constitutionally offensive, because it might be construed to include a proscription on peaceful and orderly opposition to government. *Id.* at 369-70, 51 S.Ct. at 535-36, 75 L.Ed. at 1123. Because it was impossible to discern from the jury's general verdict whether the jury's determination of Stromberg's guilt rested on a finding of genuine incitement or threats of violence, or instead on the mere brandishing of the symbol of opposition alone, the Court held that the entire conviction must be overturned. *Id.* at 367-68, 51 S.Ct. at 1122, 75 L.Ed. at 535.

[29]538 U.S. at 366-67, 123 S.Ct. at 1551, 155 L.E.2d at 556-57 (quoting Gerhard Casper, *Tribute to Professor Gerald Gunther: Gerry*, 55 STAN. L. REV. 647, 649 (2002) (internal quotation marks omitted)).

[30]538 U.S. at 367-68, 123 S.Ct. at 1552, 155 L.E.2d at 557. Justice Stevens issued a brief concurring opinion stating that he continued to adhere to his views in his separate opinion in *R.A.V.*, and for those reasons, concurred in the plurality opinion. *Id.* at 368, 123 S.Ct. at 1552, 155 L.E.2d at 557 (Stevens, J., concurring) ("Cross burning with 'an intent to intimidate,' Va. Code Ann. § 18.2-423 (1996), unquestionably qualifies as the kind of threat that is unprotected by the First Amendment. For the reasons stated in the separate opinions that Justice White and I wrote in *R.A.V. v. St. Paul*, 505 U.S. 377, 112 S.Ct. 2538, 120 L.Ed.2d 305 (1992), that simple proposition provides a sufficient basis for upholding the basic prohibition in the Virginia statute even though it does not cover other types of threatening expressive conduct. With this observation, I join Justice O'Connor's opinion.").

[31]Elliot v. Commonwealth, 593 S.E.2d 263 (Va. 2004).

[32]538 U.S. at 388, 123 S.Ct. at 1562, 155 L.E.2d at 570 (Thomas, J., dissenting).

[33]*Id.* at 368, 123 S.Ct. at 1552, 155 L.E.2d at 557 (Scalia, J., concurring in the judgment in part, concurring in part, and dissenting in part). Justice Thomas joined Justice Scalia's opinion.

Let us return to the initial inquiry. Do oral arguments matter?

The answer "it depends" seems vindicated by the saga of *Virginia v. Black*. Looking back at the argument through the prism of the final opinions that emerged, I discern quite clearly how the positions staked out by Justice O'Connor emerged as the final product of the plurality. I see in the written dissent of Justice Thomas all the passion that exploded from him during oral argument. The three Justices who would have accepted all of the arguments our team advanced, Justices Souter, Ginsburg, and Kennedy, certainly appeared at many stages of the argument to be more *simpatico* with the state of Virginia than with those challenging the law. Did the argument turn them around? Did it help convince them? No advocate ever knows, and in the complexity of factors that influence the resolution of our great constitutional conflicts, it is unlikely that any one cause is ever entirely determinative. I come away totally convinced, however, that whatever the linear influence of an argument may be, it does indeed "matter" in a broader more profound sense. A Supreme Court argument exploring the great constitutional issues of the day remains for me the most dignified and serious ritual of American government. And I'd do it again tomorrow.

Chapter 7

A FIRST AMENDMENT LIFE

Bruce S. Rogow*

EDITOR'S INTRODUCTION

The paths taken to reach 1 First Street, N.E., in Washington, DC, to argue one or more cases before the U.S. Supreme Court are as varied as the cases themselves. Bruce Rogow has walked those paths 11 times. But it never becomes routine, he says. He was asked what familiarity breeds when it comes to the U.S. Supreme Court.

"It breeds respect. It's important to recognize your role there, which is to help them along. I view it as a very civilized, high-level discussion. It can be a bit of a debate now and then with some of the justices, depending upon the questions. But basically it's a discussion."

Being at the U.S. Supreme Court, Mr. Rogow says, is the pinnacle of an attorney's career. "If you think about what a lawyer does, being in the Supreme Court is being on Broadway. But it's only for a half-hour, and you don't get to do it again. In some of my arguments, I've had 40 or 50 questions in those 30 minutes. So it's happening pretty quickly. So you just do as best you can. And you can't do it that well without having done the dry runs before."

In preparation for their arguments, most attorneys subject themselves to several mock presentations. "The dry runs are very important. If you've done a great job at the dry runs, it will rarely occur that you will have a question asked of you that you haven't heard before. And that's really very important."

---

*Professor of Law, Nova Southeastern University, Fort Lauderdale, Florida.

As part of the presentation process, Mr. Rogow likes to call the justices by their name. "I like to do that because it gives you a fraction of a second more to think about what you want to say, and it's more conversational to call a justice by his or her name." It is a technique, however, that he has seen backfire on others. "A nervous lawyer called Breyer Souter, and called Ginsburg O'Connor. When Justice Scalia asked him a question, the justice said, 'I'm Scalia.'"

Familiarity with the "cast" is but one component in a series of events leading to the Supreme Court. In this chapter, Mr. Rogow describes some of the twists and turns of his First Amendment career, including representing an array of clients from rap musicians to a Ku Klux Klan leader to the designer of Florida's "butterfly ballot" in the 2000 presidential election.

* * *

Forty years of lawyering, nearly 400 reported cases, and more than 40 major First Amendment cases have brought me no closer to understanding why the 44 words of the First Amendment cause such ferment. More than 800 Supreme Court decisions address First Amendment issues, and most of them are not unanimous. Indeed, many of the decisions are five-to-four and rife with separate opinions reflecting differences in political, economic, religious, and social philosophy, differences that are often exacerbated by the historical period in which the cases arise.

I tell my law students to look at the date of the First Amendment decisions they study and to think about what was happening in the country at that time because that will provide the backdrop for the Court's approach to its application of the Amendment. The lessons are easy to see: A fear that words and assembly will threaten interests a government (national, state, local) believes to be important drives the suppression of speech, and the schizophrenic tension between the free exercise and establishment clauses makes the religion cases so hard to divine.

One thing that practicing and teaching First Amendment law has taught me is that my mother lied to me. She told me that "sticks and stones will break my bones, but names will never hurt me." But that is not true. Although I have never been called names, I have learned that the sting and zing of words wounds psyches in enduring ways; people do not easily recover from verbal assaults. The mind takes longer to heal than a bruise or a broken bone. The power and force of speech is so strong that its repression becomes important to governments and governing bodies. Those entities composed of people who believe they know what is best for their respective constituencies, or driven by their constituencies, can be threatened by challenges to their views, which prompts legislation to quiet their critics or to try and ensure the image of the life they believe is "right" is maintained or not attacked.

Everyone has a First Amendment blind spot. Bar associations do not like lawyers who advertise. People do not like folks who burn the American flag. Jews do not like to see Nazis marching. African Americans do not like to witness Ku Klux Klan parades. Homeowners do not like door-to-door solicitations. Tourist towns do not like begging on their sidewalks. No government tolerates "obscenity." The list is as long as the thousands of cases that have addressed statutes, ordinances, administrative regulations, and court injunctions that seek to achieve the goals of the government within the restraints of the First Amendment.

Thus, the classic First Amendment lawyer places him or herself in the midst of political, social, economic, and psychological maelstroms, seeking to persuade a court that the Amendment prohibits the governmental entity from discouraging speech or assembly. (I address the religion clauses later, and I recognize that newspaper and media lawyers are First Amendment lawyers too, but that is not the genre relevant to my experience.) That takes me to me: How did I find myself in the world of the First Amendment and why have I had so much fun in that world?

As a boy I knew nothing about the First Amendment. I remember that sports and girls were my abiding interests, and then, late in high school I knew that sports would not be my field of success. How did I know? One wet soggy day at soccer practice a long, high kick came floating toward my defensive position. I could see the mud and water flying off the ball; as it approached it looked so heavy that I could not imagine it colliding with my head, so I turned and fielded it with my backside—a "butter" instead of a "header." The coach blew the whistle, then screamed at me and banished me for a week. I thought I would never get to break in my new soccer shoes but even when I did, I knew that I was afraid when the ball came toward my goal. My baseball experience was similar. I played first base and when a left-handed batter came up, threatening to pull the ball on the ground down the first-base line, I found myself hoping he would hit it elsewhere, lest I have to field a vicious grounder. Years later, when I realized that as a lawyer I wanted every hard case to come to me, and that I was delighted and excited to field questions from judges, I understood that I had found my milieu.

The freedom to assemble was my introduction to the First Amendment. I do not remember anything I learned in Constitutional Law (although my professor later became a friend and colleague and I became the executor of his estate after I promised him that if his much younger wife wanted to spend her modest inheritance on a world cruise, I would not object), but I do remember Bracky Rice.

I worked my way through law school from 1961 to 1963 as a desk clerk at a motel in Gainesville, Florida, and Bracky Rice was the 18-year-old motel bellboy. We had plenty of time to waste, and he told me about the NAACP (National Association for the Advancement of Colored People) meetings at a Gainesville funeral home, inviting me to attend. Sitting around on the caskets I got the message that law could be used in a socially beneficial way and the personal exposure, combined with news reports of the civil rights activities happening throughout the South, led me to a career. In the summer of 1964 I went to the Democratic Party Convention in Atlantic City and met Fannie Lou Hamer and members of the Freedom Democratic Party who were trying to unseat the regular Mississippi Democrats. I realized that Mississippi was where the action would be, and that lawyers would be needed.

There were two lawyer groups with offices in Jackson, Mississippi: the National Lawyers Guild and the NAACP Legal Defense Fund (LDF). The Guild was an activist, left-wing organization and the LDF was focused on school desegregation. I thought the Guild was a better fit for me and I went to see George Crockett in Detroit. Crockett was a lawyer, an *eminence grise* of radical lawyering, and he cautioned me that the Guild had been listed as a subversive organization by Florida's John's Committee, a Florida analogue to the House Un-American Activities Committee, and that as a Florida lawyer, I might want to consider that remnant of McCarthyism. Crockett also told me that the American Civil Liberties Union (ACLU) was planning on opening an office in Jackson, and that a fellow named Henry Schwarzchild was charged with setting up that office.

I was 24 years old and single. I had no debt except for a $75-a-month car payment. I went to New York to see Henry Schwarzchild. My life as a lawyer began that day. Henry welcomed me, hired me for $2,500 a year, and sent me to Mississippi.

The Equal Protection Clause provided the legal foundation for the Civil Rights Movement, but the First Amendment provided and protected the voice of the movement. That became my task—to make sure the voices were heard.

ACLU's Mississippi arm was the lawyer's Constitutional Defense Committee. Alvin Bronstein, an upstate New York lawyer, opened the office in Jackson, Mississippi, in January 1965. I followed quickly behind, and learned from Al that our role was to support and defend the frontline civil rights workers—local people and organizers from the Student Nonviolent Coordinating Committee (SNCC), the Congress of Racial Equality (CORE), and the Southern Christian Leadership Council (SCLC). That meant getting demonstrators out of jail, seeking to declare unconstitutional and enjoin ordinances, statutes, or regulations that limited First Amendment rights, and trying to ensure that police agencies protected demonstrators from being attacked by hostile white mobs.

Those tasks took me throughout Mississippi, to Selma and Montgomery, Alabama, and to Bogalusa and Tallulah, Louisiana. I learned a lot of law from Al Bronstein and from the lawyers who came from all around the country to volunteer for a week or two; lawyers who had already distinguished themselves in their careers and used their vacation time to participate in and witness the changes that the courageous local people and civil rights workers were bringing to the Deep South. When I left Mississippi, in late 1966 to join the Legal Service Program in Miami, I took with me an appreciation for, and devotion to, First Amendment litigation. What I did not know, nor could I ever have predicted, was that my Mississippi legal, social, and political education would lead me to other First Amendment experiences that, if not so socially and politically important, would have some impact on First Amendment law.

2 LIVE CREW

I am still surprised about the legs of the 2 Live Crew litigation. It was a terrific mix of race, sex, rock and roll, and the First Amendment—and it came to me because when I was a Legal Services lawyer I also taught at the University of Miami Law School, and one of my students was Allen Jacobi. Allen had become an entertainment lawyer, and when he called me in early 1990 to say he wanted to bring "two live crew" to see me I was surprised, because I thought he had become an immigration lawyer and was bringing two asylum-seeking Haitian or Cuban rafters who had survived the boat trip to Florida from Haiti or Cuba. Allen set me straight right away—"2 Live Crew" was a hip-hop group whose record *As Nasty As They Wanna Be* had incurred the wrath of the first Republican governor of Florida, Bob Martinez. I am embarrassed to say that I had missed any notice of the matter. Even worse, I had no idea what hip-hop was, what "sampling" was, nor had I even heard of Luther Campbell, the leader of the group.

My "know-nothingness," though embarrassing, actually makes an important point in my mind about the benefits and the beauty of practicing law. Being a lawyer requires one to keep learning, not just about the law, but about the details of other people's work, their lives (sometimes their loves), and their place in our society and culture. The constant need to listen, to learn, to educate oneself about matters that would not naturally come to one's attention, provides enormous opportunities to expand and refresh one's universe. Not many jobs provide the surprise and excitement of a client's problem opening windows on a world that was previously unknown. That certainly applied to what Luther Campbell taught me. (I should add that the copyright case I argued for Campbell in the Supreme Court—*Campbell v. Acuff-Rose Music, Inc.*[1]—is an example of learning the law on the job. I had never even read the Copyright Act before I began that case.)

Jacobi and Campbell came to my house and brought a tape of *As Nasty As They Wanna Be*, along with a lyric sheet that had been prepared by a conservative organization that was attempting to ban the record. I looked at the lyrics and saw that the language was strong and not complimentary toward women. But I knew the First Amendment test for obscenity, *Miller v. California*,[2] required that the work be "taken as a whole," so the music had to be included in the equation too, and, even without hearing the soundtrack, I was confident we could defeat any attempt to ban the record.

Campbell asked me if I thought we would win, and I told him yes, but that even if we lost, he would win. He wanted to know "what kind of jive, white man's talk" that was, and I told him that if the government sought to censor something, that would only make people want it more, so he would sell even more records. This prediction turned out to be prophetic because 7 months later, prompted by the national publicity surrounding the attempt by Broward County Sheriff Nick Navarro to ban the record and to arrest Campbell and the other members of 2 Live Crew for singing the songs on the record, Campbell was paid $5 million for distribution rights to 2 Live Crew's material.

Because I taught (and practiced) federal civil procedure and jurisdiction, I was familiar with taking the offense in litigation by asking for a declaratory judgment—a procedure that allows a court to declare the rights between parties with a dispute before the dispute erupts into a criminal case. So, I filed suit in the U.S. District Court in the Southern District of Florida asking that the court declare *As Nasty As They Wanna Be* not to be obscene. That was a novel approach, designed to put the record on trial in a civil proceeding, with Campbell the protagonist, not the defendant.

The case was assigned to U.S. District Judge Jose Gonzalez, a former state circuit judge, and a respected federal judge. Judge Gonzalez has (he still is on the bench, sitting as a senior judge) a great sense of humor and an appreciation for classical music. He did not think that *As Nasty As They Wanna Be* was funny or that it was good music. Indeed, I remember the irony of sitting a few rows away from him at the Fort Lauderdale Symphony one night during the week we were in trial. By day, rap music, heavy with harsh language; by night, Mahler and Brahms.

The trial was an extraordinary one because the *Miller v. California* test allowed us to present evidence of "contemporary community standards." The specific portion of the *Miller* standard that allowed us to introduce a collection of locally available magazines and videotapes portraying a wide selection

---

[1] 510 U.S. 569 (1994).
[2] 413 U.S. 15 (1973).

of lascivious sexual activities was this factor for determining whether a work is obscene: whether "the average person, applying contemporary community standards" would find that the work, taken as a whole, appeals to the prurient interest.[3] So we went shopping in the community to show what was tolerated. Finding sexual stuff was easy; the largest adult bookstore in Fort Lauderdale was across the street from the Sheriff's office. I still have the erotic evidence we introduced in that previously chaste federal courtroom, except for one exhibit: a videotape with three vignettes featuring women masturbating, which appealed to a court clerk's prurient interest. To Judge Gonzalez's relief, I convinced the Sheriff's lawyer to agree that all three video vignettes were similar, so we had to play only one segment. It was received in evidence, marked as an exhibit (although by a separate order Judge Gonzalez limited access to the exhibits to persons 18 years of age or older), and deposited with the clerk. When the case was finally over (see the rest of the story) I retrieved the exhibits from the clerk's office. One exhibit was missing; someone in the clerk's office, either in Fort Lauderdale or Atlanta, decided the masturbation tape was worth keeping, and apparently took it home.

Judge Gonzalez wrote a long opinion declaring the record to be obscene,[4] which surprised me because I knew that we had met the *Miller* "serious literary, artistic, political, or scientific value" standard with the testimony of a psychologist, two respected music critics, and a Columbia University professor, a Rhodes Scholar. He explained the call-and-response dialogues from African traditions, concepts that were embodied in hip-hop music, and were specifically present in *As Nasty As They Wanna Be*. Judge Gonzalez was not persuaded, and decided, using his own musical/cultural knowledge and experience, that *As Nasty As They Wanna Be* lacked serious literary or artistic value.

Reversing, the court of appeals left no doubt that Judge Gonzalez erred in simply making his own taste the arbiter of obscenity.[5] The court wrote: "A work cannot be held obscene unless each element of the *Miller* test has been met. We reject the argument that simply by listening to this musical work, the judge could determine that it had no serious artistic value."[6]

Before it was reversed, Judge Gonzalez's decision holding the record to be obscene resulted in the arrest of the four members of 2 Live Crew by the Broward County Sheriff for singing their lyrics at a nightclub in Hollywood, Florida, and the Sheriff's arrest of a record shop owner for selling the record. The Sheriff, Nick Navarro, was a wonderful character who I counted as a friend and still do. He is no longer the Sheriff of Broward County, largely as a result of the press hostility generated by his attempt to ban *As*

---

[3]*Id.* at 24.

[4]739 F. Supp. 578 (S.D. Fla. 1990).

[5]*See* Luke Records, Inc. v. Navarro, 960 F.2d 134 (11th Cir. 1992), *cert. denied*, Navarro v. Luke Records, Inc., 506 U.S. 1022 (1992).

[6]960 F.2d at 138–39.

Nasty As They Wanna Be. The arrests and subsequent prosecutions of the 2 Live Crew members and the record seller provided me with more weeks of trial work—this time criminal defense work—and resulted in jury acquittals for 2 Live Crew. One of my experts in that case was Henry Louis (Skip) Gates, now Harvard University's director of the W. E. B. Du Bois Institute for Afro-American Research, and the W. E. B. Du Bois Professor of the Humanities. Skip was an extraordinary witness, and the jury was wowed by his ability to weave African American culture, American pop culture, politics, and music into an explanation of literary, artistic, and political value. Skip's court appearance was a unique opportunity to lecture in a different venue, and he was as effective there as he has been since, writing for the *New Yorker* and public television.

The extraordinary part of the 2 Live Crew adventure is that a dozen years later, Nick Navarro, Judge Jose Gonzalez, and Luther Campbell are all still friendly faces in my world. Campbell now is a hip-hop impresario in Miami Beach, and we serve together in an organization whose goal is urging African American students to register to vote. Nick Narvarro has become both a client and a kibitzer, and Judge Gonzalez remains an acquaintance available for amusing talk. I recognize how serendipitous my experience was. Without Nick seeking to arrest the record and Judge Gonzalez's decision to declare it obscene, the record might have gone largely unnoticed. Indeed, given the literally thousands of prosecutors, sheriffs, police officers, and judges around the country who could have also tried to ban the record, the lesson is that the First Amendment's restraints on government power was transcendent. So I am optimistic about the good First Amendment judgment of the many, and appreciative of the idiosyncratic judgment of my Broward County friends.

A footnote to the case is that Bruce Springsteen subsequently gave Luther Campbell the right to adapt his *Born in the USA,* allowing Campbell to cut the record *Banned in the USA*. The first voice on the record is a sampling from one of my press interviews explaining the First Amendment, and when *Banned in the USA* went gold, Campbell gave me the gold record trophy. It hangs with pride on my office wall.

MIAMI, FIDEL CASTRO, AND FREE SPEECH

The Cuban Museum

Mississippi may have been the quintessential First Amendment battleground in the 1960s, but Miami became another example of a different kind of intolerance in the last quarter-century. Suppression of speech that was viewed as supportive of Fidel Castro led to a series of First Amendment cases that underscored how anticommunism could lead to antidemocratic actions.

The trilogy of cases that I handled was the *Cuban Museum of Arts and Culture v. City of Miami*,[7] *Miami Light Project v. Miami Dade County*,[8] and *Ohanian v. City of Miami*.[9]

The *Cuban Museum* case is one of my favorites for several reasons. The museum had leased an old fire station from the City of Miami for 9 years, and the museum directors had invested substantial sums for renovation and securing art that reflected Cuban culture. Some of the directors were the *crème de la crème* of the Miami Cuban-American *intelligentsia,* including Santiago Morales, who had been captured at the Bay of Pigs and spent over a decade as a political prisoner of Fidel Castro.

After the Miami City Commission members decided that the museum and its directors were not sufficiently anti-Castro because they had exhibited art by artists who had not denounced Castro, or had continued to live in Cuba, Morales' wife told me laughingly: "Santiago must be the stupidest man alive because if he had known for all those years in prison that he was a Communist he could have told Castro and been released. Instead, he had to find out he was a Communist when the Miami City Commission told him he supported Castro."

The museum had shown the works of Cuban artists for years, but in 1988 an anonymous message was sent to the media listing various artists, whose works were to be auctioned at a benefit, as being Communist sympathizers. The press ran with the story and the auction (which was approved by the board by a 19-18 vote) was held in the face of hostile demonstrations, including the burning of one of the paintings in the street outside the museum.

The controversy continued, going beyond peaceful demonstrations. A bomb exploded under the car of one of the museum directors; some of the conservative directors who dissented from the decision to include "pro-Castro" artists in the auction demanded the resignations of members of the museum's executive committee, including the woman whose car was bombed; a "Cuban Museum Rescue Committee" demanded that the Miami City Commission oust the museum's management; and, ultimately, after a series of city audits and investigations (which came to naught) and other actions designed to eliminate the "liberal" directors, the City ordered the City attorney to file an action of eviction against the museum. To his credit, the city attorney advised against the eviction, but just before Easter weekend in 1991, the City passed an eviction resolution.

---

[7]766 F. Supp. 1121 (S.D. Fla. 1991). The decision shows the name of a different ACLU lawyer—not me—as counsel, but that mistake is set straight in the attorney's fee decision at *Cuban Museum of Arts and Culture, Inc. v. City of Miami,* 771 F. Supp. 1190 (S.D. Fla. 1991), which reflects that I was counsel for the museum.

[8]97 F. Supp. 2d 1174 (S.D. Fla. 2000).

[9]Case No. 00-0014 (S.D. Fla.).

The embattled museum directors brought the voluminous city commission transcripts to my home, and over the weekend I reviewed them and found the reported actions, resolutions, and statements that reflected the City's decision to punish the museum for exercising its First Amendment right to decide what art it wished to show.

I could have raised the museum's First Amendment claims as a defense to an eviction action in state court, but the Miami-Dade County state trial court judges were elected, like the Miami City Commission, and like the commissioners, were not immune to the political realities of a constituency that brooked no indications of appeasement with Castro's Cuba. In addition, I knew that once a state court eviction action began, I could not enjoin it in federal court, because concepts of federalism and comity severely limit a federal court's authority to interfere with a pending state court proceeding.[10]

So, working over the weekend, I prepared a suit for injunctive relief and filed first in federal court, seeking to enjoin the City of Miami from taking any steps to evict the Cuban Museum. The case fell before James Lawrence King, an experienced and respected federal judge, and he quickly set a preliminary injunction hearing. The injunction trial was easy; the City commission minutes left no doubt of the City's hostile motivation and the cross-examination of the City's witnesses, including the mayor, revealed the disingenuousness of the City's denials of punitive motives. Indeed, the evidence was that the city had, in effect, adopted a foreign policy vis-à-vis Cuba by having denied Nelson Mandela a key to the City because he had spoken nicely of Castro when he was on a triumphant visit to the United States, and by conditioning a permit for Haitian-Americans to use Miami Bayfront Park to celebrate President Aristide's 1988 inauguration, upon Aristide not inviting Castro to Port au Prince for the inauguration—as if the local Haitian community had any control over the invitations to the inauguration process. The museum eviction was just another indication of the City's "foreign policy."

Judge King saw through the City's decision to evict:

> The court finds that the City of Miami's actions were indeed motivated by the plaintiff's exercise of their constitutional rights, and the City would not have voted to deny the plaintiff's continued use and possession of the premises but for the plaintiffs' controversial exercise of their First Amendment rights.[11]

He enjoined the eviction, and the museum continued to operate for several more years until it closed for reasons unrelated to the City's antipathy.

---

[10]*See* Younger v. Harris, 401 U.S. 37 (1971); Huffman v. Pursue Ltd., 420 U.S. 592 (1975).
[11]Cuban Museum of Arts & Culture, 766 F. Supp. at 1129.

Los Van Van

Time did not heal the City's zeal to punish those viewed as Castro sympathizers. In 2000, a vivacious Miami concert promoter, Debbie Ohanian, decided to promote a concert at the City of Miami Knight Center, featuring Los Van Van, a famous Cuban salsa band. The outcry was enormous. Los Van Van, who had, despite the Cuban embargo, secured visas to perform in the United States, was perceived as Castro's alter ego, and the conservative Miami Cuban community went into full battle mode, an attitude that the nation saw in its full glory a year later in the Elian Gonzalez episode.

Ohanian met with city officials regarding use of the Knight Center, only to find their demands to be impossible to meet: $5 million in liability insurance, security expenses of $17,000 plus extra charges if there were bomb threats and if "field forces" were necessary to maintain order, and a short timetable to meet those requirements; a timetable she could not meet and that resulted in an anti-Castro group reserving the Knight Center for the date in question in order to keep Ohanian from securing the facility.

Frustrated, scared, but not intimidated, Ohanian called the ACLU, who called me and, recognizing the First Amendment implications, we (Beverly Pohl, my law partner, and I) agreed to represent Ohanian after she had switched venues, and signed, under protest and under the duress of losing the concert, an agreement to pay for police protection of the concert-goers.

The concert was successfully held at the Miami Arena, but the success was the product of a large police presence, in full battle gear, holding back the bottle- and rock-throwing crowd. To the City's credit, it provided the means of protecting those who had assembled to attend the concert, but, to the city's discredit, it charged Ohanian approximately $37,000 for providing that protection from anti-Castro protestors of the concert. Because the operators of the Miami Arena, where the concert was held, had an agreement to withhold "security costs" from concert revenues, the City was paid from those revenues against Ohanian's wishes.

We sued the City. Years ago I had won a major First Amendment case for a group called Central Florida Nuclear Freeze Campaign, who wanted to protest an Orlando manufacturer's production of military materials, but Orlando insisted on prepayment of police protection costs. That case, *Central Florida Nuclear Freeze Campaign v. Walsh*,[12] was cited in *Forsyth County, Ga. v. Nationalist Movement*,[13] in which the Supreme Court struck down an attempt to condition a white supremacist march on payment of insurance fees and other costs associated with the police presence thought necessary to protect against violence.

---

[12]774 F.2d 1515 (11th Cir. 1985).
[13]505 U.S. 123 (1992).

Ohanian's case was of that genre. The police have a public duty to protect those who exercise their First Amendment rights. They cannot condition the exercise of those rights upon payment of the costs for protecting peaceful assemblies from counterdemonstrators threatening violence. We sued the City of Miami to recover the police expenses imposed on Ohanian, and U.S. District Judge Joan Lenard gave the City another First Amendment lesson. She wrote:

> The First Amendment is a cornerstone of our democracy yearned for by the oppressed and fiercely protected by all who embrace it. This is the canvas and framework to which we apply the underlying facts. There is no question that all persons who were involved in the Los Van Van concert and the surrounding events, including the City, elected officials, performers, organizers, administrators, police personnel and demonstrators were entitled to the full enjoyment and protections of the First Amendment. As admitted by the City, however, the security fees charged to Plaintiff by authorized and empowered public officials resulted in a chilling effect on Plaintiff's First Amendment activity … [t]he Court, as one of the protectors of our Constitution and its freedoms, has found that the City should be held responsible for those decisions that violated this protected activity and is led to observe that the First Amendment is alive and well—especially in the City of Miami.[14]

So, Judge Lenard ordered the City to pay back Debbie Ohanian, with prejudgment interest, and the City agreed to pay Ohanian's attorney's fees that resulted from its flawed approach to protecting speech and assembly.

The Miami Light Project Case

Miami Light Project v. Miami Dade County,[15] was the product of a Miami-Dade County Ordinance that prohibited county funds to be given to any organization that did business with Cuba, used Cuban products, or employed Cubans, despite the fact that not all contact with Cuba, Cuban products, or Cuban nationals is illegal under the Cuban Embargo laws. Indeed, Cuban-American art and culture exchanges were specifically permitted under those laws.

The Miami Light Project, an innovative music, dance, and art group, as well as several other Miami cultural organizations, had received grants from Miami-Dade County over the years. But the advent of the "Cuba Affidavit" law, requiring organizations to swear that they had no direct or indirect relationships with Cuba or Cubans, placed these organizations in an impossible situation. For example, the Miami City Ballet, one of the country's premier ballet troupes, often used Cuban dancers.

---

[14] The Ohanian summary judgment order is unreported. It was S.D. Fla. Case No. 00-1114.
[15] 97 F. Supp. 2d 1174 (S.D. Fla. 2000).

The inability to sign the affidavit was evident to the organizations, but the cost of compliance—avoiding any contact with Cuban artists—meant compromising their artistic principles in order to secure funding from Miami-Dade County. Or, if they refused to comply, it meant sacrificing the County monies, *and* risking the ire and loss of funds from a large segment of the Miami-Dade County philanthropic community who agreed with the County's hard-line anti-Castro policy.

The soul searching done by the organizations before deciding to participate in the lawsuit was painful to watch. Board meetings were held, divisions among directors were heated and reminiscent of the Cuban Museum directors' divisions, and fear was rampant because none of the organizations wanted to lose community support. The executive directors of the organizations were adamant about wanting to sue to declare the affidavit ordinance unconstitutional, and when their boards finally agreed to participate, the relief of some of the executive directors, who had threatened to resign if they could not stand up to the County, was palpable.

This case was also easy. It was not a pure First Amendment case in the traditional sense, because the argument was that, in addition to the First Amendment issues, the county's law intruded upon the exclusive province of the federal government to conduct foreign affairs. The final outcome was ultimately mandated by the Supreme Court's decision in the Massachusetts "no business with Burma" case.[16] But prior to the Supreme Court's decision, U.S. District Judge Federico Moreno left no doubt that in Miami and Miami-Dade County, the right to speak, assemble, and conduct business or pleasure was always at risk if the shadow of Fidel Castro appeared. Judge Moreno, in enjoining operation of the Miami-Dade County Cuba Affidavit Ordinance, liberated the arts and underscored the irony of Miami-Dade County Cuban-Americans using Castro-like techniques to suppress speech and conduct.

FLORIDA POLITICS AND THE FIRST AMENDMENT: FROM DAVID DUKE TO DEMOCRATIC PARTY POLITICS

Florida's role in the 2000 presidential election has been well documented, and I had a front-row seat as the lawyer for Theresa LePore, the Palm Beach County Supervisor of Elections who designed the "butterfly ballot," which caused enough confusion among voters to account for the 537-vote margin of victory for George W. Bush.[17] But that was not my first brush with Florida electoral politics and the Constitution.

---

[16]Crosby v. National Foreign Trade Counsel, 530 U.S. 363 (2000).
[17]*See* Bush v. Gore, 531 U.S. 98 (2000).

The two earlier cases are *Abrams v. Reno*,[18] and *Duke v. Smith*.[19] In *Abrams*, the federal court enjoined a state statute that sought to preclude political parties from endorsing candidates in primaries, and in *Duke*, we represented David Duke, the former Klansman, who was ultimately found to have been excluded from the Presidential Preference Primary election ballot in violation of his constitutional rights. The former case involved the shortest-lived statute in the history of Florida, and the latter case had us representing a Ku Klux Klansman who, it turned out, was more pleasant than other Klansmen I had met. Here are those stories.

Mike Abrams and Sergio Bendixen were leaders of the Dade County Democratic Executive Committee. They were energetic and powerful local leaders, and offended some state officials who saw them as party "bosses" who could control elections in Dade County. At that time—1978—Dade County was heavily Democratic, and, because the County was the largest in Florida, it had a disproportionate role in the outcome of statewide and presidential elections. Bendixen was a Democratic National Committeeman and a member of the State Democratic Executive Committee too. His roles made him an especially potent force in Florida politics.

The Dade County Democratic Party scheduled a miniconvention for April 15, 1978, at which Abrams and Bendixen planned to endorse Democratic candidates who would be seeking to be the Democratic nominees for seats in the Florida legislature. Because there was no Republican opposition in many of the districts, winning the Democratic primary meant winning the legislative seat. The Legislature became apoplectic at the thought of Abrams' and Bendixen's influence and on April 13, 1978, enacted a statute that said that no "committee established by a state or county executive committee shall endorse or oppose any candidate of its political party seeking nomination in any primary election."[20] The law was to become effective upon the Governor's signature, and I spent the next day doing two things. First, I tried to convince the Governor's general counsel that the bill was unconstitutional and the Governor should not sign it, and I prepared and filed the lawsuit against then-State Attorney Janet Reno seeking to enjoin enforcement of the statute. The law contained criminal penalties, so the state attorney was the potential prosecutor if Abrams and Bendixen violated the law. My filing was premature, because there would be no case or controversy if the Governor did not sign the bill, but I did not want to run the risk of the Governor signing it late on Friday the 14th, making it impossible to get to court before the Saturday morning convention. I told the judge's law clerk that if the Governor signed we would need a hearing right away, and on the

[18]452 F. Supp. 1166 (S.D. Fla. 1978).
[19]13 F.3d 388 (11th Cir. 1994).
[20]Abrams v. Reno, 452 F. Supp. 1166–67 (S.D. Fla. 1978).

judge's instructions, I kept his office informed of my efforts. At about 1:30 p.m., however, I got a call from the Governor's office saying he had signed the bill. I called the judge's office, and at 3:00 p.m. we had our hearing. The judge, William Hoeveler, wrote:

> The apparently brief legislative history of the bill, occurring on the eve of the mini-conventions it was designed to emasculate, made sufficiently clear the danger of violation presented to plaintiffs and the others participating. The timing of the legislation was such that the plaintiffs would have been caused to withdraw on Saturday, April 15, from engaging in constitutionally protected activities which, until approximately 1:30 p.m. the preceding day, had been legal and non-criminal.[21]

Judge Hoeveler did not mince words: "It seems clear that the act in question imposes a direct prior restraint on the exercise of free speech—the right to endorse or oppose; in sum, on the important right of free political expression. In other terms, a substantial burden on First Amendment rights is presented." He concluded: "It is the opinion and finding of the Court that Florida Statute 103.091(6) is unconstitutional."

Thus, by 5:00 the statute was gone—3½ hours after it became law. Subsequently the court of appeals affirmed Judge Hoeveler's decision.[22] The convention was held; candidates were endorsed. Abrams later became a state legislator himself. Bendixen went on to become a successful political campaign consultant. Janet Reno became Attorney General. The Governor—Bob Graham—became a U.S. Senator.

David Duke did not meet with any success in his political candidacy, but we were successful in declaring unconstitutional his (and others) exclusion from the Florida Presidential Preference Primary Ballot in 1992.[23]

Like the *Abrams* case, time was of the essence too in *Duke,* because the Presidential Preference Primary Ballots were to be printed by February 4, 1992, and the Presidential Candidate Selection Committee had, on January 16, 1992, refused to place Duke's name on the ballot. The Chairman of the Republican Party "specifically cited Duke's former activities with the Ku Klux Klan, Nazis, and his association with the National Association for the Advancement of White People" as the reason for keeping him off the ballot, saying that "his political views were inconsistent with traditional Republican values."[24] President George H. W. Bush and Patrick Buchanan were the only Republican candidates allowed on the ballot, although Duke was a nationally declared Republican candidate for president, who had gained bal-

---

[21]*Id.* at 1169.
[22]Abrams v. Reno, 649 F.2d 342 (5th Cir. 1981).
[23]Duke v. Smith, 13 F.3d 388 (11th Cir. 1994).
[24]Duke v. Smith, 784 F. Supp. 865, 867 (S.D. Fla. 1992).

lot access in at least 10 other states, and who had filed his declaration of candidacy with the Federal Elections Commission.

It was common knowledge in Florida that the Republicans did not want Duke on the ballot because they would have been embarrassed by the number of votes he would have received in the state, an embarrassment that the party and President Bush did not want to suffer. The State Republican Party Chairman admitted that "there are no criteria set forth in the statute governing procedures for selecting candidates or reconsidering denial of access, or delineating Republican values."[25]

It was against that background that, as cooperating lawyers for the ACLU, and on behalf of Republican and Democratic presidential candidates who were excluded from the 1992 Florida Presidential Primary Election Ballot, and registered voters who wished to vote for those candidates in the March 10, 1992, primary election, we brought suit against the Florida Secretary of State, the speaker of the Florida House of Representatives, the President of the Florida Senate, the minority leader of the Florida House of Representatives, the minority leader of the Florida Senate, the Chairman of the Florida Democratic Party, and the Chairman of the Florida Republican Party, in their capacities as members of the bipartisan Presidential Candidate Selection Committee. The suit was a facial challenge to § 103.101, *Fla. Stat.*, which created the exclusive mechanism for placing names on the Presidential Primary Election Ballot, and sought declaratory and emergency injunctive relief: getting the unfairly excluded candidates on the ballot.

The prominent set of defendants was represented by a prominent group of attorneys, whose deposition of our most infamous plaintiff, David Duke, was an "event." I was unavailable due to teaching, and my now-partner, Beverly Pohl, who defended the deposition, was a new attorney then with, as she describes it, "15 minutes of experience." Her initiation into the practice of law was memorable.

She arrived at the Miami location, which was abuzz with reporters and photographers anxious to capture the moment and the candidate. The deposition conference room was long, and the table was filled with big lawyers from big firms, all ready to pounce on the unwanted candidate/plaintiff and expose his unsuitability for the Florida ballot. The first skirmish dealt with whether the press, who outnumbered the numerous attorneys, could attend the deposition. That prompted an emergency telephone hearing with a federal magistrate judge, and some accommodation was reached (a mini First Amendment moment in and of itself).

The star of the show, however, had not arrived. Hours passed, and David Duke was feared to be a no-show, although his campaign headquarters repeatedly reassured his novice lawyer (who was feeling outnumbered and

[25]*Id.* at 867.

somewhat embarrassed by the empty chair next to her), that he was en route. Eventually he arrived, professing that he had needed to detour to buy a razor and freshen up for the event, and without further explanation for delaying a roomful of attorneys who had gathered on short notice, began his deposition. He was reported to be a pleasant, articulate, and cooperative witness, who acknowledged his unsavory past but disavowed any residual discriminatory predilections. But although sartorial savvy was not required of either plaintiffs or putative presidential candidates, he lost points in my partner's eyes when she looked under the table and saw that David Duke was wearing thick woolen socks and beat-up shoes, arguably not commensurate with a bona fide candidate for the office of president. But it is not uncommon for proponents of First Amendment freedoms to be social pariahs in one way or another, and my partner observed that lesson, too, from David Duke.

The district court judge who heard the testimony of David Duke and our arguments was looking for a way to avoid putting Duke on the ballot, and he found it by deciding that the decision regarding who could appear on the ballot "is made by the political party's leadership" and that "interference with the internal functions and decisions of the political parties would be a violation of the parties own rights of association."[26] In effect, he used the theory that won *Abrams v. Reno* to rule against us in *Duke v. Smith*. David Duke was not on the Florida ballot.

The court of appeals saw it differently, first finding that the issue was "capable of repetition yet evading review" and could be decided even though the election was over. Most important, it found that the Presidential Preference Primary Selection Committee is "inextricably intertwined with the process of placing candidates' names on the ballot, and the state created procedures, not the autonomous political parties, make the *final* determination as to who will appear on the ballot in each primary election."[27] On the merits, the court of appeals found for Duke because the committee's "unfettered discretion to exclude candidates" permitted arbitrary and discriminatory actions that deprived Duke of his right not to be eliminated from the ballot "because of his political beliefs and expressions (free speech)" and "voters' rights to vote for the candidate of their choice."[28]

The victory was too late for David Duke (and some Democrats who had also been excluded), and for us, because in a later order the court called the victory "pyrrhic," and refused to award attorneys' fees. So, though David Duke may not have had much virtue, for us, the virtue of protecting First Amendment rights was our only reward.

---

[26]*Id.* at 871.
[27]Duke v. Smith, 13 F.3d 388, 393 (11th Cir. 1994) (emphasis in original).
[28]*Id.* at 394.

COMMERCIAL SPEECH

Although political speech is at the pinnacle of First Amendment protected speech, I have always thought that commercial speech was more important to the masses than political speech. We make so many important daily decisions based on advertising, and so few based on what politicians say, that commercial speech should receive more respect than it does. Indeed, commercial speech is probably more honest than political speech—those people and organizations that pay big dollars have more reason to provide truthful information to customers than do politicians whose assurances seem to last only through the next election.

My commercial-speech career began when the Florida Bar decided to severely restrict lawyer advertising, a decision based on antipathy to distasteful lawyer advertising and disrespect for lawyers seen as "ambulance chasers," not silk-stocking, large-firm, elegant, and proper practitioners. Perhaps no one fit the "improper" mold more than Stewart McHenry, whose case I ultimately argued in the U.S. Supreme Court.[29]

McHenry came to me after I had litigated a series of cases seeking to challenge, or at least narrow the Florida Bar's attempt to severely restrict lawyer advertising. The Bar, offended by excesses in Yellow Page, print, and television advertising, formed a task force to study the issues and ultimately enacted a litany of rules designed to discourage the excesses. Among the problem areas were lawyers changing the names of their firms to monikers like "AAA Aaron" to get first listings in the Yellow Pages; dramatizations that showed lawyers working all night to solve personal injury clients' problems; reenactments of car and motorcycle crashes; and other over-the-top efforts to attract viewers' attention. The Bar conducted polls of judges, sought feedback from the public, and commissioned focus groups to tell it what it wanted to know: that the advertisements contributed to disrespect for the legal profession.

I did not doubt that some lawyers had engaged in advertising that was, at best, tacky and in bad taste, but I thought the Bar missed two important concepts in its zeal to improve the image of lawyers. First, it overlooked the importance of alerting people to their rights and saving them "search costs." Most people have no idea about where to go if they are injured in an accident or by a defective product. The upper middle class may know lawyers or have access to those who can recommend a lawyer for a certain type of problem, but the vast majority of people are not knowledgeable about either their rights or who may be available to give them legal advice about certain kinds of issues. A lawyer advertisement has two purposes: You may need a lawyer if you have a certain kind of problem and you should consider me if you think you have that certain kind of problem.

---

[29]*See* Florida Bar v. Went For It, Inc., 515 U.S. 618 (1995).

The challenges to the various Florida Bar Rules went though various courts—the Florida Supreme Court, the U.S. District Court, the U.S. Court of Appeals for the Eleventh Circuit—but the one rule that was not initially challenged was the rule prohibiting personal-injury lawyers from immediately sending direct-mail solicitation letters to persons who had been in automobile accidents. The rule required a 30-day waiting period and the Bar sought to justify it as a protection of the right to privacy and as a means of decreasing disrespect for lawyers and the judicial system.[30] I thought the rule was vulnerable because a Supreme Court case,[31] had declared a direct mail *ban* to be unconstitutional, saying that a recipient could just throw an unwanted letter in the wastebasket, so privacy was not really invaded.

The personal-injury lawyers who used direct-mail advertising were not held in high esteem by the lions of the personal-injury bar, and none of them came forward to challenge that particular rule until G. Stewart McHenry, a successful Tampa personal-injury lawyer, called me. He asked if he could fly over from Tampa to talk to me about two things—a Bar proceeding seeking his disbarment on grounds he would disclose to me when we talked in person, and the challenge to the direct-mail 30-day-wait rule.

McHenry's disbarment problem was substantial. The Bar had brought proceedings against him based on allegations by two female personal-injury clients that he masturbated while interviewing them, and the hearings on those charges had resulted in a finding that he had indeed done so. McHenry maintained that the clients were lying because they were angry with him about how their cases were handled. The judge appointed by the Florida Supreme Court to hear the case credited the women's testimony and recommended disbarment. The appeal was directly to the Florida Supreme Court and McHenry, who was a very likeable fellow, made me this offer: He would retain us to challenge the 30-day no-direct-mail rule if he could also retain us to represent him before the Florida Supreme Court on the disbarment issue. I immediately told him that the chances of success in the disbarment proceeding were slim to none, and that if he were disbarred he would no longer have standing to challenge the 30-day rule because if he

---

[30]Rule 4-7.4, Direct contact with prospective clients, provided:
   (b) Written communication.
      (1) A lawyer shall not send, or knowingly permit to be sent, on behalf of himself, his firm, his partner, an associate or any other lawyer affiliated with him or his firm, a written communication to a prospective client for the purpose of obtaining professional employment if:
         a. The written communication concerns an action for personal injury or wrongful death or otherwise relates to an accident or disaster involving the person to whom the communication is addressed or a relative of that person, unless the accident or disaster occurred *more than thirty days prior to the mailing of the communication* (emphasis added).
[31]Shapero v. Kentucky Bar Association, 486 U.S. 466 (1988).

were not a lawyer, the restrictions could not affect him. It was then that he told me he also had a lawyer referral company —"Went For It, Inc."—which obtained accident reports from the public records to sell the names to other lawyers so they could do their own direct-mail solicitations, and that he would continue that business if he was disbarred. Because a related rule also precluded lawyer referral services from sending targeted direct-mail solicitations in personal-injury cases for 30 days after the injury, that solved the standing issue that loomed on the legal horizon. We initiated an action for declaratory judgment and injunction against the Florida Bar, bringing it in Tampa in the U.S. District Court for the Middle District of Florida.

In the disciplinary action, we wrote the brief in the Florida Supreme Court and I argued the disbarment case there—it was not an easy argument. My predictions proved correct. The Florida Supreme Court disbarred McHenry.[32]

The U.S. District Court held that the Bar's 30-day ban on personal-injury targeted direct-mail lawyer advertising was unconstitutional, based on *Shapero v. Kentucky Bar Association,* although the U.S. magistrate judge who initially was assigned to make a recommendation on the matter distinguished *Shapero* as a total across-the-board ban on direct mail, a position that proved to be prescient when the case reached the Supreme Court. The U.S. Court of Appeals for the Eleventh Circuit affirmed the district court decision, finding *Shapero* to be binding precedent, although the author of the opinion, Judge Susan Black, voiced dissatisfaction with the outcome, writing:

> We are disturbed that *Bates* and its progeny require the decision we reach today. We are forced to recognize that there are members of our profession who would mail solicitation letters to persons in grief, and we find The Florida Bar's attempt to regulate such intrusions entirely understandable. Although the Bar may not formally restrict such behavior, an attorney's conscience, self-respect, and respect for the profession should dictate self-restraint in this area. To preserve the law as a learned profession demands as much.[33]

At that point, given the limited number of cases that the Supreme Court takes each year, we felt confident that Florida's 30-day rule was history, although we were sensitive to the fact that at least four Supreme Court justices—Chief Justice Rehnquist and Justices O'Connor, Scalia, and Thomas—were not fans of lawyer advertising and indeed even questioned the wisdom of the foundational decision for lawyer advertising.[34] However, we also knew that the Bar was willing to see its commitment through to the end, and that its counsel was well aware that the "Rule of Four" con-

---

[32] *See* The Florida Bar v. McHenry, 605 So. 2d 459 (1992).
[33] McHenry v. The Florida Bar, 21 F.3d 1038, 1045 (11th Cir 1994).
[34] Bates v. State Bar of Arizona, 433 U.S. 350 (1977).

trols certiorari review; if four justices vote in favor of granting review of a case, the case will be heard by the whole Court. The Bar did seek certiorari, and while the petition was pending an aircraft crash occurred in Washington, DC—the loss of a U.S. Airways plane—which resulted in lawyers vigorously soliciting wrongful-death and personal-injury cases. The *Washington Post* published a long article detailing, unfavorably, the efforts of those lawyers just weeks before the first Monday in October, the day the Supreme Court term begins and the Court announces the cases it has decided to hear. I knew then that review was likely and, in an unusual departure from the "first Monday" practice, on the Thursday before the first Monday we received a call from the clerk of the Supreme Court telling us that certiorari had been granted and that there would be an expedited briefing schedule and oral argument.

The Florida Bar v. Went For It, Inc. oral argument went swimmingly; the justices joked about lawyers, the antipathy to lawyers, and the thin-skinned nature of the Florida Bar's reaction to public opinion, and I walked away from the courtroom thinking we had as much as a seven-to-two majority affirming the decision striking the 30-day rule.

I was wrong. In a five-to-four opinion, the Court reversed the Eleventh Circuit and upheld the 30-day rule. The majority opinion found that the Bar had advanced substantial interests—privacy and the dignity of the legal profession—and that the 30-day rule was narrowly tailored because it was not a total ban on direct mail and that there were alternative advertising methods available, including billboards, television, and print to apprise people of the availability of lawyers. The majority credited the Bar's "record" of polls and anecdotal comments relating to the public's perception of advertising lawyers, leading Justice Kennedy, writing for the dissent, to say of that "record":

> It is noteworthy for its incompetence ... Our cases require something more than a few pages of self-serving and unsupported statements by the State to demonstrate that a regulation directly and materially advances the elimination of a real harm when the State seeks to suppress truthful and nondeceptive speech ... Today's opinion is a serious departure, not only from our prior decisions involving attorney advertising, but also from the principles that govern the transmission of commercial speech. The Court's opinion reflects a new-found and illegitimate confidence that it, along with the Supreme Court of Florida, knows what is best for the Bar and its clients. Self-assurance has always been the hallmark of a censor.[35]

Justice Kennedy's recognition of the "paternalism factor," that the state knows what is best for its citizenry, is at the heart of every attempt to limit

---

[35]Florida Bar v. Went For It, Inc., 515 U.S. 618, 640-45 (1995) (Kennedy, J., dissenting).

speech and assembly, and although I lost the case, I was pleased to be in the company of those who rejected the notion of the all-knowing state.

The dissenters, Justices Kennedy, Stevens, Ginsberg, and Souter, were deprived of majority status because Justice Breyer, who had been recently appointed to replace the retiring Justice Harry Blackmun, sided with the four justices whose antipathy to lawyer advertising was unrelenting. The rumor I heard was that the chief justice and Justices O'Connor, Scalia, and Thomas wanted to overrule *Bates,* and Justice Breyer would not agree to that, but he would agree to join them if they receded from their anti-*Bates* position. If true, that means that the 30-day rule was sacrificed on the altar of saving *Bates;* given that choice, I cannot complain. The Court's delicate balance on lawyer advertising was brought home to me some months later when I saw Justice Blackmun and he told me that if he had not retired I would have prevailed because he would have joined the dissenters and held the 30-day rule to be violative of the First Amendment's protection of commercial speech.

That was not the first time I had heard from a justice that a five-to-four decision could or should have been different. Years before I had lost the school corporal punishment case[36] with Justice Lewis Powell writing the bare majority opinion holding that the Eighth Amendment's cruel-and-un-usual-punishment clause did not create a cause of action for public school students who were viciously paddled by school officials. That outcome came before the sensitivity to violence toward children became a national cause. A retired Justice Powell later told me that perhaps he was wrong in *Ingraham*.

But wrong or right, a five-to-four majority in the Supreme Court is "right" because it is final, at least until, or unless, the Court decides to change its mind. I think that accepting and acknowledging that concept underscores the excitement of practicing law, especially in as dynamic an area as First Amendment constitutional law. The outcome of First Amendment cases is dependent on a complicated set of principles that do not have much precision, and on the social and political climate extant at the time of the decision. No wonder our jurisprudence struggles with resolving these cases, and will continue to do so unless Justice Douglas' literal approach prevails: "Congress shall make no law" ends any inquiry—any restraint on speech or assembly is unconstitutional.

CONCLUSION

A First Amendment lawyer's life is an opportunity to participate in the most vibrant aspects of American life. Speech, assembly, petitioning for redress, and the free exercise of religion are at the heart of our democratic process. When

---

[36]Ingraham v. Wright, 430 U.S. 651 (1977).

and how those constitutional guarantees are to be respected will provide work for lawyers not yet born. But I am happy that my life has provided me the chance to be involved in the cases I have described here (and others), whether I have won them or lost them. The important part was to be in the game.

THE FIRST AMENDMENT IN THE AGE OF THE INTERNET

THE U.S. SUPREME COURT TAKES ON THE CHALLENGE OF A NEW COMMUNICATION MEDIUM

Paul M. Smith*

EDITOR'S INTRODUCTION

The Internet and the future of communication technology are the focus of the next two chapters. Attorneys who are among those who litigated the seminal and foundation-establishing case in Internet regulation, Reno v. ACLU, *author each of these chapters. Not surprisingly, each author examines that case, though, from different perspectives.*

*Beyond that, in chapter 8 Paul M. Smith also provides a front-row seat with his analysis of the post-*Reno *congressional efforts to regulate Internet content. From home and office computers to those in public libraries, the laws attempted to protect children from smut on the Internet. But the laws were challenged on the basis of infringing on First Amendment values. Did the technological structure of this new medium allow for limiting children's access to certain content while not infringing on the rights of adults? If not, then is it constitutionally permissible to restrict the rights of adults in order to protect children? Mr. Smith examines those cases with an eye on Supreme Court dynamics and where its rulings left the law in this area.*

---

*Paul M. Smith practices law at Jenner & Block LLP in Washington, D.C., where he cochairs the firm's Media & First Amendment and Appellate & Supreme Court practice groups. He was among the counsel for the American Library Ass'n plaintiffs in *Reno v. ACLU* and lead counsel for the American Library Ass'n plaintiffs in *United States v. American Library Ass'n*, both of which are discussed in this chapter.

Because the Internet is still a relatively new medium of communication, the "history" of laws regulating the Internet—and of court decisions reviewing those laws—goes back only a few years. The story begins in the mid-1990s, when members of Congress came to the realization that the Internet had emerged as a vehicle for delivering directly into the home any and all content that someone somewhere in the world might want to put there. This included an unprecedented degree of access to sexually explicit materials. Congress responded with three laws: the Communications Decency Act, the Child Online Protection Act, and the Children's Internet Protection Act. The U.S. Supreme Court has in turn reviewed each under the First Amendment.

As a result, we now have a relatively clear sense of how the First Amendment will be applied in this new context and the limits that will apply to efforts by lawmakers to regulate content there. As a general matter, speakers on the Internet enjoy constitutional protection comparable to that accorded to print publications like books and magazines. Beyond certain recognized categories of unprotected speech, they, like their print brethren, generally cannot be censored based on legislators' views that their content is potentially harmful. Web *users,* on the other hand, face more difficult challenges when they assert a right to have uncensored access to the content on the Internet at terminals provided by the government in a library, school, or other setting. The fate of such a claim will turn on a whole variety of context-specific factors that are hard to predict in advance.

As a participant in the constitutional challenges to two of the three statutes listed earlier, I can testify that the story of how the courts responded to a dramatic new medium of communication has some interesting twists and turns.

LAYING THE GROUNDWORK: THE COMMUNICATIONS DECENCY ACT

Congress' first attempt to regulate content on the Internet was in the Communications Decency Act (CDA),[1] passed as a part of the landmark Telecommunications Act of 1996. The CDA would have imposed very substantial restrictions on sexual content transmitted over the Internet. It made it a crime to transmit or display any words or images using an "interactive computer service" if the words or images were available to minors under 18 and were indecent or patently offensive. It was an affirmative defense if the speaker could show that access to the material required a user to provide a credit card number or an electronic adult ID. As a result, any portions of the Internet not segregated and screened in one of these ways would have been required to exclude content not satisfying the "decency" standards applied by the Federal Communications Commission to daytime broadcast television. Those standards, of course, are

---

[1]7U.S.C. § 223.

far more restrictive than those that may constitutionally be applied to sexual material appearing in print publications.

When I, along with others in my law firm and elsewhere, sat down to try to figure out how to challenge the CDA, we faced great uncertainties. We knew that the act would dramatically transform the free-wheeling new world of "cyberspace" by demanding a great deal of self-censorship by the millions of persons speaking through Web sites, "bulletin boards," "chat rooms," and the like. After all, the broadcasting indecency standard can be violated merely by use of one of the "seven dirty words" made famous by George Carlin in the monologue broadcast by Pacifica Radio in 1973, as well as by graphic images included in posted works with very clear literary, artistic, scientific, or educational value.[2] That means that all kinds of Web speakers faced criminal liability if they failed to segregate and screen access to material that was then currently available to all comers. This would have had a major impact on Web sites providing any form of sexually explicit information—no matter how valuable—as well as libraries, booksellers, and myriad other speakers using the Internet. It was this broad kind of potential impact that led to challenges being filed by a very broad coalition, including such "establishment" corporations as America Online, Apple Computer, and Microsoft.

What we did not know was how to go about communicating about this harm to judges who at that point likely remained completely unfamiliar with the Internet and its potential. (Looking back only a few years, it is hard to remember how recent the Internet really is—and how new and different it was from anything that had come before.) Nor was it at all clear how the First Amendment categories developed in case law involving quite different media would be adapted and applied to the Internet. Several possibilities existed:

First, the courts might accept the analogy to broadcast television with its very intrusive regulatory standard allowing very substantial limits on content. The analogy to broadcast television was not fanciful given that the Internet is delivered into the home through an electronic screen resembling a television set and was likely to be accessible to unsupervised minors in that setting. The reality was that the Internet had made "adult" material vastly more available to children in the home than had previously been the case. On the other hand, the constitutional case law upholding application of the indecency standard to broadcast television rested not just on the fact that the medium is easily accessed in the home but also on the fact that broadcasters use a share of a scarce resource—the broadcast spectrum—that is owned by the public and allocated by the federal government in return for commitments to serve the public interest. Capacity on the Internet, by contrast, was anything but scarce. There was no apparent limit

---

[2]*See* FCC v. Pacifica Foundation, 438 U.S. 726 (1978).

to the number of Web sites that could be created. Nor was the government involved in licensing access to this resource.

A second possible way to view the matter was to analogize the Internet not to television but to retail stores and rely on the case law allowing intrusive zoning of retail businesses purveying "adult" materials. In a series of cases culminating in *Renton v. Playtime Theatres, Inc.,*[3] the Supreme Court had held that it was permissible for a municipality to confine adult businesses to one small area of town or, instead, to require that they be widely dispersed. The theory was that such businesses cause "secondary effects" like crime and urban decay that are an appropriate basis for locational regulation, if not banning. As applied to the Internet, the argument would have been that adult sites cause a comparable sort of harm when accessible to children and can be "zoned" into a space behind screens for credit cards or adult IDs. But this analogy, too, had its potential flaws. It was not at all clear that the harm of exposure of minors to adult Web sites could be viewed as "secondary" in the sense used in *Renton*. Moreover, the burdens on adult recipients of speech caused by zoning adult businesses were different in kind from those that would be caused by mandated use of credit cards or adult IDs that provide a record of the identity of everyone accessing a site.

Our position was that content-based regulation of the Internet should instead be analogized to content-based regulation of print media, which is subject to strict scrutiny under the First Amendment and thus very seldom upheld as constitutional. The argument was that the Internet provided various ways in which individuals and groups could communicate electronically that were much like letters (e-mail), newspapers (Web sites), and public meetings (chat rooms). But even this favorable analogy was no guarantee of a favorable outcome. Indeed, it crystallized the bottom-line question raised by the Internet and Congress' response to it in the CDA.

In the print media, the Supreme Court had made clear that most "adult" material is nonobscene and thus constitutionally protected for adults. But in *Ginsberg v. New York,*[4] it had also held that much material depicting nudity and sexuality could be banned from sale to children as "harmful to minors." It was clear that a large amount of the sexual material on the Web fell in that category but was available to minors on sites that did not require credit cards or adult IDs. That seemed to point to an ultimate question: whether a legislature could act to protect minors if the choice was between (a) substantially burdening adults' constitutionally protected access to sexually explicit material in cyberspace by requiring them to identify themselves and (b) allowing open access to material that is not only not constitutionally protected for minors but presumed to be "harmful" to them.

---

[3]475 U.S. 41 (1986).
[4]390 U.S. 629 (1968).

In 1996, it was far from obvious how the Court would answer that question. After all, even under strict scrutiny, a content-based regulation of protected speech can be upheld if it is the least restrictive means available to the government to pursue a compelling state interest. Ultimately, because of how the CDA defined the scope of the speech it was regulating, the issue was not resolved in *Reno v. ACLU*. Indeed, the question was not finally resolved even in 2004 when the Court again addressed it in *Ashcroft v. ACLU II*, involving a challenge to the subsequently enacted Child Online Protection Act.[5]

The first CDA challenge was filed in Philadelphia on February 8, 1996, the day the act took effect. The plaintiffs were the American Civil Liberties Union (ACLU), several other organizations concerned about free speech on the Web, and a number of operators of Web sites. The case was assigned to Judge Ronald Buckwalter, who a week later granted a temporary restraining order barring enforcement of the CDA, basing this ruling on the conclusion that the act was unconstitutionally vague. The act mandated that further proceedings would be heard by a three-judge district court, followed by an immediate appeal to the U.S. Supreme Court. Accordingly, on the same day the temporary restraining order was issued, then-Chief Judge Sloviter of the Third Circuit Court of Appeals appointed herself and another federal district judge—Stewart Dalzell—to join Judge Buckwalter to make up the three-judge trial court. Within a few days, the Department of Justice had agreed not to enforce the CDA pending the full consideration of a forthcoming preliminary-injunction motion. A day or two later, a second group of plaintiffs, represented primarily by my firm of Jenner & Block, joined the case. The lead plaintiff in this second group was the American Library Association, which was joined by associations of booksellers, newspapers, and the like, along with America Online, Inc., Apple Computer, Inc., and Microsoft Corp. among other companies. Counsel for both groups ended up working together very cooperatively.

Within a month, the three-judge court began hearing testimony relevant to the constitutional claims presented by the plaintiffs. This testimony focused on (a) the ways in the which the Internet operates, including the barriers preventing most speakers from assuring that their speech will go only to adults, (b) the nature of the material on the Web potentially covered by the CDA, (c) the burdens on Web speakers if they were forced to comply, and (d) less restrictive alternative methods of achieving the congressional goal of protecting children. Although this hearing was relatively short, we did take the time to educate the judges with actual demonstrations. The government, though showing the court sexually explicit material from the Web, also did not contest the fact that the statute reached a much broader set of materials. Its expert conceded, for example, that a speaker could violate the

---

[5]*See* text accompanying notes 32–60.

act by posting on a Web site a text containing a "four letter word."[6] And the government did not seriously contend that persons seeking to convey valuable messages, such as through sexual-education materials, could do so without fear of running afoul of the CDA.

On June 12, 1996, the district court granted plaintiffs' motion for a preliminary injunction barring enforcement of the act.[7] The lengthy opinion began with detailed findings of fact made by all three judges jointly. The judges then offered three separate legal analyses, all of which arrived at much the same conclusion: The CDA imposed too great a burden on speech protected for adults in a rather clumsy and overbroad effort to protect minors. As Chief Judge Sloviter explained in her opinion, the terms "indecent" and "patently offensive" covered a very large amount of constitutionally protected content—some of it quite "valuable"—and the facts showed that "it is either technologically or economically prohibitive for many of the plaintiffs to comply with the CDA without seriously impeding their posting of online material which adults have a constitutional right to receive."[8]

Judge Buckwalter agreed with this conclusion, while reiterating his view that the term "indecent" was unconstitutionally vague.[9] He added that he was not willing at that early stage to say that the government could not come up with an alternative statute that could address the problem of sexually explicit material on the Internet in a constitutionally permissible way.[10]

In this he disagreed with Judge Dalzell, who wrote a remarkable opinion in which he stated that any attempt to regulate speech on the Internet that is constitutionally protected requires the highest level of First Amendment scrutiny. The CDA, he noted, would have had little impact on commercial pornographers—because they already typically used credit cards or adult verification—but would substantially affect other forms of adult use of the Internet:

> The CDA's wholesale disruption of the Internet will necessarily affect adult participation in the medium. As some speakers leave or refuse to enter the medium, and others bowdlerize their speech or erect the barriers that the Act envisions, and still others remove bulletin boards, Web sites, and newsgroups, adults will face a shrinking ability to participate in the medium. Since much of the communication on the Internet is participatory, i.e., is a form of dialogue, a decrease in the number of speakers, speech for a, and permissible topics will diminish the worldwide dialogue that is the strength and signal achievement of the medium.[11]

---

[6]*See* Reno v. ACLU, 521 U.S. 844, 878 (1997).
[7]ACLU v. Reno, 929 F. Supp. 824 (E.D. Pa. 1996).
[8]*Id.* at 854.
[9]*Id.* at 858.
[10]*Id.* at 859.
[11]*Id.* at 879.

Judge Dalzell ultimately concluded that the power of the government to regulate speech based on its content in this medium is limited to speech unprotected even for adults—obscenity and child pornography—explaining:

> True it is that many find some of the speech on the Internet to be offensive, and amid the din of cyberspace many hear discordant voices that they regard as indecent. The absence of government regulation of Internet content has unquestionably produced a kind of chaos, but as one of plaintiffs' experts put it with such resonance at the hearing:
> "What achieved success was the very chaos that the Internet is. The strength of the Internet is that chaos." Just as the strength of the Internet is chaos, so the strength of our liberty depends upon the chaos and cacophony of the unfettered speech the First Amendment protects.[12]

The case proceeded to the Supreme Court as everyone had always expected it would. There, the government, now represented by the Solicitor General's office (the division of the Department of Justice that practices in the Supreme Court) refined both the broadcast television and the zoning analogies as it struggled to find a way to uphold a law in the face of findings that it would substantially interfere with a vast amount of protected speech on the Internet. We as plaintiffs had the benefit not just of those findings but also of the three district judges' separate but complementary legal analyses that so strongly supported our position.

Oral arguments were held on March 19, 1997. It was understood by all concerned that this would be a landmark case, because it would write on a clean slate about the nature of the First Amendment protection to be accorded to an entirely new medium of communication. Arguing for the United States as appellant was Seth Waxman, the eloquent principal Deputy Solicitor General who would soon be elevated to Solicitor General by President Clinton. Arguing for the multitude of plaintiffs was my law partner, the late Bruce Ennis, a veteran Supreme Court advocate and First Amendment crusader, who was then at Jenner & Block but had previously been the National Legal Director at the ACLU. Bruce, formerly a novice when it came to the Internet, had by then become quite conversant with the technical issues involved. Lined up to hear the argument were a host of experts and VIPs, included members of Congress. The Court signaled the importance of the case when, for the only time in my experience, the Chief Justice stated on taking the bench that the Court had spontaneously decided to grant each side 35 instead of the usual 30 minutes.

Mr. Waxman attempted to convince the Court that the CDA covered an identifiable and narrow category of speech and that even noncommercial Web speakers could require users to produce adult IDs before accessing in-

---

[12]*Id.* at 883.

decent material without imposing an excessive burden on speech rights. This attempt foundered due to the breadth of the statute, which as the justices pointed out, would criminalize even a typical conversation among high school students—via e-mail or in a chat room—about the details of their real or imagined sexual experiences. Along the way, Mr. Waxman dismissed filtering at the user end as an inadequate substitute for speaker regulation, arguing that there are too many sites to establish comprehensive lists of sites to block and too many computers where minors might obtain unfiltered access.

Mr. Ennis started by pointing out that it was conceded that screening for adult IDs was possible only for Web sites and thus could not be done for other parts of cyberspace like "listservs" and chat rooms. He then fended off questioning from Justice Scalia about why it was not sufficient that indecent communication could continue on Web sites if not elsewhere —pointing out that Web sites were not interactive in the same sense and often themselves were designed in a manner that precluded checking adult IDs. Ennis went on to point out that the scope of the speech affected was much broader than that allowed in prior cases involving "harmful to minors" speech. The justices seemed interested in ways to narrow the act, possibly to a smaller category of speech or to a smaller category of speakers, like "commercial pornographers." Ennis then lauded the alternative of use of filtering at the recipient end as a better alternative. Mr. Ennis was then quizzed about who should bear the burden of justification in a case where the main claim is that a statute permissibly limiting distribution of speech to minors will in practice inhibit distribution to adults as well. Finally, he pointed out that as a practical matter the act would not affect the multitude of foreign-based sites and thus would accomplish little to protect children. That notion was met with skepticism typified by Justice Kennedy's comment that it is a "weak argument to say that the United States, if it has a strong public policy, cannot lead the way, and maybe other nations would follow."

The Supreme Court's ruling came on June 26, 1997, and—in what was then a novelty—was posted on the Web within minutes. The Court unanimously held that the CDA violated the First Amendment. In an opinion by Justice Stevens, the Court quickly dispatched every argument offered by the government for application of some lower level of First Amendment scrutiny than the strict scrutiny applied to content-based regulations of protected speech. First, it held the *Ginsberg* "harmful to minors" approach inapplicable to a statute not limited to sexually explicit and offensive speech lacking any serious literary, artistic, political, or scientific value for minors.[13] Second, it held that the *Pacifica*/broadcasting analogy did not ap-

---

[13]521 U.S. 844, 865 (1997).

ply to a medium that had no history of pervasive governmental regulation, required a user to take "affirmative steps" to access sexually explicit material, and (unlike the broadcast spectrum) was in no sense a "scarce expressive commodity." Finally, the Court held that the *Renton*/zoning analogy applied only to regulations seeking to mitigate the "secondary effects" of adult establishments, whereas the CDA was clearly directed at the effects of the *content* of speech—that is, its "primary effects."

Turning to the application of strict scrutiny, Justice Stevens began by emphasizing how vague and therefore broad the CDA was in terms of the scope of the speech covered. He noted that the terms "indecent" and "patently offensive" covered "large amounts of nonpornographic material with serious educational or other value, including any work containing one of the seven "dirty words" at issue in *Pacifica*.[14] He concluded for the Court that:

> [The] CDA lacks the precision that the First Amendment requires when a statute regulates the content of speech. In order to deny minors access to potentially harmful speech, the CDA effectively suppresses a large amount of speech that adults have a constitutional right to receive and to address to one another. That burden on adult speech is unacceptable if less restrictive alternatives would be at least as effective in achieving the legitimate purpose that the statute was enacted to serve.[15]

In so concluding, Justice Stevens did two things. First, he effectively invited Congress to come up with a new statute covering a narrower category of speech, while refusing to rewrite the CDA in that way to make it constitutional. And he repeatedly refused to answer the hard question that would be posed if another statute could not be rejected on the basis of available "less restrictive alternatives"—that is, whether the need to protect children would justify interference with communication of protected speech to adults, if the two were shown to be in irreconcilable conflict. Instead, several times he left that question open by stating that the Court was only saying that the goal of protecting children "does not justify an *unnecessarily broad* suppression of speech addressed to adults."[16] As explained below, with the Child Online Protection Act Congress attempted to force the Court's hand by narrowing both the scope of speech regulated and the type of speakers covered. But as it happened, the next relevant case to reach the Court involved another law mandating filtering of the Internet in the library.

---

[14]*Id.* at 878.

[15]*Id.* at 874.

[16]521 U.S. at 875 (emphasis added). Justice O'Connor's partial concurrence, joined by Chief Justice Rehnquist, was similar in that it merely emphasized that the constitutional calculus would come out differently if and when technology allowed real "zoning" of cyberspace to allow the free flow of "indecent" material to adults while protecting children. *Id.* at 886–97.

A SIDE TRIP TO THE LIBRARY

In the Children's Internet Protection Act (CIPA), passed several years after the invalidation of the CDA, Congress tried to find a constitutional method of addressing the perceived problem of sexually explicit content on the Internet being viewed in public and school libraries. Its solution, somewhat ironically, was reliance on the very same filtering technology that the government had condemned as insufficient when it was offered as a less restrictive alternative to the CDA. In CIPA, Congress mandated that any library accepting federal funding for its Internet connections—which included most public and school libraries at the time—was required to install on all of its terminals a "technology protection measure" to screen out obscenity and child pornography.[17] In addition, when children were using the terminals, the technology protection measure was also supposed to be designed to screen out the much broader category of images deemed "harmful to minors." The law stated that the library had the discretion to disable the filter on the request of an adult user who requested unfiltered Internet access for a "bona fide research or other lawful purpose."

Like the CDA, CIPA provided for review by a three-judge court and a direct appeal to the U.S. Supreme Court. Also as with CDA, two groups of plaintiffs brought suit in federal court in Philadelphia. I was lead counsel for one of those groups, headed by the American Library Association (ALA), but worked closely with counsel for the second group from the ACLU. Our basic contention was that a library complying with CIPA would end up screening out a large amount of constitutionally protected content ("overblocking"), while allowing through a substantial percentage of the "pornographic" sites that were the ostensible targets of the act ("underblocking").[18] We put on substantial expert testimony documenting that overblocking of protected speech—including thousands of sites with no sexual content whatsoever—would occur with installation of any commercially available filtering software and that such overblocking, in fact, was a virtual certainty with any attempt to categorize content on the vast and ever-changing World Wide Web. The examples we were able to marshal—such as sites for the Knights of Columbus, candidates for Congress, orphanages, and a large percentage of sites dealing with gay material or sex education—seemed to make a powerful impression on the trial court judges. We also showed that because of substantial underblocking, reliance on filters to prevent access to sexually explicit material in the library would be misguided. The government did not really

---

[17]The act, which is codified in a variety of places in the U.S. Code, is described in *United States v. American Library Ass'n*, 539 U.S. 194, 201 (2003).

[18]Under *South Dakota v. Dole*, 483 U.S. 203 (1987), a federal law providing funding to the states is unconstitutional if it conditions the funding on actions by the states that would themselves violate constitutional rights.

dispute these factual points, which were ultimately transformed into voluminous findings of fact by the three-judge court after a 2-week trial in 2002.[19]

Instead, the government argued that use of filters to limit access to sexually explicit sites is (a) good policy and (b) constitutionally permissible because libraries have no obligation to provide their patrons any content that
librarians have not chosen voluntarily to acquire and make available. There
was some tension between this position and the reality that prior to CIPA,
only 7% of libraries had chosen to mandate use of filters for children and
adults. The ALA was in court saying there were much more appropriate
ways to deal with the practical problems that can arise when patrons wish to
access "pornographic" material in the library setting. These alternatives include use of privacy screens and recessed monitors to minimize inadvertent
exposure of other patrons, as well as patron codes of conduct and making
filtering available as an option to be chosen by the patron or a parent. The
trial included a substantial amount of factual and expert testimony about
how libraries deal with these issues in practice. That testimony also covered
the more fundamental question of what a library's central mission is. The
government, supporting exclusion of material in the Internet, argued that
libraries seek to inculcate patrons with valuable information preselected for
that purpose. The plaintiffs, including the ALA, disagreed, arguing that libraries seek in a nonjudgmental way to provide whatever information *patrons* are asking for. Our very first witness was Candace Morgan, a librarian
from Vancouver, Washington, who made this point strongly. The government attempted to cross-examine her by showing her sexually explicit images printed from Web sites and asking if these were materials she would
want to see in a library. The effort fell flat as the three judges showed little
interest and Ms. Morgan stood fast by her position that it is not the job of a
librarian to judge the value of a text or image. The government countered
with testimony from librarians about the kinds of disruptions that had been
caused by teenagers accessing sexually explicit sites and the like.

As a legal matter, the plaintiffs' argument was that the Internet is not
comparable to the printed materials that a library has to decide whether to
acquire. Though a patron cannot claim a First Amendment right to have a
library acquire a specific book, once an Internet connection is established
and the entire universe of material on the Web becomes available, the library cannot then exclude one small category of disfavored protected
speech based on disapproval of its content. To the contrary, in that situation, the Internet terminal becomes a kind of "public forum" from which
speakers cannot be excluded based on the content of what they have to say.
Furthermore, we argued that even if librarians might have the constitutional authority to decide to install mandatory filters (and we said they did

---

[19]American Library Ass'n v. United States, 201 F. Supp. 2d 401 (E.D. Pa. 2002).

not), it was an "unconstitutional condition" on federal funding for the federal government to attempt to mandate one exercise of professional judgment on this issue in every library in America—just as it could not use the "carrot and stick" of federal money to curtail academic freedom at public universities.

The three-judge court, in an opinion by Edward Becker, the eminent chief judge of the Third Circuit, agreed with the plaintiffs on the public forum argument[20] and added a lengthy footnote apparently agreeing with us on the unconstitutional conditions point as well.[21]

The linchpin in the Supreme Court turned out to be the provision in CIPA authorizing libraries to disable the filters on request from an adult who offered a "bona fide research or other lawful purpose." In the trial court, this had not been emphasized as a potential solution to the constitutional problems presented by the law by the court or even by the government's lawyers. The problem, we argued, was that the disabling provision (a) only created *discretion* to disable, (b) implied that the librarian in exercising that discretion should inquire into the reasons why the adult patron desired unfiltered access and make a judgment about whether it was both desirable and lawful, and (c) did nothing to mitigate the stigma problem created by requiring adults in each instance to ask a librarian to disable software intended to screen out pornography. The district court concluded that even if the "lawful purpose" language did not impose any content-based limit on when and why the filter could be disabled, patrons would still be unconstitutionally burdened in their access to protected speech by the need to ask a librarian to disable the filter and by the delays inherent in that process.[22]

The disabling provision played a comparably minor role in the briefing in the Supreme Court. There the government relied primarily on the argument that if librarians could rely on content-based judgments in deciding what books to buy, they could similarly make content-based judgments about what Internet content to exclude. But when it came time for oral argument, Solicitor General Theodore Olson changed the picture substantially by asserting, early on, that in the government's view a library could accept federal Internet funds if it installed filtering software on every computer, *even if it had a policy of turning off the filter at the request of an adult patron automatically, no questions asked.*

Arguing for the plaintiffs that morning, I knew that this interpretation spelled trouble because the Court would be tempted to use it as a basis for upholding a law that probably meshed well with their basic assumption that "pornography" does not belong in the public library. I attempted to coun-

---

[20]*Id.* at 453.
[21]*Id.* at 490 n.36.
[22]*Id.* 484–89.

ter this interpretation in my argument in two ways. First, I pointed out that Congress quite clearly intended to signal to libraries that they had a duty to scrutinize patrons' purposes—to see if they were "bona fide"—before turning off the filters. Second, I noted that the government's new interpretation in no way addressed the stigma problem of requiring an adult to approach a librarian and ask to have to have the "porn filter" turned off. After all, if Congress really intended to give adult patrons a free and uninhibited choice, it could have mandated that libraries install *optional* filtering on some or all of their terminals. But it went further for an obvious purpose of attempting to coerce patrons into not asking to have the filters turned off.

Ultimately, the Court reversed the district court, upholding CIPA by a vote of 6-3.[23] Four of the justices joined in an opinion by Chief Justice Rehnquist that accepted the government's broad theory that CIPA does not demand any improper conduct by libraries, because libraries have just as much discretion to consider the content of the Internet sites they want to screen *out* as they do in considering the content of the books they want to acquire. In his words:

> A library's need to exercise judgment in making collection decisions depends on its traditional role in identifying suitable and worthwhile material: it is no less entitled to play that role when it collects material from the Internet than when it collects material from any other source. Most libraries already exclude pornography from their print collections because they deem it inappropriate for inclusion. We do not subject these decisions to heightened scrutiny: it would make little sense to treat libraries' judgments to block online pornography any differently, when these judgments are made for just the same reason.[24]

The Chief Justice added that it would be impractical for a library to affirmatively select each valuable site it wants to make available to patrons—as it does with books—because it would end up excluding much more material to voluminous to review.[25]

The Chief Justice also rejected the plaintiffs' second argument that CIPA imposes an unconstitutional condition on the exercise by libraries of their First Amendment right to decide whether to provide unfiltered Internet access. In so doing, he revived the position he had previously espoused in *Rust v. Sullivan*, that the First Amendment allows the government to limit in any way it wants the content of speech that it wants to subsidize. That holding in *Rust* had been repeatedly rejected in later cases, where the Court said that the government's ability to draw lines based on content applies only when the government or its agents are speaking, not when the government is sub-

---

[23]539 U.S. 194 (2003).
[24]*Id.* at 208.
[25]*Id.*

sidizing private speech.[26] But the Chief Justice's opinion paid no heed to these subsequent case law developments.[27]

In sum, if the Chief Justice's plurality opinion would have had a major impact on two basic First Amendment doctrines—the public-forum doctrine and the unconstitutional-conditions doctrine—if it had received support from a majority of the Court. But in fact, the final two justices voting to uphold CIPA—Justices Kennedy and Breyer—did not join in the Chief Justice's opinion or agree with his reasoning. Instead, they each said that the constitutional problems with CIPA had largely disappeared once the government interpreted the act as allowing libraries to give adults unfettered access to the Internet on request "no questions asked." As Justice Kennedy put it in the first line of his concurring opinion, "If, on the request of an adult user, a librarian will unblock filtered material or disable the Internet software filter without significant delay, there is little to this case. The Government represents this is indeed the fact."[28]

Justice Stevens wrote one of the dissenting opinions, taking the view that a library could choose to require filters on its terminals but cannot be forced to make the choice that Congress prefers through a condition on federal funding.[29] Justice Souter, joined by Justice Ginsburg, agreed with Justice Stevens about the unconstitutional-conditions argument, but disagreed about whether libraries on their own may impose filtering. He would have agreed with the district court and the plaintiffs on both points.[30]

Where this left matters was not entirely clear. But there is now a strong argument that five members of the Court would find CIPA unconstitutional if adults were not in fact given "no questions asked" unfiltered access. For that reason, our legal team and our clients who put substantial time and resources into this effort took some comfort that we had achieved a partial victory limiting the ability of the government to engage in selective content-based filtering when it provides a portal to the Internet. Future litigation is thus likely to be focused on particular library policies and practices.

Minors, however, are left with little in the way of a constitutional argument for a right to access materials that a library has chosen to filter out. As the testimony at the trial made clear, that will be detrimental in some cases to those teenagers seeking to learn about controversial topics, because commercially available filters tend to filter out not only "pornography" but also sites dealing with homosexuality, sex education, and the like. Indeed, two

---

[26]*See* Legal Services Corp. v. Velazquez, 531 U.S. 533, 541 (2001) (reviewing later cases analyzing meaning of Rust).
[27]*See Id.* at 210–13.
[28]*Id.* at 214.
[29]*Id.* at 220–31.
[30]*Id.* at 231–43.

young witnesses who talked about how important it had been for them to be able to obtain confidential and uncensored Internet access during times of private crisis clearly impressed the district court, which referred to them several times in the opinion.[31] Some libraries, noting this potential problem, have refused federal Internet funding in order to avoid the strictures of CIPA. Others, however, have agreed to comply with Congress' judgment that the need to protect children outweighs the resulting interference with their access to important information.

A RETURN TO REGULATING WEB SITES DIRECTLY: THE CHILD ONLINE PROTECTION ACT

As noted earlier, the Congress reacted to the invalidation of the CDA by attempting to fix the problems identified by the Court. It did so in the Child Online Protection Act (COPA),[32] which paralleled the CDA by making it a crime to making certain "adult" content available on the Internet without putting the content behind a screen requiring a credit card number or an adult ID. The difference is that the new law applied only to commercial Web sites and only to content sufficiently explicit and sufficiently lacking in redeeming value to fall in the category called "harmful to minors."

More specifically, COPA provides in relevant part:

(1) PROHIBITED CONDUCT—Whoever knowingly and with knowledge of the character of the material, in interstate or foreign commerce by means of the World Wide Web, makes any communication for commercial purposes that is available to any minor and that includes any material that is harmful to minors shall be fined not more than $50,000, imprisoned not more than 6 months, or both.

A "communication for commercial purpose" is made only "if such person is engaged in the business of making such communication."[33] A person is "engaged in business" if:

[The] person who makes a communication, or offers to make a communication, by means of the World Wide Web, that includes any material that is harmful to minors, devotes time, attention, or labor to such activities, as a regular course of such person's trade or business, with the objective of earning a profit as a result of such activities (although it is not necessary that the person make a profit or that the making or offering to make such communications be the person's sole or principal business or source of income). A person may be considered to be engaged in business of making, by means of the World Wide Web, communications for commercial purposes that include material that is harmful to minors, only if the person knowingly causes the

---

[31]*See, e.g.,* 201 F. Supp. 2d 401, 406 (E.D. Pa. 2002).
[32]47 U.S.C. § 231.
[33]*Id.* at § 231(e)(2)(A).

material that is harmful to minors to be posted on the World Wide Web or knowingly solicits such material to be posted on the World Wide Web.[34]

Material harmful to minors is defined as:

Any communication, picture, image, graphic image file, article, recording, writing, or other matter of any kind that is obscene or that—
(A) the average person, applying contemporary community standards, would find, taking the material as a whole and with respect to minors is designed to appeal to, or is designed to pander to, the prurient interest;
(B) depicts, describes, or represents, in a manner patently offensive with respect to minors, an actual or simulated sexual act or sexual contact, or an actual or simulated normal or perverted sexual act, or a lewd exhibition of the genitals or post-pubescent female breast; and
(C) taken as a whole, lacks serious literary, artistic, political, or scientific value for minors.[35]

COPA provides the same basic affirmative defenses that appeared in the CDA—allowing the defendant who the offending material was screened from access by a requirement that the user supply an adult ID or a credit card number.[36]

As it happened, I did not have a substantial amount of personal involvement with the challenge to COPA, which was handled by the same able lawyers from the ACLU with whom we teamed so well in the CDA and CIPA cases. It is an understatement to say that the courts have had major difficulty figuring out what to do with this new attempt to regulate sexually explicit content on the Web. In 1999, Internet content providers and other plaintiffs represented by the ACLU challenged COPA under the First Amendment, once again in the Eastern District of Pennsylvania. That same year,[37] the district court entered a preliminary injunction against the enforcement of COPA. As a content-based restriction on speech, the Court deemed COPA presumptively invalid and subject to strict scrutiny. The district court held that plaintiffs were likely to prevail on arguments that COPA "imposes a burden on speech that is protected for adults,"[38] and that there were fewer speech restrictive alternatives available—particularly filtering and blocking software.[39] Furthermore, the court held that plaintiffs had demonstrated irreparable harm if denied a preliminary injunction:

---

[34]*Id.* at § 231(e)(2)(B).

[35]*Id.* at § 231(e)(6).

[36]*Id.* at § 231(c).

[37]ACLU v. Reno, 31 F.Supp.2d 473 (E.D. Pa. 1999).

[38]*Id.* at 495 ("The plaintiffs are likely to establish at trial that under COPA, Web site operators and content-providers may feel an economic disincentive to engage in communications that are or may be considered to be harmful to minors and thus, may self-censor the content of their sites.").

[39]*Id.* at 497.

The plaintiffs have uniformly testified or declared that their fears of prose-cution under COPA will result in self-censorship of their online materials in an effort to avoid prosecution, and this Court has concluded in resolution of the motion to dismiss that such fears are reasonable given the breadth of the statute. Such chilling effect could result in the censoring of constitutionally protected speech, which constitutes an irreparable harm to the plaintiffs.[40]

In 2000, the Third Circuit affirmed the district court's grant of a prelimi-nary injunction.[41] That court held that COPA's use of "contemporary com-munity standards" to determine whether materials would be harmful to minors renders the statute overbroad as applied to the Internet. "Pub-lishers would be compelled to abide by the 'standards of the community most likely to be offended by the message.'"[42] This would "impose an over-reaching burden and restriction on constitutionally protected speech."[43] The court further held that COPA was not "readily susceptible" to a narrow-ing construction that would make it constitutional.[44] Two possibly limiting interpretations—assigning a narrow meaning to the language of the statute itself, or deleting the portion of the statute that is unconstitutional—were rejected by the court as unfeasible.[45]

In 2002, the Supreme Court reviewed the Third Circuit decision in *Ashcroft v. American Civil Liberties Union I.*[46] A plurality vacated the decision by the Third Circuit and remanded, holding that use of "contemporary community standards" to identify material that is harmful to minors does not, by itself, render the statute substantially overbroad under the First Amendment. Justice Thomas announced the opinion of the Court. Unlike the CDA, COPA incorporates a definition of harmful material that "paral-lels" the *Miller* test for obscenity.[47] "When the scope of an obscenity statute's coverage is sufficiently narrowed by a 'serious value' prong and a 'prurient interest' prong, we have held that requiring a speaker disseminating mate-rial to a national audience to observe varying community standards does not violate the First Amendment."[48] Justice Thomas stressed that the "unique characteristics" of the Internet do not justify adopting a standard of review different from speakers in more traditional media.

Justice O'Connor concurred in part, and in the judgment. Justice O'Connor would have preferred that the Court adopt a national standard for judging obscenity on the Internet, however she agreed that the ACLU

---

[40]*Id.*

[41]ACLU v. Reno, 217 F.3d 162 (3d Cir. 2000).

[42]*Id.* at 177 (citing Reno v. American Civil Liberties Union, 521 U.S. at 877–78).

[43]*Id.*

[44]*Id.*

[45]*Id.* at 179.

[46]535 U.S. 563 (2002).

[47]*Id.* at 578.

[48]*Id.* at 580 (citing Hamling v. United States, 518 U.S. 87 (1974)).

failed to demonstrate substantial overbreadth on the face of the statute based "solely on variations between local communities."[49]

Justice Kennedy, joined by Justices Souter and Ginsburg, concurred in judgment. Justice Kennedy agreed with the majority that the use of "contemporary community standards" language does not *by itself* render the statute overbroad. However, "the extent of the speech covered and the variation in community standards with respect to that speech" may *in fact* render the statute overbroad.[50] Thus, the Third Circuit was asked to undertake a comprehensive analysis in the first instance.

Justice Stevens, in dissent, argued that the "unique characteristics" of the Web medium—namely the inability of Web speakers to limit access to specific communities—renders COPA "substantially overbroad regardless of how its other provisions are construed."[51]

On remand in 2003, the Third Circuit once again affirmed the district court's issuance of a preliminary injunction against the enforcement of COPA.[52] The court held that plaintiffs had demonstrated a substantial likelihood of prevailing on claims that COPA was not narrowly tailored to a compelling government interest and that the statute was overbroad.

Several provisions of COPA, the court found, were insufficiently tailored. The term "minor," defined as "any person under 17 years of age,"[53] "applies in a literal sense to an infant, a five-year old, or a person just shy of age seventeen."[54] This creates great uncertainty for Internet speakers in determining whether their speech can be considered "harmful to minors," and chills a large body of protected speech. The limitation to "commercial purposes" was found to subject "too wide a range of Web publishers to potential liability."[55] Finally, the affirmative defenses were held to overburden protected speech, and lacked narrow tailoring because of the availability of less restrictive filtering and blocking technology.

The court then held that the statute was substantially overbroad because it "encroaches upon a significant amount of protected speech beyond that which the government may target constitutionally."[56] The court used a museum Web site and an informational safe-sex Web site as examples of speech protected under the First Amendment but deemed "harmful to minors" under COPA.[57] Again the Third Circuit determined that no narrowing construction was available.

---

[49]*Id.* at 589 (O'Connor, J., concurring).
[50]*Id.* at 597–98 (Kennedy, J., concurring).
[51]*Id.* 1726–27 (Stevens, J., dissenting).
[52]322 F.3d 240 (3d Cir. 2003).
[53]47 U.S.C. § 321(e)(6)(C)
[54]322 F.2d at 254.
[55]*Id.* at 256.
[56]*Id.* at 266–67.
[57]*Id.* 267–68.

In 2004, for the second time in three years, the Supreme Court had occasion to review COPA. Once again, the issue facing the Court was whether to affirm a Third Circuit decision upholding the issuance of a preliminary injunction against the enforcement of the statute. It looked like we would finally get a definitive answer to the question whether the rights of adults to access protected speech anonymously on the Internet could be abridged in order to protect minors from inadvertent or unsupervised access. And as I sat there in the courtroom that day listening to the able oral arguments of Ann Beeson from the ACLU and Solicitor General Olson, I thought the answer was clear as well. Justice Breyer made it very clear during the argument that the answer for him was already decided. He believed that adults could constitutionally be required to give up some degree of free access to sexually explicit material in order to protect minors. Given the clarity of this announcement it was difficult for me at least to forecast a way for the plaintiffs to muster five votes to affirm.

But as often happens with the Supreme Court, my prognostications proved wrong. In a five-to-four decision, the Court affirmed the preliminary injunction and remanded the case so that it may be returned to the district court for trial, as Justice Thomas somewhat surprisingly joined the majority.[58]

The majority opinion, authored by Justice Kennedy and joined by Justices Stevens, Souter, and Ginsburg as well as Thomas, reached the same result as the Third Circuit but on narrower grounds. It thus did not fully resolve the question we had all been debating since the passage of the CDA back in 1996, although it came awfully close. The Court held that the district court did not abuse its discretion in deciding to preliminarily enjoin the enforcement of COPA pending a full trial, and it remanded for such a trial. The Court reasoned that the government had failed to meet its burden of proof that there were no plausible, less restrictive alternatives to COPA. Justice Kennedy reasoned that available blocking and filtering software may turn out after a trial to be both less speech restrictive and more effective at restricting children's access to harmful materials. Filters allow users to impose restrictions on the receiving end of speech, rather than allowing the government to place a blanket restriction on the source of speech. Furthermore, filters can be applied to all forms of Internet content including e-mail, and internationally posted materials, whereas COPA protects only against access to domestically posted materials on the World Wide Web. Although Justice Kennedy suggests that the Congress could not require families to use filtering software in their homes, it could pass legislation encouraging them to do so. The case was remanded to the district court for both sides to litigate the issue of whether blocking or filtering software is truly a less restrictive alternative to COPA.

---

[58]124 S. Ct. 2783 (2004).

Interestingly, in the course of saying that optional filtering may be a more effective means of dealing with minors' access to adult material than censorship of Web speakers, Justice Kennedy made the very same argument that he had previously rejected on the bench during the CDA argument. There Bruce Ennis argued that attempting to censor Web speakers would be futile because a large percentage of Web sites were already operating from overseas and more could be shifted there almost instantly. Justice Kennedy indicated he found that argument singularly unpersuasive, but he made precisely the same point in the course of saying why COPA was probably a wrong-headed approach.[59] As one who had strongly urged that argument back in 1996–1997, I found some vindication in that switch—particularly because the problem of foreign sites now appears to present an insoluble problem to those who would defend this kind of content-based regulation of Web speakers.

Justice Stevens, joined by Justice Ginsburg, filed a concurring opinion. Justice Stevens would have upheld the preliminary injunction on the additional basis that criminal prosecutions are an "inappropriate means to regulate the universe of materials classified as 'obscene.'" According to Justice Stevens, the line between obscene and nonobscene material is too blurred to support a criminal charge.

Justice Breyer wrote a dissenting opinion joined by Chief Justice Rehnquist and Justice O'Connor. Justice Breyer reasoned that COPA imposes only a modest burden on protected speech. The language of the statute very closely traces the test for obscenity in *Miller v. California*[60] and therefore regulates "very little more" than unprotected obscene speech. At the same time, it significantly helps to achieve a compelling congressional goal—protecting children from exposure to commercial pornography. Applying the least restrictive means test, Justice Breyer finds that filtering and blocking software "does not solve the 'child protection' problem," because it suffers from four serious inadequacies: It underblocks, imposes a cost upon each family that uses it, fails to screen outside the home, and lacks precision. Under Justice Breyer's reasoning, the government has established that COPA is the least restrictive means to protect children from harmful material on the Internet, and therefore the district court's preliminary injunction was inappropriate.

Justice Scalia wrote a dissenting opinion, arguing that COPA only regulates commercial pornography—an area of speech not protected under the First Amendment.

SO WHERE ARE WE NOW?

The latest COPA ruling, by its very nature, is not conclusive with regard to how the Supreme Court will draw the balance between protecting minors and

[59]*Id.* at 2792.
[60]413 U.S. 15, 24 (1973).

preserving the freedoms of adults. But the Court went a long way toward a final decision that, in this area, parents must take responsibility and utilize the tools that are available to establish limits on access to controversial material that satisfy the family's own standards. The primary tool is some form of filtering software. Although the evidence on remand at the COPA trial will no doubt show that filters are imperfect—that they still underblock adult material and overblock a great deal of innocuous material—it will also show that regulating Web speakers will be much more ineffective. Difficulties of enforcement, compounded by the fact that a Web site can be posted anywhere in the world and be immediately accessible everywhere, mean that this will likely never be a fruitful approach. Moreover, efforts to extend American law to foreign-based Web sites are bound, ultimately, to lead to problems when other countries attempt to apply to American Web speakers limitations that would never be tolerated under the First Amendment.

So the way of the future is training parents to do a better job and training children to protect themselves and respect limits on where they will go on the Web, while tailoring environments in schools and libraries so children cannot evade parental supervision in those locales. There simply is no other practical alternative. It is not a perfect solution, but technology in this instance will have the final say.

Chapter 9

THE PAST, PRESENT, AND FUTURE OF INTERNET CENSORSHIP AND FREE SPEECH ADVOCACY

John B. Morris, Jr.*

EDITOR'S INTRODUCTION

So where will the future battleground(s) of the First Amendment be? As suggested by the previous chapter, Internet expression may be the issue that attracts the most attention in the first half of the 21st century. As a new medium, the Internet is a setting likely to be the focus of a tug-of-war attempting to shape the boundaries of acceptable content. At the conclusion of the previous century and into the present, repeated efforts were made to proscribe specific kinds of content on computer-mediated communication formats. Virtually without exception, these legislative efforts were ruled unconstitutional. And virtually without exception, lawmakers were unrelenting in their endeavors to craft measures that could withstand constitutional challenges.

Among those intimately familiar with this struggle is John Morris. He was not only a member of the team of attorneys involved with some of the cases at the heart of these issues, he is now the Director of the Internet Standards, Technology and Policy Project at the Center for Democracy & Technology (CDT) in Washington, D.C.

---

*Director, Internet Standards, Technology and Policy Project, Center for Democracy & Technology, Washington, DC. Prior to joining CDT in April 2001, Mr. Morris was a partner in the law firm of Jenner & Block, where he litigated groundbreaking cases in Internet and First Amendment law, including *American Library Association v. U.S. Dep't of Justice*, the companion case to *ACLU v. Reno*.

CDT, in its own words, works to promote democratic values in the digital age. It seeks to enhance free expression in global-communication technologies.

In this concluding chapter, Mr. Morris traces the history and contemplates the future of this First Amendment conflict. The history extends all the way back to the mid-1990s when the Internet was in its infancy and faced its first attempt of content regulation. The future is now and beyond. As with other media (U.S. broadcasting, for example), it is the technology itself and how its ramifications are interpreted, he suggests, that may ultimately drive the debate—and the resolutions.

*   *   *

In the 1996 district court decision in the landmark *Reno v. ACLU* case overturning the Communications Decency Act (CDA), Judge Stewart Dalzell aptly characterized the nature of the Internet as a medium of free speech:

> It is no exaggeration to conclude that the Internet has achieved, and continues to achieve, the most participatory marketplace of mass speech that this country—and indeed the world—has yet seen. The plaintiffs in these actions correctly describe the "democratizing" effects of Internet communication: individual citizens of limited means can speak to a worldwide audience on issues of concern to them. Federalists and Anti-Federalists may debate the structure of their government nightly, but these debates occur in newsgroups or chat rooms rather than in pamphlets. Modern-day Luthers still post their theses, but to electronic bulletin boards rather than the door of the Wittenberg Schlosskirche. More mundane (but from a constitutional perspective, equally important) dialogue occurs between aspiring artists, or French cooks, or dog lovers, or fly fishermen.[1]

As Judge Dalzell concluded, the "Internet is a far more speech-enhancing medium than print, the village green, or the mails."[2] In his decision, he identified the key aspects of the Internet that has made it such a speech-enhancing medium:

> Four related characteristics of Internet communication have a transcendent importance to our shared holding that the CDA is unconstitutional on its face. We explain these characteristics in our Findings of fact above, and I only rehearse them briefly here. First, the Internet presents very low barriers to entry. Second, these barriers to entry are identical for both speakers and listeners. Third, as a result of these low barriers, astoundingly diverse content is available on the

---

[1]American Civil Liberties Union v. Reno, 929 F. Supp. 824, 881 (E.D. Pa. 1996) (available at http://www.ciec.org/victory.shtml).

[2]*Id.* at 882 (Dalzell concurring).

Internet. Fourth, the Internet provides significant access to all who wish to speak in the medium, and even creates a relative parity among speakers.[3]

The Internet is in the process of truly revolutionizing global society. Although there are enormous economic, societal, and technical hurdles that must be overcome to eliminate a "digital divide" separating Internet-haves from Internet-have-nots—both across the country and around the world—the Internet has already had a huge impact in terms of facilitating free speech.

But as with every communications medium throughout history,[4] free speech on the Internet has been closely followed by efforts to regulate and censor speech on the "Net." And the censorship of the Internet has led, in the United States, to First Amendment challenges to keep speech on the Internet free from governmental interference. But just as the Internet itself has grown and evolved by leaps and bounds over a very short period of time—at the high speed of "Internet time"—so have the legal and nonlegal efforts to defend free speech on the Internet evolved. And perhaps not surprisingly for a communications medium that is so inherently based on *technology,* the defenses of free speech have increasingly had to focus on and address the technology on which the Internet is built.

This chapter looks at three different "defenses" of Internet free speech in which I have been involved, focusing first on the early precedent-setting *Reno v. ACLU* litigation in 1996 and 1997. The *Reno* case is then contrasted with a 2004 case overturning a Pennsylvania state regulation of the Internet, and with a wholly different kind of defense of Internet free speech, taking place not in a courtroom but within the engineering community responsible for designing the "protocols" on which the Internet is based.

In looking at these three efforts to protect free speech, the increasingly technical nature of the challenges to the First Amendment becomes clear. Coupled with this reality is the fact that to defend free speech in the future, advocates need to move beyond the courtroom to ensure that the Internet of tomorrow is as open and unfettered as the Internet of today.

THE COMMUNICATIONS DECENCY ACT LITIGATION: DEFINING THE FIRST AMENDMENT STANDARD FOR THE INTERNET

Signed into law as a part of the broader Telecommunications Act of 1996, the Communications Decency Act (CDA) was the first attempt by the U.S. Congress to directly regulate speech on the Internet. The most problematic pro-

---

[3]*Id.* at 877 (Dalzell concurring).
[4]*See, e.g.,* TOM STANDAGE, THE VICTORIAN INTERNET: THE REMARKABLE STORY OF THE TELEGRAPH AND THE NINETEENTH CENTURY'S ON-LINE PIONEERS (1999).

vision of the CDA made it a crime to "display" on the Internet "in a manner available to" minors, certain content deemed to be "patently offensive."[5] Although "patently offensive" was not defined, the term clearly covered material that was wholly lawful for adults to publish and receive. Web site operators, however, had (and still have today) no effective way to prevent minors from accessing their Web sites while still making those Web sites broadly available to the global Internet. Thus, the effect of the CDA would have been to reduce the content of the Internet to a level suitable for children.[6]

The Legal Challenges to the CDA

The day the CDA was signed into law—February 8, 1996—the American Civil Liberties Union (ACLU) filed a constitutional challenge in the U.S. District Court for the Eastern District of Pennsylvania, in Philadelphia. The plaintiffs in *ACLU v. Reno* sought and, on February 15, obtained a temporary restraining order (TRO) blocking enforcement of key portions of the CDA.[7] In his memorandum decision on the TRO application, Judge Ronald Buckwalter recognized that the ACLU plaintiffs published a wide range of protected expression on the Internet, including "communications [that] deal with issues involving sexuality, reproduction, human rights, social responsibility, environmental concerns, labor, conflict resolution, as well as other issues, all of which have significant educational, political, medical, artistic, literary and social value."[8] Judge Buckwalter concluded that the ACLU plaintiffs' free speech would in fact be chilled by the CDA, and that the plaintiffs were likely to succeed in their legal challenge of the law.[9]

The plaintiff group in the ACLU lawsuit represented a broad range of 19 organizations and speakers, many of them with Web sites that address topics

---

[5]The critical statutory language is:
   (d) Whoever—
      (1) in interstate or foreign communications knowingly—
        ...
      (B) uses any interactive computer service to display in a manner available to a person under 18 years of age, any comment, request, suggestion, proposal, image, or other communication that, in context, depicts or describes, in terms patently offensive as measured by contemporary community standards, sexual or excretory activities or organs, regardless of whether the user of such service placed the call or initiated the communication; ... shall be fined under title 18, United States Code, or imprisoned not more than two years, or both.
   CDA § 502(2).
[6]Other provisions of the CDA raised similar constitutional problems and were invalidated in the legal challenges. Still other provisions—criminalizing the sending of "obscene" material over the Internet—were not challenged and thus remain in force.
[7]*See* Order, ACLU v. Reno, No. 96-963 (E.D. Pa. Feb. 15, 1996), available at http://www.aclu.org/CriminalJustice/CriminalJustice.cfm?ID=14099&c=49.
[8]*See* Memorandum, *ACLU v. Reno*, No. 96-963 (E.D. Pa. Feb. 15, 1996), available at http://www.aclu.org/CriminalJustice/CriminalJustice.cfm?ID=14099&c=49.
[9]*Id.*

that some segments of society would view as controversial or offensive. In addition to advocacy groups such as the Electronic Frontier Foundation and the Electronic Privacy Information Center, the ACLU plaintiffs included, for example, the Critical Path AIDS Project (operating a Web site with information on safe sex and AIDS), Human Rights Watch (documenting, among other issues, sexual abuse around the world), the Queer Resources Directory (linking online resources for the gay and lesbian community), Stop Prisoner Rape (addressing rape of people while incarcerated), and the Wildcat Press (an independent publisher of gay and lesbian literature).[10]

At the same time that the ACLU legal challenge was gearing up, a second challenge to the CDA was coalescing. The initial and primary focus of the ACLU's complaint and its motion for a TRO[11] was on the important, yet sometimes controversial, speech that would be suppressed by the CDA. Other opponents of the CDA had a significantly different priority: concern about governmental interference with the Internet as an emerging communications medium. Two groups of organizations in particular were concerned primarily about the unfettered development of the Internet: the mainstream American publishing and content distribution community, and the Internet industry itself. These and other groups came together as the "Citizens Internet Empowerment Coalition" (CIEC) to initiate a second legal challenge to the CDA.

CIEC was organized and managed by the Center for Democracy and Technology (CDT), the American Library Association (ALA), and America Online (AOL).[12] Joining the ALA as named plaintiffs in the legal challenge were, among others, the American Booksellers Association, the Association of American Publishers, the Magazine Publishers of America, and the Newspaper Association of America. From the Internet industry, in addition to AOL, Apple Computer, CompuServe, Microsoft Corporation, Prodigy, and others joined as named plaintiffs.[13]

In seeking to hire attorneys for their legal challenge, the CIEC organizers looked for both significant experience in First Amendment challenges as well as technical knowledge of the Internet. CIEC retained Bruce Ennis, Ann Kappler, and me—from the Washington office of Jenner & Block—to bring a second challenge to the CDA. Ennis, who passed away in 2000, was

---

[10]*See* Complaint, ACLU v. Reno (filed Feb. 8, 1996), available at http://www.epic.org/ free_speech/censorship/lawsuit/complaint.html.

[11]*See* Plaintiffs' Memorandum of Law in Support of a Motion for a Temporary Restraining Order and Preliminary Injunction, ACLU v. Reno (filed Feb. 8, 1996), available at http://www.aclu.org/Privacy/Privacy.cfm?ID=14101&c=252.

[12]*See* CDT Policy Post 2.7 (Feb. 26, 1996), available at http://www.cdt.org/publications/ pp_2.7.html.

[13]Although CompuServe and Prodigy are no longer household names, in 1996 AOL, CompuServe, Microsoft, and Prodigy represented the leading online-services providers in the United States.

one of the leading Supreme Court and First Amendment lawyers in the country, having argued numerous cases before the High Court, including important free-speech cases. I had worked with computers since the early 1970s, had co-founded a successful computer company in 1985, and had used the Internet since the mid-1980s. The Jenner & Block team also had significant experience challenging federal government efforts to suppress sexually oriented expression.[14]

The second challenge to the CDA, titled *American Library Association v. U.S. Dep't of Justice,* was filed on February 26, 1996, in the Philadelphia U.S. District Court, the same court before which the *ACLU v. Reno* challenge was pending. The differing focus of the *ALA* challenge was clear from the first paragraph of the complaint:

> 1. During much of this century the mass media, particularly radio and television, have been characterized by a limited number of speakers transmitting programming and information to essentially passive audiences. The communications medium of the twenty-first century—the Internet and "cyberspace" generally—is changing that, and will allow hundreds of millions of individuals to engage in interactive communication, on a national and global scale never before possible. The public square of the past—with pamphleteering, soap boxes, and vigorous debate—is being replaced by the Internet, which enables average citizens to participate in national discourse, publish a newspaper, distribute an electronic pamphlet to the world, and generally communicate to and with a broader audience than ever before possible. It also enables average citizens to gain access to a vast and literally world-wide range of information, while simultaneously protecting their privacy, because in this new medium individuals receive only the communications they affirmatively request.[15]

One day later, the two legal challenges were consolidated by the Eastern District of Pennsylvania for purposes of trial.

From that point on, the Jenner & Block trial team worked closely with the lead ACLU lawyers, Chris Hansen, Ann Beeson, and Margorie Heins (the author of this volume's chap. 4). Although the two groups of plaintiffs had somewhat differing interests and agendas, and not all legal claims were raised in both cases, the two teams of lawyers had a very symbiotic and successful working relationship, with the work being roughly divided between two groups of lawyers consistently with the focuses of the two complaints. The ACLU lawyers had primary responsibility for establishing that important speech was directly threatened by the CDA, whereas the ALA lawyers

---

[14]*See, e.g.,* PHE, Inc. v. United States Dep't of Justice, 743 F. Supp. 15 (D.D.C. 1990); United States v. P.H.E., Inc., 965 F.2d 848, 856 (10th Cir. 1992).

[15]*See* Complaint, ALA v. U.S. Dep't of Justice (filed Feb. 26, 1996), available at http://www.ciec.org/trial/complaint/complaint.html.

had primary responsibility for establishing the technical nature of the Internet and the threat to the Internet posed by the CDA.[16]

Because Congress knew that the CDA would spark legal challenges, it created special procedures to resolve the cases.[17] The consolidated actions were set for an expedited hearing before a three-judge panel consisting of Judge Dolores Sloviter, then Chief Judge of the Third Circuit Court of Appeals, and Judges Ronald Buckwalter and Stewart Dalzell of the Philadelphia District Court. The decision of this three-judge panel could be appealed directly to the U.S. Supreme Court.

Introducing the Court to the Internet

A paramount goal was to educate the three-judge panel about how the Internet worked, and how the CDA would impact speakers on the Internet. Although today many judges (and virtually all judicial law clerks) are familiar with the Internet, in 1996 the Internet was a much newer phenomenon, and none of the three judges had "surfed" the World Wide Web (Judges Sloviter and Dalzell had used e-mail). To address the plaintiffs' concerns about the CDA, the judges needed to understand how communications over the Internet took place, and the limited ability of publishers on the Internet to control who accesses content on the World Wide Web.

More fundamentally, however, the very nature of the Internet as a communications medium was directly at issue in the case. In analyzing the constitutional validity of Congressional efforts to restrict speech, the Supreme Court has made clear that "differences in the characteristics of [particular communications] media justify differences in the First Amendment standards applied to them."[18] Over the years, the Supreme Court had concluded that a less stringent standard of First Amendment analysis could be applied to regulations of television and other broadcast media.

From its initial substantive filing in the case, the U.S. Department of Justice had staked out its argument that the Internet should be regulated like broadcast, and should thus receive a lower level of constitutional protection. According to the government, Congress had made clear its view that any court interpreting the CDA could be "guided by a substantial body of First Amendment case law in the area of broadcasting (radio and television), cable television, and telephone communications."[19] Thus, the most critical question for the courts to decide was whether the Internet could be

---

[16]Within the ALA litigation team, I had primary responsibility for the development and presentation of the technical evidence placed before the court.

[17]*See* section 561 of the CDA, Pub. L. No. 104-104, § 561, 110 Stat. 143.

[18]Red Lion Broadcasting v. Federal Communications Comm'n, 395 U.S. 367, 386 (1969).

[19]Defendant's Opposition to Plaintiffs' Motion for a Temporary Restraining Order, *ACLU v. Reno* (filed Feb. 14, 1996), available at http://www.law.miami.edu/~froomkin/seminar/ACLU-Reno-TRO-Justice-brief.htm.

regulated like the broadcast media, or whether speech on the Internet would receive the same level of constitutional protection as that afforded to printed speech (and thus be essentially unregulated).

The effort to educate the court began with the complaints filed in the two consolidated cases. Although the ACLU complaint emphasized the speech harmed by the CDA, it also introduced the court to the Internet. The ALA complaint, filed about 3 weeks later, was at its core a technical introduction to the Internet. The 73-page ALA complaint—which the *Washington Post* called "wonkish"[20]—traced the historical development of the Internet, and set out in detail how users access the Internet, what methods of communication they have available on the Internet, and how the CDA would impact on Internet communications. This complaint formed the foundation of what became the parties' joint stipulations of fact, and ultimately a major part of the three-judge panel's formal findings of fact.

Following the late-February consolidation of the two cases for purposes of the evidentiary hearing, the parties entered into an intense 4-week period of expedited depositions and other discovery.[21] Also during this period, the CIEC coalition arranged to "wire the courtroom" by bringing a high-speed Internet access line into the courtroom and linking seven video screens so that the three judges, the two sides of the litigation, and the public could see the Internet content displayed during live testimony. Although "technology courtrooms" are now common around the country today, to our knowledge this case was the first time a courtroom was wired to provide all participants direct viewing of testimony demonstrating Internet access. With joint factual stipulations submitted by the parties but discovery continuing interspersed with the trial days, the three-judge court received 5 days of testimony from March 21 to April 15, 1996.

A critical element of the plaintiffs' case was the technical explanation of how the Internet works, conveyed primarily through the testimony of a variety of expert witnesses. Plaintiffs' first witness and lead technical expert was Scott Bradner, an early pioneer of the Internet and a leader within the Internet Engineering Task Force, the technical engineering body that manages the development of the key technical standards and protocols on which the Internet is based. Bradner provided a detailed written declaration explaining Internet communications and the likely impact of the CDA on those communications, and he testified on both March 21 and 22, 1996.[22]

---

[20]John Schwartz, *Coalition to File Suit Over Internet Rules: Action Targets New Law as Unconstitutional*, WASH. POST, Feb. 26, 1996, at A4.

[21]"Discovery" is the period of time early in litigations when both sides in a case can learn the facts about the other side's arguments, and can usually interrogate the relevant witnesses (through "depositions").

[22]Bradner's declaration is available at http://www.sobco.com/papers/cda.html, and his (and other's) trial testimony is available at http://www.ciec.org/transcripts/.

From early in Bradner's testimony, it became clear that the judges were eager to gain as good an understanding of Internet communications as possible, and Bradner provided precisely the type of testimony needed. With a bushy white beard and a gentle, precise, and professorial manner, Bradner both looked and sounded like the archetypal Internet geek. He and the judges established the type of rapport that litigators dream of, and Bradner was able to answer all of the questions raised by the court. In particular, Judge Stewart Dalzell was the judge most actively exploring the technical details of the Internet, and consequently most active in dialogue with Bradner.

Other technical, industry, and academic witnesses filled in the factual picture of the Internet and the CDA's likely impact on Internet communications. Albert Vezza, chairman of the World Wide Web Consortium, testified on behalf of plaintiffs to explain the fundamentals of the World Wide Web and possible approaches for parents and other Internet users to prevent the display of sexual or other unwanted content on the Internet. Similarly, Ann Duvall, the president of Surfwatch Software, testified about user controls over Internet content, as did William Burrington of America Online. Professor Donna Hoffman testified about the experience of "surfing" the World Wide Web from a user's perspective, and explained the negative impact that the CDA would have on that experience.

On top of this technical and factual introduction to Internet communications presented to the three judges, plaintiffs also presented the critical other half of the evidentiary picture—the valuable speech that would be suppressed by the CDA. This testimony ranged from the operators of specific web sites with important but controversial content to the director of the Carnegie Library in Pittsburgh, which would be unable afford to screen all of its online material for compliance with the CDA. The chief executive of the online publication *Hotwired* explained how the user verification requirements of the CDA would directly inhibit many of *Hotwired*'s readers, and would thereby reduce the publication's viability as an ongoing concern.

Fundamentally, the consolidated team of litigators representing the ACLU and ALA plaintiffs achieved four fundamental goals in the evidentiary hearing. First, the plaintiffs gave the judges a crash course in the Internet and the nature of communications over it. Second, the court understood the vital speech that would be harmed by the CDA. Third, plaintiffs showed how, in technical and practical terms, the CDA would in fact harm speech. And finally, the ALA plaintiffs in particular highlighted alternative ways for parents, and ultimately the government, to shield users from undesired Internet content.

The Decision and Appeal

In a 175-page decision issued on June 12, 1996 (after mid-May closing arguments), the three-judge panel of the U.S. District Court for the Eastern

District of Pennsylvania unanimously declared the CDA to be unconstitutional and granted plaintiffs' motion for an injunction against the law.[23] As
one journalist described the decision:

> Hunched behind computer terminals, they presided over what was probably
> the first Internet surfing session in a Federal courtroom.
>
> They sat through days of dense testimony littered with cutting edge com-
> puter jargon—phrases like "uniform resource locator" and "hypertext
> markup language."
>
> They even endured a courtroom computer crash.
>
> For almost three months, three Federal judges, all neophytes to the world of
> on-line communications, took an unusual journey to learn the ins and outs of
> cyberspace. So it was only appropriate that they should bring their trail-blaz-
> ing constitutional case to an unusual conclusion: Instead of taking the typical
> path of writing one opinion that spoke for the court, the judges ruled unani-
> mously that the Communications Decency Act was unconstitutional—and
> then each wrote an individual opinion explaining why.[24]

For somewhat differing but overlapping reasons, each of the three
judges concluded that the CDA was unconstitutional, holding that the CDA
would chill protected expression on the Internet. Of the three judges,
Judge Dalzell's focus was most directly on the potential of the new communications medium of the Internet to democratize free speech and to allow
small speakers to reach vast global audiences.

One of the threshold, and most pivotal, legal determinations made by
the three-judge district court panel would become a key issue in the government's direct appeal to the U.S. Supreme Court: whether the Internet
should receive the full protection of the First Amendment (like printed
speech) or whether it could be more easily regulated along the lines of the
broadcast media. Judge Dalzell and Chief Judge Sloviter most squarely addressed this question, and declared that speech on the Internet should be
protected at least as much as speech in print (and to Dalzell's thinking, possibly even more).

On the government's appeal to the U.S. Supreme Court, this was the central question, and the answer turned most fundamentally on the technical
facts that the lower three-judge panel had found. The government continued to press its argument that the Internet was most closely analogized to
the broadcast media, in part simply because both the Internet and television had the capability to display video and sound. But unlike broadcast
spectrum, communications over the Internet did not use a scarce resource
that could appropriately be regulated by the government. Moreover,

---

[23]The trial court decision, ACLU v. Reno, 929 F. Supp. 824 (E.D. Pa. 1996), is available at
http://www.ciec.org/decision_PA/decision_text.html.

[24]Pamela Mendels, "3 Judges. 3 Voices. 1 Conclusion.," NYTimes.com, June 13, 1996,
available at http://www.nytimes.com/library/cyber/week/0613decency.html.

Internet content does not flow "unbidden" into a user's home simply by turning on a computer—users must take action to access Internet content. The Supreme Court declared that the lower court was correct in deciding that "our cases provide no basis for qualifying the level of First Amendment scrutiny that should be applied to this medium."[25]

The Legacy of the Communications Decency Act

In two largely unrelated ways, the CDA has played a crucial—and ongoing—part in the development of free speech on the Internet.

First, as discussed previously, the CDA set the stage to answer the most important threshold question of what First Amendment standards would apply to the Internet. At a simplistic level, analogizing the Internet to television seemed plausible, but first the three-judge court in Philadelphia and then the nine Justices of the Supreme Court were able to take the time to understand Internet technology, and understand how fundamentally different the Internet is from any prior means of electronic communications.

In retrospect, the challenged parts of the CDA were so clumsy and overreaching, and were enacted by Congress with so little thought or analysis, that the plaintiffs were able to focus on making sure that the courts understood the technical realities of the Internet and how the medium differs from broadcast. Once the courts understood as a technical matter how communications flowed over the Internet, they were able to conclude that Internet communications warranted a high level of protection. Once armed with the appropriately high standard of constitutional protection, it became a fairly easy matter for the courts to conclude that the CDA failed to meet those constitutional standards.

The second way in which the CDA has proved to be vital to free speech on the Internet has nothing to do with the litigation discussed earlier, but instead relates to a different—and unchallenged—section of the original CDA. Section 230 of the CDA declared, simply stated, that Internet Service Providers (ISPs) cannot be held liable for content posted to the Internet by third parties.[26] Thus, if a customer of an ISP defames someone over the Internet, the ISP is immune from liability. Similarly, if someone places illegal content on a Web site, the Web hosting company that simply provides space on a Web server will not be liable for the illegal content.

Section 230 has been upheld and applied by numerous courts to protect ISPs,[27] and the immunity that flows from Section 230 has allowed ISPs to provide service to customers without any need or incentive to create private

---

[25]Reno v. ACLU, 521 U.S. 844, 869 (1997).

[26]*See* 47 U.S.C. § 230.

[27]The leading case is Zeran v. America Online, Inc., 958 F.Supp. 1124 (E.D. Va.), *aff'd*, 129 F.3d 327 (4th Cir. 1997).

systems of censorship in which the ISP reviews and approves all content or communications posted by customers. Without this immunity, it is likely that service providers would be far more cautious about potential customers, and controversial and unpopular speakers would be less able to speak over the Internet. But, as we see in the following sections, the pressures on and incentives of private service providers will continue to be a concern for free speech on the Internet.

THE "PRESENT" OF FIRST AMENDMENT AND FREE-SPEECH CHALLENGES ON THE INTERNET

Just as the Internet has evolved very quickly—on "Internet time"—so has Internet-focused free-speech litigation and advocacy significantly evolved in less than a decade since the *ACLU v. Reno* case. The Internet is now ubiquitous in many parts of society—including in the federal and some state judicial systems. Whereas cases involving "online" issues were very rare in 1996, now they are common. Judges today are far more aware of the Internet and far more likely to use access it personally. Moreover, it is now a virtual certainty that law clerks who work for the judges are Internet-aware. Indeed, courthouses and courtrooms are now often wired for the Internet.

But the First Amendment cases have also progressed, and are now turning on technical questions about the Internet that are radically more detailed and specific than what was discussed in *ACLU v. Reno*. This is vividly illustrated in a 2004 case in which I was lead counsel. *Center for Democracy & Technology v. Pappert,* filed in 2003, challenged a Pennsylvania state law that attempted to control content on the Internet by imposing obligations on ISPs to block illegal content and making the ISPs subject to criminal liability if they do not block the content.[28]

The challenged Pennsylvania statute had an unquestionably laudable and important goal: The law sought to combat the serious problem of child pornography on the Internet. The statute did not, however, take any action against the child pornographer or any company that is itself "hosting" the child pornography on the Internet. Instead, it required ISPs that provide Internet access to Pennsylvania residents to block access to alleged child pornography sites that are located *elsewhere* on the Internet (even halfway

---

[28]*See* Center for Democracy & Technology v. Pappert, 337 F. Supp. 2d 606 (E.D. Pa. 2004). Jerry Pappert was the Attorney General of Pennsylvania, and was responsible for enforcing the challenged statute. The trial court's 102-page decision is available at http://www.cdt.org/speech/pennwebblock/20040910memorandum.pdf. The litigation case is discussed in detail at http://www.cdt.org/speech/pennwebblock/ and the major litigation documents, including expert reports, are available at http://www.cdt.org/speech/pennwebblock/penndocs.shtml.

around the world). Thus, in effect, the Pennsylvania law attempted to force ISPs to become a "traffic cop" over Internet content, even content the ISPs have no direct connection to or knowledge of.

But because the Pennsylvania legislature had no understanding of how communications over the Internet work, the statute had the practical effect of blocking massive amounts of perfectly lawful speech, wholly unrelated to the alleged child pornography. Thus, the evidence established that in an effort to block access to fewer than 400 child pornography Web sites, Pennsylvania *also* blocked access to more than 1.5 *million* other, lawful Web sites. The constitutional problems were compounded by the fact that the blocking happened in a secret process that did not involve any judicial review, and allowed no notice whatsoever to the blocked Web sites (whether the alleged child pornography sites or the wholly innocent sites that were also blocked).

Although the constitutional problems with the Pennsylvania statute were (in the plaintiffs' view) both clear and strong, the evidentiary proof of the unconstitutional impact of the statute required a very detailed exploration of how communications on the Internet take place. The evidence presented in the *CDT v. Pappert* case was orders of magnitude more complex and at a much greater level of detail than that required in the *ACLU v. Reno* case discussed earlier. As one imperfect comparison, the CDA litigation required 5 days of trial, about half of which focused on technical evidence, whereas the evidentiary hearing in the *CDT* case ran into 12 days of trial with at least 75% of the focus on technical evidence.

The three trial judges in the *ACLU v. Reno* case were required to get a clear understanding—at a fairly broad-brush level—of how information flows over the Internet. The *CDT* trial judge, Jan E. DuBois, received detailed evidence on precisely how Internet Web browsers take an Internet "URL" (or Uniform Resource Locator) such as http://www.example.com, and convert that URL into a numeric "Internet Protocol address" such as 123.45.1.104, and then what the routers and switches that exist within ISPs' networks do with that "IP address." To be able to evaluate the assertions of the defendant (claiming that ISPs could easily block access to illegal content without also blocking lawful content), the court received extensive evidence about the capabilities and limitations inherent in ISPs' operations. Thus, the level of detail for which the *CDT* court received expert testimony was far deeper than that in the *ACLU v. Reno*.

Moreover, to be able to provide the court with a quantification of the risk that requiring an ISP to block access to one Web site would also block access to other Web sites, an expert witness for the plaintiffs had to conduct a massive data collection and analysis process. The expert researched more than 30 million Internet "domains" to determine what "IP address" the Internet Web sites use, and was able to demonstrate that it is very common for many Web sites to share a single IP address (which in turn creates significant risk that blocking access to one Web site will block access to other, unrelated Web sites).[29]

In September of 2004, Judge DuBois decisively held—on a variety of grounds—that the Pennsylvania statute was unconstitutional, declaring that "there is an abundance of evidence that implementation of the [statute] has resulted in massive suppression of speech protected by the First Amendment."[30] Two thirds of the court's 102-page decision focused on the technical details of how communications flow over the Internet and how the challenged statute effectively forced ISPs to block access to protected speech. A critical issue decided by the court was whether the Pennsylvania law was unconstitutional even though it only targeted wholly unprotected speech (child pornography). The court concluded that the technical actions taken by private actors (the ISPs) to comply with the law almost inevitably led to the blocking of protected speech, and thus the law could not withstand constitutional scrutiny.[31] Judge DuBois found multiple constitutional defects with the law, and the state of Pennsylvania did not appeal the court's decision.

As the *CDT* case illustrates, claims about free speech on the Internet can turn on very detailed questions about the technical inner-workings of the network. The *CDT* case also highlights the pivotal role that ISPs play in battles about free speech on the Internet. In *CDT*, the evidence revealed that ISPs facing potential criminal liability would take technical actions necessary to avoid liability, even if those actions also had the unintended consequence of blocking innocent Web sites on the Internet. Although the court in *CDT v. Pappert* acted to protect free speech, the case makes clear that highly technical aspects of the Internet can have massively harmful impacts on speech on the Internet.

THE "FUTURE" OF INTERNET FREE-SPEECH ADVOCACY: CONSIDERING TECHNICAL DESIGN DECISIONS IN THE TWENTY-FIRST CENTURY

As illustrated previously, defending the First Amendment on the Internet can require advocates and ultimately the courts to grapple with increasingly technical details about Internet communications. But advocacy for free speech on the Internet has also jumped out of the courtroom and into an even more technical (and far less well-known) environment—the technical engineering efforts that underlie the Internet itself. Because speech on the Internet is so inherently intertwined with the technology that facilitates the

---

[29]The relevant expert report is available at http://www.cdt.org/speech/pennwebblock/20031121clarkrpt1.pdf.

[30]CDT v. Pappert, 337 F. Supp. 2d 606, 611 (E.D. Pa. 2004), available at http://www.cdt.org/speech/pennwebblock/20040910memorandum.pdf.

[31]*Id.* at 649–52.

speech, the design of the technology itself is becoming vitally important to permit and enhance free expression on the Internet.

On the Internet, it is said that "code is law."[32] Seemingly narrow technical choices can have a broad and lasting impact on public policy and individual rights. These technical design decisions are often made in the private bodies—such as the Internet Engineering Task Force and the World Wide Web Consortium—that set technical standards for the Internet. These and other key standards bodies operate largely outside of the public eye and with little input from public interest groups and free speech advocates. It is well understood that technical standards, from building codes to "generally accepted accounting principles," can have important impacts on public-policy concerns. But in the last decade no field has had the shape of its future as broadly influenced, in complex and sometimes arcane ways, by technical standards choices than the field of Internet technology. Once the sole province of engineers, academics, and industry, technical decisions about Internet design can have far-reaching implications for public-policy concerns, including free speech.[33]

Many of the technical design bodies are "open" to new participants, and free speech and public interest advocates can participate in the design discussions and effectively raise policy concerns—albeit using quite different approaches than are used in the courtroom. One example can illustrate both the risk to free speech posed by technical design decisions, and the potential for effective input by advocates.

The Internet Engineering Task Force (IETF) is the leading standards-development organization responsible for the creation and evolution of the technology on which the Internet is based. Over the course of more than a year starting in 2000, the leadership of the IETF grappled with whether to sanction a proposed working group to create technology for "Open Pluggable Edge Services" (OPES). The proposed OPES protocol would permit ISPs and other providers in the middle of the Internet to modify or block content in midstream from a server to a user. In other words, someone in the middle of an Internet communication would, with the proposed OPES technology, be able to easily interfere with (and censor) the communications between, for example, an Internet user and a Web site. Moreover, in the original OPES proposal, the midstream modification (or

---

[32]LAWRENCE LESSIG, CODE AND OTHER LAWS OF CYBERSPACE (2000).

[33]Technical design decisions can impact a wide range of public-policy concerns, such as privacy and security. The issues raised in this section are discussed in more detail in John Morris and Alan Davidson, "Policy Impact Assessments: Considering the Public Interest in Internet Standards Development," Aug. 2003, available at http://intel.si.umich.edu/tprc/papers/2003/248/CDT_Standards.pdf; Alan Davidson, John Morris, and Robert Courtney, "Strangers in a Strange Land: Public Interest Advocacy and Internet Standards," Aug. 2002, available at http://intel.si.umich.edu/tprc/papers/2002/97/Strangers_CDT_to_TPRC.pdf.

censorship) could take place without either the knowledge or consent of the sender or recipient of the communication.

Some engineers within the IETF community raised concerns about the OPES proposals. In August 2001, as part of an extensive project focused on the policy impacts of technical standards, sponsored by the Center for Democracy & Technology, I submitted detailed comments about the issues raised by OPES to the leadership of the IETF.[34] In response to the concerns raised, in late 2001, the Internet Architecture Board, which provides architectural guidance to IETF, undertook an extensive review of the OPES proposals. In November 2001, that board released its recommendations, urging that any work on OPES include strong protections against unauthorized or secret interference with Internet communications, and subsequently those recommendations were implemented within the IETF.[35]

To be effective, this type of public-policy input must be tailored to the standards bodies' unique needs and expectations. The organizations that develop Internet standards have organizational structures, expectations, and priorities that will be unfamiliar to many public-interest advocates, and the style of public-policy advocacy and lobbying that is effective in the traditional public-policy venues of legislatures and government agencies is particularly unsuited to the atmosphere of most Internet standards-setting bodies. Although aggressive assertions that something is problematic (and unconstitutional) is often exactly how litigators proceed in court, such an approach is often precisely the wrong way to be effective in standards-setting discussions. A new approach, combining respect for technical procedures and goals with clear thinking about public-policy effects, must be adopted for the new type of forum.

This is not to suggest that lawsuits and litigators will become obsolete in the Internet age—they certainly will not. First Amendment claims will continue to be the primary guard against governmental infringement of free speech. But free speech advocates also need to pay close attention to questions of technical design. In some cases, in particular, a lawsuit or even a proposed law may simply be too late. Had OPES technology been created without any constraints on its use, technology perfect for censorship would have become widely available, and it would have been hard to fully put the genie back into the bottle (especially in places like China where U.S. laws and lawsuits have little or no effect).

Of course, historically, public interest advocates have in fact paid close attention to technical details about broadcast and other electronic media, most often in the United States in the context of proceedings before the

---

[34]The comments are available at http://www.imc.org/ietf-openproxy/mail-archive/msg00827.html.

[35]A more detailed discussion of OPES and the issues it raises can be found in Standards Bulletin 1.02, Aug. 7, 2002, available at http://www.cdt.org/standards/bulletin/1.02.shtml.

Federal Communications Commission. But with the Internet, government agencies play a far less relevant role in technology development and oversight, and thus the Internet age will require some new focuses for free speech advocates. To ensure that free speech continues to flourish on the Internet, advocates cannot only be responsive to censorship and other First Amendment challenges. Instead, advocates must proactively work to ensure that the openness, low barriers to speech, and lack of ready tools for censorship that characterize the origins of the Internet continue to be features of the network as its technical underpinnings evolve.

Whether in the courtroom or the engineering meeting, the defense of and advocacy for free speech on the Internet will require an increasing attention to the fine details of the technology. It is, ultimately, technology that has made the Internet, in Judge Dalzell's words, "a far more speech-enhancing medium than print, the village green, or the mails." And thus, to protect and promote the Internet as a medium for free speech, advocates will need to pay close attention to technology itself.

Table of Cases

INDEX